ECONOMICS
AND THE
DREAMTIME

ECONOMICS AND THE DREAMTIME

A HYPOTHETICAL HISTORY

N. G. BUTLIN

CAMBRIDGE
UNIVERSITY PRESS

CAMBRIDGE UNIVERSITY PRESS
Cambridge, New York, Melbourne, Madrid, Cape Town, Singapore,
São Paulo, Delhi, Dubai, Tokyo, Mexico City

Cambridge University Press
The Edinburgh Building, Cambridge CB2 8RU, UK

Published in the United States of America by Cambridge University Press, New York

www.cambridge.org
Information on this title: www.cambridge.org/9780521438209

© L. J. Butlin 1993

First published 1993

A catalogue record for this publication is available from the British Library

Library of Congress Cataloguing in Publication Data
Butlin, N. G. (Noel George)
Economics and the dreamtime: a hypothetical history/N. G. Butlin.
Includes bibliographical references and index.
ISBN 0-521-43236-7. - ISBN 0-521-43820-9 (pbk)
1. Australian aborigines - Economic conditions. 2. Australian
aborigines - History. 3. Australian aborigines - Government
relations. 4. Economic history. 5. Australia - Economic conditions.
I. Title.
GN666.B883   1993
330.994'01-dc20   92-35937
                                             CIP

ISBN 978-0-521-43236-8 Hardback
ISBN 978-0-521-43820-9 Paperback

CONTENTS

PREFACE

Perhaps all books should be preceded by a confession. This book most certainly warrants one. For most of my working life I was committed to what I believed to be a forward-looking type of economic history of Australia. My object was to exploit above all what I regarded as 'hard statistical evidence' and to build history around it. (This did not include high-level model building and econometrics.) Where a relatively simple portrayal of statistical evidence was insufficient, I preferred to fall back on institutional records to confirm or deny the relevance of statistical inference. I continue to sustain that protestation.

But the statistical condition imposed a limitation on all my work — it had essentially to be related to experience after 1860, for which reasonably coherent Australia-wide data are available. From this came my estimates of Australian national income after 1860 and my studies of investment in growth and, in general, of growth conditions leading to the present. The work was designed to track the longterm path of the Australian economy and in the process to throw light on the present and the future — how far the past constrains the present, how far history does or does not repeat itself, how far we continue to replicate past mistakes, how far we took false fits and starts and continue to do so.

In all this I was inadvertently trapped in an ignorance of what had happened before 1860 and hence committed the blunder of seeing the progression of a successful European development of Australian resources, particularly during 1860 to 1914, gradually enmeshed in doubts and uncertainties as the nature of our position in the world economy came to greater prominence — where selling the product became at least as important as producing it.

I decided to deviate backwards in time and experienced a revelation. My object was to try initially to extend the national income estimates back to the very beginning of European settlement. This may seem to be a strange approach to a future-looking economic history! However, it took me into many unexpected corners and to a vast reading undertaking, and then to a new view of my own country and its place in the world.

One of the aberrations in this exercise was to write a jocular article, 'Yo Ho Ho and How many Bottles of Rum?' (*AEHR*), to investigate one major component of consumer expenditure in early Australia. The conclusion — early Australians were not as inebriated as historians would have us believe. But a niggling question remained: was it possible that Australian Aborigines — as in the case of the Amerindians — became substantial consumers of alcohol? If they did, the colonists might have been relatively abstemious. That question demanded another answer: how many Aborigines were there? The answers available on that point were so unsatisfactory that I could not resist an attempt at a type of re-estimation, with quite radically different suggestions (*Our Original Aggression*, 1983). But with the conclusion of most probably very much larger numbers precontact, it followed that very extensive use had been made of Australian resources by Aborigines, and that there had been massive depopulation and a large-scale transfer of beneficial resources from Aborigines to Europeans. Moreover, that transfer occurred in conditions in which Aborigines had supplied, through millennia of resource use, ideal conditions for the domesticated animals and other technology of a European economy. We had been the inheritors of enormous Aboriginal effort, most of which was adapted and discarded and their society destroyed. Many remain degraded, their condition a disgrace to our humanity.

This book is not written with a sense of guilt. We cannot now be guilty about what was done so long ago. But we need to be aware of the conditions of our success; that is what the book is about.

My rediscovery took me far afield, far beyond economics into prehistory and the ancient world, into oceanography and climatology, into geomorphology and anthropology, in what was to me a fascinating if possibly inept process of learning. So much for carefully designed research plans! Nevertheless, economics is deeply embedded in this volume, even though often only in the form in which economists might ask questions of different disciplines. If Australian history is about human existence in Australia, it begins now at least 60 000 years ago and probably millennia earlier. We are dealing with one of the very longest settled countries on earth, so far as *Homo sapiens* is concerned — not the longest but a very long history indeed. We can no longer approach Australia as an 'area of recent settlement'.

This volume attempts to outline the arrival and settlement of Aborigines and the structuring of their economy; the likely precontact (pre-destruction) numbers, the intrusion of the first settlement of Europeans during the first two decades and the different processes of absorbing Aboriginal resources that were adopted.

My forthcoming book, *Forming a Colonial Economy: Australia 1810–1850* (Cambridge University Press), takes account of European 'success' — and it was a success from this perspective — to 1850. In this approach, 1788–1809 is a preliminary step (equally destructive to Aborigines) giving obscure shape to the early Australian colonial economy. By 1810, when the local colonial story (as distinct from the British background) begins, a new mould began to be stamped with full constitutional authority, made firmer after 1821. Substantially, even though convict-based, it starts with the formation of a more conventional mixed economy of public and private sectors, and gradually absorbs an increasing and conventional private form. But by 1840 its prospects become shrouded and it is a relevant question in the later part of the forthcoming volume as to whether there was a net 'productivity' success when both Aboriginal and European performance is taken together. This is not an easy question to tackle and many will disapprove of the answers suggested.

N. G. Butlin

ACKNOWLEDGEMENTS

I have many debts. I cannot list them all. My wife Joan and my children Janet, Matthew and Andrew have been a source of unqualified and unquantifiable support in all sorts of ways. To my good medical friends Dr Reg Lam-Po-Tang and Professor Fred Hollows I owe the continual association of body, soul and eyesight. Many thanks are due to Ms Kyra Suthern for unfailing research support and to Messrs Wayne Naughton and Douglas White for programming help. The typing staff of my old Department of Economic History at the Australian National University — particularly Barbara Gramza and Winnie Pradela — have been invaluable in backing up my work and word processing efforts.

I have also received a great deal of encouragement outside my specialty, particularly from Professors Mulvaney and Chappell, Dr Singh and others too numerous to list.

For material in Part I I have to thank Commodore Compton of the Australian Navy, Mr Bruce Willington and Mr Ben Searle, Professors Horridge, Lambeck, Mulvaney, Nix and Walker, and Drs Chappell, Creswell, Fandry, Flenley, McKnight, Pope, Singh and Wolanski for guidance to literature, helpful comments, criticisms and so on. None of these has seen the final draft and hence none is responsible for its contents. I also owe a great debt to Douglas White for programming efforts, particularly in relation to mapping and contouring. I also acknowledge with thanks advice received from the UN Co-ordinating Committee for Offshore Prospecting in South-east Asia, the Union Oil Company and British Petroleum, all in Bangkok.

Finally, while the work was begun before retirement, I have to thank the Australian National University for a continuing appointment, first as a University Fellow and subsequently as a Visiting Fellow. This has provided me with a much needed base and facilities.

I also acknowledge financial support from the Reserve Bank of Australia and from the Australian Research Grants Committee that has helped in sustaining necessary support and without which the book could not have been written.

Postscript
Noel Butlin completed the manuscript of this book, in its current form, shortly before his death in April 1991. Completion was an extremely difficult task, but he

won the race and left his literary executor with strict instructions that 'no word be changed'. I would like to thank Cambridge University Press, in particular Robin Derricourt and Yvonne White, for the spirit in which the publisher has honoured that last injunction. Thanks are also due to Noel's former colleagues at ANU for their assistance in finalising data and maps.

M. W. Butlin

Figures

Maps

Tables

INTRODUCTION

W hat is Australian history and economic history about? Is Australia to be seen as an offshoot of Britain and Europe that is gradually, if reluctantly, moving towards Asia? Is it the product of a special socio-imperial experiment, with the initial convict colonies gradually emerging as freed and free societies with deeply engrained ideas of class relations? Is the economy one focused on natural resource development, with a brief interlude in the twentieth century when urban industry and services were given some primacy in policy decision-making? Is the economy a small appendage of the trading world, tied by trade, capital, migration and technology to one or two major countries (most notably, for much of its history, to Britain)? How far is there an 'internal dynamic' to be identified in Australian economic development, most obviously but not exclusively arising from the high degree of urbanisation achieved at an exceptionally early date?

These are some of the themes that run through writings on Australian history and economic history. This volume, *Economics and the Dreamtime*, suggests some possible differences in emphasis. One does not simply throw away established historical traditions and elements in an attempt to present a revised picture, but there is a fundamental difference of approach in this volume as compared with most past general histories. Prominence is given to the Aborigines — their presence over many millennia, their role in shaping the local environment, the form of their economy, their contribution and resistance to eventual colonial occupation and their substantial demise.

Pre- and post-Columbian history

Not much more than a millennium ago, the Vikings managed to settle North America. That initiative did not persist. It is now almost exactly the five-hundredth anniversary of Christopher Columbus' crossing of the Atlantic. If he did not actually discover America, his successful passage established the finger of contact between the advanced societies of Western Europe and the indigenous people of the New World, people who had arrived in the Americas far earlier, perhaps 20000 or more years ago. Columbus' voyage was not the only one to push inquisitive mariners on, but it dramatised the potential and the beginning. In due course, the challenge of the perimeter of the Afro-Eurasian continent was met, opening up other points and modes of contact between the West and other less 'advanced' societies. Cook's 'discovery' of the east coast of Australia was among the last of the world's great maritime feats that might be dated as the modern beginning, 500 years ago (*pace* Eric the Red).

These European achievements followed long after the passage of other earlier peoples to the 'new' worlds. The history of the Americas might be seen as the process whereby these early indigenous peoples, whose numbers grew to be very large even by comparison with Europe, occupied the hemisphere, established societies there and in due course gave way to occupation by Europeans. Whatever internal conflicts may have occurred amongst early peoples, here then is a story of grand achievements over thousands of years and of the eventual massive transfer of resources between opposing cultures. It is doubtful if few or any of the ancient conquests of the past have matched this scale of redistribution of assets that was the post-Columbian heritage for Western Europe. Though archaeologists and his-torians have established some of the outlines of this early indigenous achievement, any attempt to delineate the 'expansion of Europe' as a massive resource transfer seems to be inadequate.

Cook's penetration of the Pacific less than 300 years after Columbus' passage was followed quickly by actual settlement of Australia by penal colonies in 1788. What is accepted in Australian history, but not adequately integrated in it, is that other migrants had preceded these settlers by many tens of thousands of years. Early Aborigines were the first discoverers and occupiers of the Australian continent, the first to establish functioning societies and economies, and the first to make the large-scale adaptations required to use almost every type of ecological condition in Australia. As in the case of the Americas, the arrival of Europeans meant not merely 'contact' with Aborigines but the destruction of Aboriginal society and populations and the transfer of their resources *to the benefit of both the new arrivals and those who remained in Britain*.

If, hypothetically, Amerindians began to occupy the American hemisphere as far back as 25 000 years ago, post-Columbian history spans perhaps 1.6 per cent of total human history in the hemisphere. Mere time lapse is not necessarily impressive. The scale and pace of change in resource use, demographic expansion and integration with the rest of the trading world are pointers to a speeding up and change in the nature of development in the post-Columbian world. This may suggest that the long time during which human beings occupied pre-Columbian America is not as interesting as it might sound.

The Australian case is even more striking. A mere two centuries of occupation had been added to the certainly 40 000, probably 60 000, and possibly longer period of Aboriginal settlement. Post-European 'contact' then accounts probably for a mere 0.3 per cent of Australian human history. Once again — although the speed and scale of resource transformation does not match that in the United States — acceleration of development appears to have followed British settlement.

Settlement and resource transfers

The allotment of interest on a temporal versus developmental basis depends, of course, on a value judgement. Most modern Americans and Australians would opt for the developmental criterion. Yet there is an issue that might prompt at least some amendment of the conventional allocation of interest. This is the inbuilt and massive transfer of resources between indigenous and immigrant societies. Europe found several modes of imperial organisation and methods of colonisation. Not all depended on 'settlement', and even within the process of settlement there were variants. In the American and Australian cases, at all events, settlement meant eventually and substantially the total displacement of the indigenous populations and the acquisition by immigrants of their resources.

This is not the place to pursue any grand counterfactual on the assumption that such a transfer did or did not occur. We have, in any event, comparative history to guide us to the options of conquest and partially coerced trade between imperial centres and colonies, together with the international spread of slavery as an intermediate alternative. The Americas had plenty to offer in the way of trade and the Europeans, in principle, goods to exchange with the local inhabitants. It is possible that the Australian case was almost unique — there appear to have been very few British objects, at least on first encounter, that the Aborigines valued.

What settlement meant in this case was the cheap acquisition of Aboriginal resources, just as it did, essentially, in the Americas. In other cases, overt conquest which led to comparatively little settlement provided a mechanism for imperial access to resources without such an overt asset transfer. It improved the terms of trade for the conquerors, opened up opportunities for imperial development and to some extent ameliorated the imperial process by a sharing of the benefits of development. In the process it acknowledged prior property rights, but this option did not apply in the Americas or Australia (though some contemporary groups joined the different immigrants in short- but not longterm benefit). Indeed, in Australia great care was taken to avoid claims of conquest because of the property implications for the conquered.

The lack of obvious instruments for trade may have been important in prompting settlement. But there was another and fundamental reason for differences in imperial modes that Marxist concepts of imperialism have not effectively incorporated. The Eurasian continent was by the time of Columbus, and certainly of Cook, a common pool of disease, to a large extent due to the presence of concentrated population nuclei. Centuries of experience built, for several crucial diseases, endemic conditions and large segments of populations that were immune by virtue of prior infection. Once plague disappeared there remained the potential for some large-scale epidemics, with massive population losses. But for several diseases the common manifestation became childhood infection with consequential immunity for survivors. What this meant was that contact between different groups on the Eurasian mainland could occur, if not with impunity, at least with greatly limited risk of disease transfer. (There were some special transfer problems from tropical areas to Europe that need not concern us here.)

This condition did not apply to the Americas. There must be some doubt about Australia but, for reasons given in this volume, it appears that Aborigines represented, at least in the main, an exposed population nucleus for a considerable variety of diseases that had become attenuated largely to diseases of childhood in Western Europe. Indigenous populations could not tolerate contact with the West. Introduced diseases meant infection of all age groups and heavy mortality. Moreover, small points of contact between newcomers and the indigenous populations could spread diseases far along human chains and over large areas beyond the points of immediate contact. Resource transfer was achieved dominantly by depopulation. The local populations had little that was lethal to render in exchange.

So in, for example, Peru and Mexico, in the United States and Canada, and in Australia, there were differences in detail but the same fundamental demographic disaster. Until recently, the sizes of indigenous populations have been taken to be too few to make this a momentous change in world terms. More recently, in the Americas and in Australia, this demographic evaluation has been challenged with increasing force. Recent suggestions are that indigenous populations were relatively numerous, their modes of resource use relatively efficient and, at times, their technology far from primitive. So the story in both Australia and America is one of a mass exchange of ownership and the replacement of indigenous productive practices with new ones.

One may feel that this mass resource transfer is old and long ago, with little present relevance. But is this the case? One has only to ask how economists attempt to explain 'modern economic growth' for Western Europe in particular to suggest that the process of resource transfer had a longterm relevance and may have significant implications for the present.

Thus Robert Solow in chapter 1 of *The Cambridge Economic History of Europe*, vol. 7, follows the well established economists' routine of explaining economic development in the industrial nations of Europe in terms of the growth of inputs of land, labour and capital plus residual contributors (technology, etc.). What does 'land' for any given nation mean? Should we not incorporate in one nation's 'land' its share in 'land' acquisitions in areas of settlement? Should we not also include the interactive benefits that each European state obtained from each other's acquisitions? And should we not also recognise that these acquisitions did not merely imply food but included all natural resources, such as wealth under the surface?

Looked at in this light, the nature, speed and scope of European economic development over the past three to four hundred years would have been very different indeed had it not been for the peculiar conditions of their 'success' in colonial settlements. Asset transfers and the ability to use those assets were not one-off events. Their benefits persisted over centuries and, it might be suggested, continued with declining effect towards, if not right to, the present day.

No doubt there are plenty of unused resources in the modern world — just as there is a rapidly expanding population to press on those resources. But one great historical mode that served to advantage Western Europe is now closed off, at least for all practical purposes. Displacement by relatively easy settlement is no longer a practical possibility. It would be a fascinating thesis to explore how far that condition has weighed in generating the increasing resource scarcity, inflation and instability that emerged shortly before World War I and has intensified into the present.

From the very beginning, for very peculiar reasons, the Australian settlers faced a crucial question. From a British perspective, this can be seen as the successful establishment of a penal settlement. Gradually, that British perspective gave way to the establishment of free colonies in a continent in which Aborigines were regarded as irrelevant. Certainly, this was one of the criteria of success. That the settlers were successful in their own lights and by their own standards can scarcely be doubted. High and rising living standards in the Americas and Australia are simple testimonies to that fact.

But there was another policy issue, already summarily indicated. This was a core issue for the settlers: how far should available resources be diverted to natural resource exploitation and how far to the other potential of available and acquired human (skilled) capital? Initially, that implicit policy option revolved around sheer survival and the ability of a few individuals to gain command of resources. The specifics of that policy changed but the substance of the options remained. Driven by outside flows of capital and labour from an increasingly industrialised and urbanised Britain, Australian settlers confronted opportunities to acquire control of large-scale natural resources and also to develop urban industrial–service communities. They chose both.

They chose both partly because of the relevance of basic comparative advantage in natural resources but partly also because of the predilections of many immigrants to exploit their skills in urban environments, predilections encouraged by the importance of ports, governing centres and their British urban habits, now set in a position of isolation.

The dominance of skilled immigrants was at first gradually and then, after 1830, rapidly watered down by the rising number of colonially born. So a different tension entered, in which the colonies had either to accept lower urban skills or to generate their own through local training. It is doubtful whether they have ever succeeded in the latter. Yet the basic policy option remained and remains today — natural resources versus urban development. It has hung over the whole of Australian colonial history and remains possibly the crucial problem at the end of the twentieth century.

PART I

THE PALAEOECONOMIC HISTORY OF ABORIGINAL MIGRATION

1

INTRODUCTION

In Australian history, Aboriginal migration is exodus and genesis — exodus from South-east Asia and genesis of the first society and economy in Australia. Economic historians tend to treat countries such as Australia, Canada, New Zealand and USA as 'areas of recent settlement'. They generally ignore the fact that prehistorians have demonstrated that all these countries (New Zealand is a qualified exception), far from being 'recent', are areas of very ancient settlement. The incorporation of Aboriginal history is of interest in a more general record of human presence in Australia. But even for those with no interest in Aborigines as such, the influence that Aborigines had on British settlement (and vice versa) is far from being a minor consideration in the 'success' of European settlement after 1788. Indeed, one important way to look at Australian history in the nineteenth century is to view it in part as a takeover bid.

Here, the focus is on migration. Many Aborigines adopt the position that they have 'always' been in Australia. As Europeans perceive the origins of *Homo sapiens*, this is contrary to the evidence. To the extent that Aborigines have been present in Australia for many millennia, perhaps somewhere between 50–100 000 years, the distinction between 'always' and this extraordinarily long timespan becomes, as a practical matter, shadowy. Exploration of Aboriginal migration may, then, be of interest to Aborigines for at least two reasons. First, it may help to indicate the exceptionally long period over which they and their ancestors, as representatives of *Homo sapiens*, have occupied and exploited Australian resources. Secondly, accepting their original passage from mainland through island South-east Asia to Australia many millennia ago, and given the exceptional maritime potential of island South-east Asia, it is likely that Aborigines could be hot contenders to claim the title of the world's first mariners, the persons who broke the dependence of *Homo sapiens* on continental land masses and led to the eventual global mobility of human beings.

From a scientific perspective, Aborigines have been recognised as present in Australia (Mulvaney and White, 1987), including the southern mainland, for at least 40 000 years. Very recent, evidence at Alligator River in northern Australia suggests that this timespan may have to be pushed back to 60 000 years. This dating is based on evidence of human remains back to 30 000 BP (before present) and of other physical objects, chiefly campsites, for a further 10 000 years. This timespan is almost certainly an underestimation, given the limitations of radio carbon dating. Different prehistorians have speculated about the time likely to have been taken to occupy the Australian continent, yielding estimates that range up to as long as 15 000 years from the date of first arrival and down to a very short period. Several estimates suggest a first arrival around 55 000 BP; some prehistorians would not rule out as far back as 130 000 BP (Singh and Geissler, 1985); and, at the other extreme, it is suggested that the first arrival may not have been much before 40 000 BP. Nevertheless, in this context, it is important to stress that '40 000 BP' really means, most probably 'before 40 000 BP'. Limitations on carbon dating, ignorance about much of South-east Asia before 40 000 BP and, more recently, Aboriginal resistance to archaeological investigation obstruct efforts to push dates back earlier.

The minimum date of 40 000 BP and certainly that of 60 000 BP is a very long time. The identification of this record is the very considerable achievement of Australian prehistorians in recent decades.[1] The dating compares with a first arrival in USA at 20 000 and New Zealand about 2000 BP. The Australian date may be compared with about 40 000 BP for Java (where some very much older dates also exist), Borneo and New Guinea, about 32 000 for New Ireland (Allen *et al.*, 1988) and 28 000 BP for the Solomons (Wickler and Spriggs, 1988).

The series of dates might hint at a process of human movement out of the Eurasian continent in what is possibly the greatest human migration that has ever occurred. Perhaps the migration to Australia was an integral early part of this movement leading to the settlement, out of Asia (Kirk and Szathmary, 1985), of most of the Pacific Islands and North and South America. Perhaps the settlement of Australia was a distinct early movement. We do not know. In any event, the migration out of Asia was a remarkable achievement of human adaptation, courage and technical innovation. Whether other factors intervened is a central issue; in particular, it would be interesting to know whether the flow was partly driven by economic factors.

This is not a technical contribution to prehistory. The object, after reading some of the literature and attempting a little new investigation, is to pose questions, many of them speculative and counterfactual, about some of the processes of Aboriginal migration as an economic historian might nominate them. This means far more than a merely economic analysis and one must bring in a great variety of considerations. In contrast with the tendency of prehistorians throughout the world to encompass (with good reason) vast masses of undifferentiated time, I have tried, despite the risks, to build in a sense of human action and reaction sequentially in response to changing circumstances. Attention is limited to approximately the 100–120 000 years and related ice age fluctuations that might define the limits of Aboriginal migration.

The order of treatment

The structure of the discussion is deeply influenced by the widespread — not universal — view that prehistorians throughout the world have of hunter gatherers. Basically, any reader of the literature will be impressed by its fundamentally non-Malthusian perspective. It is true that some limited efforts have been made to explore possible 'population pressure' conditions but generally the picture is of humanity not subject to scarcity. Hence attempted investigations of Aboriginal migration have tended to pay limited attention to economic considerations.

The first part of the discussion here, then, gives a highly condensed (and possibly a little unfair) outline of prehistorians' approaches to Aboriginal migration, juxtaposed with an alternative in which economics is more prominent. The second part accepts provisionally the non-Malthusian perspective and examines prehistorians' comments on Aboriginal migration on their own terms. It focuses accordingly on two matters — pathways of migration and technical innovations to achieve maritime capability. The third part departs from this convention and attempts to explore the possibilities of changing scarcity conditions, population pressures and 'push' as well as 'pull' factors in migration. At the end, an attempt is made to combine the two sets of approaches in presenting several migration scenarios.

Because there is a major difference of approach, parts II and III are separated by what is essentially a methodological interjection. In moving between parts II and III, it is necessary to consider alternative views of the meaning of optimum population levels and to introduce ways of thinking about the demographic and migration implications of changes in aggregate and relative productivity and of reallocations of the workforce.

Note

1 Whatever explicit or implicit criticisms of prehistorians may appear below, they relate to the question of migration, not to studies within Australia.

2

CONVENTIONAL VIEWS
AND ALTERNATIVE
APPROACHES

Prehistorians' views on Aboriginal migration

Given their reliance on empirical evidence, prehistorians have generally — but not always — been cautious in their statements about Aboriginal migration. The few comments here do not do justice to differences of opinion between some individuals but very briefly indicate what appears to be a prevailing view. It is agreed that Aborigines arrived by sea; their ancestors passed out of South-east Asia through the islands; and the ultimate immigrants arrived not less than 40 000 years ago. Since New Guinea was joined physically to Australia for about 100 000 years before around 8000 BP, the most common belief now seems to be a first arrival in New Guinea and then land passage to the present Australian mainland (e.g. Jones, 1977; Mulvaney and White, 1987; Walker, 1972; White and O'Connell, 1982).

In exploring migration to New Guinea/Australia, given a lack of interest in economics, most attention has been paid to pathways across the islands (Allen et al., 1977); the question of means has dominated over those of motive and opportunity. Indeed, insofar as opportunity has entered the debate, prehistorians' observations on ice age conditions and consequent lowering of seas (which reduced the length and frequency of sea trips) have sometimes appeared contrary to present understanding.[1] Any likely economic motivation has generally been submerged under an essentially non-Malthusian and culture-driven view of the world of hunter gatherers (Birdsell, 1972; Hassan, 1981). There are occasional suggestions of a possible flow of migrants over time (Allen et al., 1988; Fox, 1980), but the efforts at demographic modelling have tended to lead to extreme proposals ranging from a bare handful of ever-arriving migrants to, at the extreme, one pregnant female! Though the last suggestion may originally have been jocular, it has not prevented efforts to reconstruct the possible rate at which such an Aboriginal Eve may have succeeded in populating the whole of Australia. In all this, there is a strong suggestion of preoccupation with the First Migrant and the Oldest Inhabitant rather than attention to an historical process.

Alternative approaches

One can adopt the common prehistory assumption of a non-Malthusian state for early hunter gatherers and pursue its implications for migration. In this event, one is indeed concerned with migration paths and the technology necessary to travel by sea. Even then, one should treat the migration process as one of numbers of mobile human beings and explore the possibilities of levels of and variations in migrant flows over time. Motivation to move, to take risks and to innovate would be prominent, even without much concern for economic issues.

The alternative is to investigate the process of migration from the perspective of economic history. In this event, we would like to deal with such questions as: what determined the source, level and fluctuations of Aboriginal migration, the modes and costs of transfer, their skill characteristics and the consequences for the recipient area? We cannot expect to answer these questions in the way that we might hope to do for recent times. But there may be some profit in investigating their implications.

After reading some of the literature, I roughed out the beginnings of a 'model' of Aboriginal migration as an economic historian might perceive some of the issues in an ice age context. This is here relegated to appendix 1 because I do not propose to develop it further and certainly not to estimate it. Nevertheless, it provides a useful set of boxes that one would need to fill in pursuing an economist's approach. It rests fundamentally on the standard notion of push and pull factors in migration, of a succession of 'regions' into which early human beings flowed and temporal segments over which migration movements may have been made. It tries to recognise the massive exogenous factors to which early human beings in ice age conditions were exposed and the potential for significant changes in net reproduction rates as people moved into particular regional conditions. It tries to accommodate to the limited scope for changes in production functions for hunter gatherers. It gives some prominence to the likelihood of conflict and competition between groups, the risks to which humans may have been exposed in passing into the volcanic and earthquake-affected area of island South-east Asia and, in particular, the innovatory activity required for continental people to become sea-goers. It also raises the issue of whether explicit pull factors to an unseen Australia might have been relevant.

In both approaches, the fact that Aboriginal migration occurred during the last ice age is basic. It is important to appreciate that the last ice age, beginning about 115–120 000 years ago, was predominantly a northern hemisphere phenomenon in terms of glaciation and, even at the climax, also probably in terms of temperature and ecological change. Moreover, even in the northern hemisphere, large areas escaped the direct effects of glaciation. Views on the last ice age are often Eurocentric because Europe (and Canada) was most severely affected. It is relevant to the present issue that the eastern side of the Eurasian continent escaped heavy glaciation. In terms of migration, one might be tempted (as I was) to think of the ice age as prompting a movement from the cold northern hemisphere to the warmer southern one. This is a misconception. Nevertheless, Siberia and Alaska were subject to severe periglacial influences and it seems probable that northern and central China experienced periods of desert development. Not only in the southern hemisphere but also in mainland and island South-east Asia, temperature changes were relatively limited as was vegetational adaptation. Substantial temperature, aridity and vegetational change may have been limited in these areas to the climax of the ice age at about 17 000 BP. However, there was one global phenomenon — declining sea levels. This feature more than any other appears as the dominant issue in Aboriginal migration. Nevertheless, it is necessary to consider whether more far-flung ice age changes, conforming to the Eurocentric picture, may have indirectly affected Aboriginal migration.

This adumbration of an economic history 'model' is exploited here in a purely literary mode, to provide a checklist of empty boxes and some possible forms of relationships. The discussion is not, in the end, structured around it, though it has helped to inform some of the sections. Those who are interested may wish to relate various sections of the book to appendix 1. In the event, I have found it more meaningful to explore the implications of several variables in different equations rather than focus on the 'model' itself. It is convenient instead to take up, first, a couple of issues that are central to the non-Malthusian prehistory literature: pathways and innovations.

Note

1 White and Lampert in Mulvaney and White (1987) refer to sea levels of about 130 metres bp at around 55 000 BP. This is not present understanding. The date is taken to 'fit' a presumed time required for Aborigines to occupy the Australian continent derived from the period taken by Amerindians to settle North America. The implied analogy is open to question. Amerindians approached North America from the north-west in the worst glacial conditions and from the most difficult direction. The analogy misses the point of the concentration of ice age conditions on the northern hemisphere and the geographical configuration of North America.

3

NON-MALTHUSIAN ISSUES: PATHWAYS AND INNOVATIONS

Sea and land passages

Birdsell (in Allen *et al.*, 1988) has made the most detailed attempt to investigate the sea and land pathways through island South-east Asia (map 1, p. 00). Assuming that the migrants and their ancestors travelled during the last ice age, it is argued that changes in sea levels during the past 100 000 years significantly altered the obstacles to passage from mainland South-east Asia to Australia/New Guinea. In economists' terms, the costs of transfer were affected by the lowering of sea levels and consequent reduction of sea distances.

Ice age sea levels

Estimates of sea level changes from 135 000 BP to date have been made, with significant amendments, during the past decade. Sea level changes are, subject to some time-lag problems, good proxies for the progression of and fluctuations in ice age conditions. Graph 1 (page 15) presents estimates by Chappell and Shackleton (1988). These give for specific 'dates' (subject to variable margins of error) the sea level reductions in metres (also qualified by margins of error) below present levels at the Huon Peninsula in New Guinea over the past 135 000 years. Prehistorians have tended to opt for some extreme lowering of the sea or some supposed average. The graph strongly suggests that we should be concerned with fluctuations around a trend. Non-prehistorians might note that the graph should be read from right to left.

Manifestly, present sea levels are abnormal — as they were at around 125–115 000 BP. The ice age contains long periods not radically different from today but with deep changes, most obviously at the climax in the vicinity of 17 000 BP. But there are also less pronounced but exceptional troughs of the order of −65

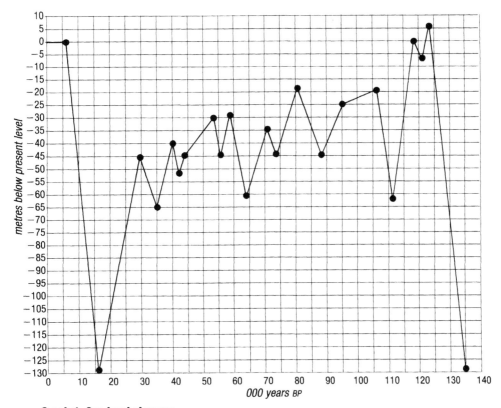

Graph 1: Sea level changes

metres bp (below present [levels]) at around 112 000, 64 000 and 35 000 BP (these 'dates' should not be taken literally and, indeed, the line linking of the points may give a spurious impression). Chappell suggests (personal communication) that the higher levels are more securely founded and that possibly larger margins of error apply to the trough levels. However, he also suggests that the low level at about 64 000 BP is more likely to be somewhat lower rather than higher.

Land and sea stages: a comment on maps, geomorphology and oceanography

From mainland to island South-east Asia, human beings were able during most of the past 100 000 years to walk from the Malay Peninsula through Sumatra and Java to Bali. Over more limited but extensive periods, they could walk to Borneo. At Bali and eastern Borneo, they confronted the sea and, indeed, a series of sea gaps to reach Australia and New Guinea. Thus a western, land-accessible section of island South-east Asia is offered as one distinct region, with the islands attainable only by sea trips as another.

Birdsell accepts present maps of islands and present seabed contours as risky guides but the only ones we have. We need to be aware of the risks. In an area as tectonically active as island South-east Asia, it is improbable that the sea and land relationships that we see today have remained unchanged. Experts I have consulted from Port Hedland to Canberra and from Hobart to Townsville generally believe that one is not taking great risks in assuming that the configurations of the two great shelves of Sunda and Sahul have remained basically as they are today back over the limited timespan of 100 000 years. The island array beyond the shelves is more exposed to change, but within this limited timespan distances between islands are probably no more subject to change than we have experienced within the period of available written records, and seabeds are not likely to be altered outside a range of the order of 100 kilometres from an exploding volcano.[1] Erosion of exposed land and siltation of parts of the seabed may affect other matters but not sea distances or depths (at least not significantly) over the specified timespan. These other matters will become prominent on several occasions. With some qualms, I am prepared to follow Birdsell to the extent of accepting present land structures and seabeds as a guide, while recognising that we are literally on somewhat shaky ground.

Maps are another matter. Here there are two questions that are immediately relevant. We cannot measure distances with any precision, even on the best of maps. Hence, only approximate measurements are proposed (for scale adjustments see appendix 2). The second question concerns the vital matter of sea depth contours. Prehistorians have been accustomed to using the most general indicators, sometimes merely the 200 metre contour line, as broadly indicative of distances from the islands to the Sahul Shelf. Birdsell adopted two contours — the 130 metre level supplemented by the single 50 metre contour. These contour lines are derived from generalised representations of sea soundings over centuries and brought together in such representations as the General Bathymetric Chart of the Oceans (GEBCO) maps from Monaco. The immediate alternative is the specific soundings entered on the so called Admiralty Charts. These charts have grown like Topsy and their regional quality varies enormously, praise as one may the charting feats of early mariners. Perhaps most relevant for present purposes is the fact that in many important areas the soundings are far apart and tend, apart from close inshore, to follow the frequent paths of ships. There are important gaps in the record. Most importantly from the present point of view there are large holes in the Admiralty soundings, particularly above north-west Java and in the Gulf of Thailand; and in water secure for the early shipping of shallow draft vessels, it is possible that soundings were not very precisely carried out. Moreover, given the longevity of some of the soundings, one may be a little uncertain as to the accuracy of some of the coordinates.

There are two other sources that were not available to Birdsell and a third will soon be relevant. The third, not used, is the satellite photography that discloses many subsea features. The other two (that have been used) are, first for the whole area, the computer tapes of the Digital Relief of the Surface of the Earth produced by the US National Oceanographic and Atmospheric Administration (NOAA) and second, for the Australian (Sahul) Shelf, the bathymetric measurements carried out originally by Australian National Mapping and now produced as AUSLIG Bathymetric Maps by the Australian Navy. I have to thank the Navy for making available digitised data and some unpublished dyelines to complete the record of the north-west Australian shelf.

Micro-bathymetry is not satisfactorily covered by the NOAA tapes. These are a composite of satellite and sonar soundings combined with data from Admiralty Charts laid out in a coarse 5 minutes latitude by 5 minutes longitude grid. This implies, for the relevant area, an array of actual or interpolated soundings (corrected for sea conditions) at roughly 9 kilometre intervals. Such a coarse grid will miss many detailed points and may grossly oversimplify. In areas where physical conditions alter rapidly, it may be seriously misleading. On the other hand, it can provide a simple strategic picture, subject to micro-qualifications, and has, in this case, pointed to a number of critically important features. Insofar as we are concerned with some comparative issues related to the island South-east Asia seabed and the Australian Shelf, it is a very convenient, if coarse, reference source. NOAA has produced three editions and the 1988 version has been used here.

The Australian bathymetric data are extremely detailed, the product of recent sonar soundings, covering the entire Shelf to the dividing line between the declared Indonesian and Australian seabeds. With this source, this part of the area can be examined in detail and the strategic picture presented by NOAA checked and corrected. Unfortunately, no comparable data are available elsewhere in the region.

Notwithstanding the variety of sources, there are two problems in using them. First, we assume that present seabed characteristics extend back over the past 100 000 or so years. Apart from siltation and erosion, this is probably not a severe obstacle. The second point arises from the fact that, as sea levels fell and the weight of the ocean on the earth's crust was reduced, the seabed rose slowly (the isostatic effect). This raises much more problematical and variable effects in interpreting current sub-sea contours. Though this might be discussed at length, the issue crops up in different ways in different places and times, and comment is best left to particular sections below. It is, however, important to note in general that present seabed contours tend to understate the seabed exposure when used in relation to the Chappell chart (graph 1, p. 15); and that the lagged effects mean that seabed exposure was almost certainly longer at cyclical troughs than is implied in the chart.

Implied likely pathways

Based essentially on a complex of sea distances between stepping stones, visibility of destination points and 'target size' of islands, Birdsell concluded that the Aboriginal pathways lay primarily from Borneo and Sulawesi through the islands to their east and eventually to New Guinea. This was true, for him, whether one used a 50 or 130 metre contour line. In his view, only at the climax of the ice age at around 17 000 BP, when the 130 metre contour became relevant, was a route direct from Timor to mainland Australia a reasonable probability. At 130 metres, he nominated eight to ten sea trips to New Guinea from Borneo and eight from Bali to Australia via Timor. But the latter was taken to include one very long sea trip of several hundred kilometres until the climax seafall to 130 metres. In effect, the mainstream of early Aboriginal migration lay through New Guinea; and Australia was largely approached through the north, at least until the ice age climax approached. At or near that climax, the Timor route might have been preferable, but only late in the migration process (see map 1, p. 18).

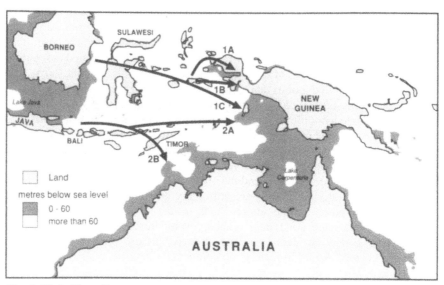

Map 1: Birdsell's pathways

I would suggest that on all the criteria — sea distances, visibility and target size — Birdsell's conclusion is open to serious doubt. It seems likely that all his routes were used but that the route marked 2A on the map was the least plausible at any time. So far as the other specific options (1A, 1B, 1C and 2B) go, route 2B via Timor offered the best chance of success and may have been the one most regularly used until about 25 000 BP. This suggestion rests partly on the bathymetric evidence, partly on the fact that Timor was more readily accessible throughout the whole ice age than was Borneo and partly on the proposition that the Timor route for much of the ice age required less navigational skill. After about 25 000 BP it is possible that improved directional control and the likely buildup of population would have led to greater flows to New Guinea. Very tentatively, it might also be suggested that as the climax approached, the Timor route may, from some points of view, have become a little less rather than more acceptable to migrants.

In general, it seems likely to have been much more feasible to travel via Timor to the Sahul Shelf than Birdsell represented or could represent on the basis of the evidence available to him. Two preliminary points are:

• The attainment of New Guinea depended on first reaching Borneo. Populations may have existed there before the last ice age but it is assumed that the main flow came initially from mainland South-east Asia. Even if we think of eventual migrants as merely inquisitive wanderers, direct flow from the mainland to Borneo was interdicted for substantial periods. It is possible that until maritime skills were developed this direct flow to Borneo depended on a seafall to close to 40 metres bp. This would suggest that for something like 90–87 000, 76–62 000, 57–55 000 and continuously after 47 000 BP, access to Borneo was not dependent on sea movement. Alternatively, Borneo may have been cut off for trickling movements out of the mainland for 34 000 or so years during 100 000 to

47 000 BP — to be cautious, say for half or rather more of the time. So long as human beings could manage a trip maximum of about 35 kilometres, Timor was accessible throughout the whole ice age and, indeed, the preceding interglacial.

- Access to Timor at the eastern end of the Lesser Sundas depended on seven trips from Java/Bali. But of these, four did not exceed 6 kilometres, a distance swimmable in slack water between tides. None of the remaining trips was as long as the one from Borneo to Sulawesi. Variations in sea level had little significance for sea distances and Timor was relatively easily attained at all sea levels after 115 000 BP.

Two crucial considerations follow. First, although we know little of the population of Borneo, its potential as a source of migrant supply seems far lower, prior to about 25 000 BP, than that of mainland South-east Asia, Sumatra and Java during the periods when Borneo was not easily attained. Secondly, the detailed conditions of transfer from Timor to and across the Australian Shelf, compared to the transfer conditions from Sulawesi to New Guinea, need to be examined thoroughly at various sea levels and not merely at the climax.

Comparing Sulawesi and Timor as base points for migrant departure, the direct

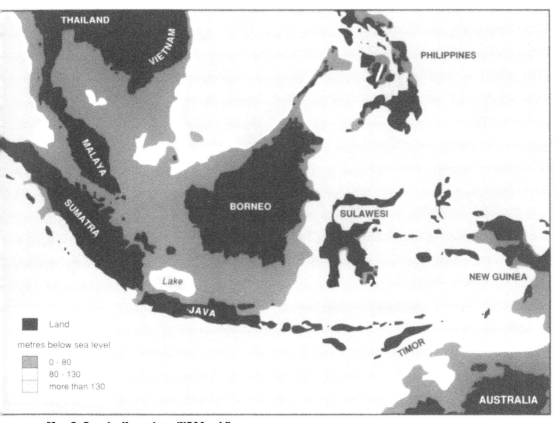

Map 2: Sea depth contour (NOAA grid)

distance from Sulawesi to New Guinea was much longer than that from Timor to the present Australian coastline. Sea level changes did not affect the Sulawesi to New Guinea route significantly except at the New Guinea end. Similarly, the Timor–Australian distance was determined by events at the Sahul Shelf. A reappraisal of the latter transforms one's view of the migration process.

First, let us take the coarse NOAA grid (map 2, p. 19). This conforms to Birdsell's view of the Sulawesi–New Guinea route, though more detailed bathymetric measures around New Guinea might produce some qualifications. By contrast, the NOAA tapes (map 3, below) suggest very important changes occurring between Timor and north-west Australia at crucial sea levels of −40 and −60 metres bp. These levels are very relevant to the fluctuations shown in the Chappell diagram (graph 1, p. 15). Remembering that the Timor–Australia route was much shorter than that from Sulawesi to New Guinea, the NOAA tapes suggest:

- a seabed exposure not very far from the mid-point of the Timor–Australia sea distance; and
- a massive land exposure with two tongues of land extending at either side of the Bonaparte Gulf towards Timor at −60 metres bp, reducing the transfer from Timor to a single sea trip not much longer than the maximum single one (of eight

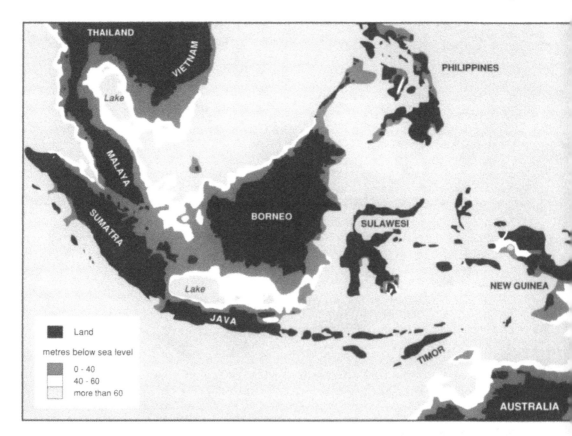

Map 3: Sea depth contour (NOAA tapes)

or so) from Sulawesi. This would suggest maximum success probability by movement from East Timor to Troubadour Shoal at about 9 degrees 30 minutes south and 128 degrees 30 minutes east.

We are, then, invited to investigate this different NOAA picture by reference to detailed bathymetric data. These show the NOAA grid to be highly deficient in detailed terms and indeed point to easier transfer paths at these relatively high sea levels. Nevertheless, they confirm the importance of the issue raised by the NOAA tapes.

The AUSLIG map, as presented (map 4, p. 23), shows in comparatively great detail the seabed contours at 60, 80 and 150 metres and, at certain points, also includes some sections of 70 metre contours. It also shows, as specific numbers beside many locations, the contour level closest to the present surface. This picture should be considered, bearing in mind that it is bounded on the Timor side by the legal delimitation of the boundary between the Australian and Indonesian seabed and that only the Australian section is covered. Admiralty Charts show that some (but not much) shallow water exists on the Timor side of this boundary and also that there appears to be a large section of deep water between Troubadour Shoal and the islands running to the east from East Timor.

Three observations follow from an inspection of the 60 metre contour levels. At a seafall to −60 metres bp with no adjustment for seabed uplift:

- a long chain of islands would extend about 750 kilometres along the full length of Timor and Roti, with most of these islands very close together so that transfer along the full length of the chain should have presented little difficulty to people capable of reaching the islands. Set at distances as close, in certain locations, as about 90 kilometres from Timor/Roti, they would have been visible from Timor. *Most of them lie beyond the 150 metre contour.* The NOAA tapes (map 3, opposite) missed most of these areas.
- Two broken and divided land masses would indeed extend out from the Australian coast north and south of Bonaparte Gulf, as indicated in a simplified way by NOAA.
- Between the outer chain of islands and these two broken tongues of land would lie a large variety of stepping stones providing many possible routes for migrants to a continental landfall. The two that appear most direct are (a) Roti–Ashmore Reef–Cartier Island–South Bonaparte and (b) East Timor–Troubadour–Marie Shoal–Bathurst Island. But there are many other variants, somewhat more demanding. The presence of these alternatives might have been important to the extent that they would have limited conflict between different groups of stragglers *en route* to Australia. (Though it does not seem to be a primary alternative, there was a possible line from Cartier Island through Heywood Shoal, Browse Island and on to a third tongue of land at Lynher Bank. This would have taken Aborigines well south of Bonaparte Gulf and moving towards the point about Rowley Shoal where the Leeuwin Current might have influenced their fortunes.) A search of the bathymetry to North-west Cape does not suggest any promising routes by sea further south.

The 60 metre contour is given greatest prominence because Chappell proposes three occasions at 'about' 112 000, 64 000 and 35 000 BP when the seas fell to this level or a little lower (indeed Chappell suggests that the '64 000 BP' occasion is probably underestimated). Using the unadjusted 60 metre contour line is already conservative on this basis.

Continuing with this constraint, the map shows, as numbers, important locations where substantial land areas would have surfaced at sea levels higher than −60 metres bp. The great majority of the islands close to Timor would have existed as such at −40 metres bp. In other words, they would have been exposed and with much the same surface dimension as at −60 metres bp, during very long periods. The Chappell graph (graph 1, p. 15), read literally, would imply such an exposure during 114–110000, 89–87000, essentially 77–62000, 57–55000 and continuously from 47000 BP until 8000 BP during the last great sea rise. As indicated in relation to numbers shown beside some emerging seabed areas between these islands and Australia, there would also be substantial numbers of stepping stones towards Australia at this relatively high sea level. We do not need to depend on reading Chappell's data literally to conclude that there were several very long periods when a variety of pathways were available from Timor to Australia. Aborigines did not have to await seafalls to −60 metres bp. The crucial question becomes one of the likely time at which they might have had the maritime capability to travel about 90–100 kilometres by sea — not very different from the maximum distance requirement for the Sulawesi–New Guinea route.

At about −60 metres bp, however, the task may have been easier than that shown by the 60 metre contour level. This is because of the isostatic effect of sea lowering — the consequential seabed uplift. The AUSLIG map (map 4, opposite) includes, therefore, the 80 metre contour mark and, in some strategic locations, a dotted 70 metre contour level. This is not the place to discuss the technicalities of isostatic adjustment. What is clear is that the transfer task beyond the island chain was significantly easier than is implied by the simple 60 metre contour. Seabed uplift was slow. It is relevant, therefore, that apart from the first lowering to this level, a great deal of the isostatic adjustment had occurred long before the lowering to the −60 metres bp level.

In distance terms, then, it was no more difficult to travel from Timor to Australia at −40 or −60 metres bp than it was to move from Sulawesi to New Guinea. In terms of visibility, the same conclusion follows. So far as target considerations go, the matter is strongly in favour of the Timor–Australia route. The islands east of Sulawesi were a relatively narrow line oriented in an easterly direction. This route required significant directional capacity. Though individual islands south-east of Timor were small, the likelihood of missing landfall in a 750 kilometre chain presented front-on was minimal. Only maritime capability to stay afloat and move in a south-easterly direction over the initial stage was essential. Minimal navigation and quite crude floating platforms were needed. It seems plausible, therefore, that, given these conditions and given the interruptions to access from mainland South-east Asia to Borneo, the Timor–Australian route was the more likely ancestral and long-sustained path to Australia.

This is not to rule out the Sulawesi–New Guinea route. But it does suggest that until about 47000 BP, after which flows from the mainland through Borneo were unimpeded for several millennia, and until significant directional control was achieved, the Sulawesi–New Guinea route was less significant. Once directional control was achieved, there may have been little to choose between the two. It is indeed possible that, with improving sailing capability, other flows of people from the north towards New Guinea may have exceeded those passing through Timor. But this was relatively late. And the question remains: if such people, with such

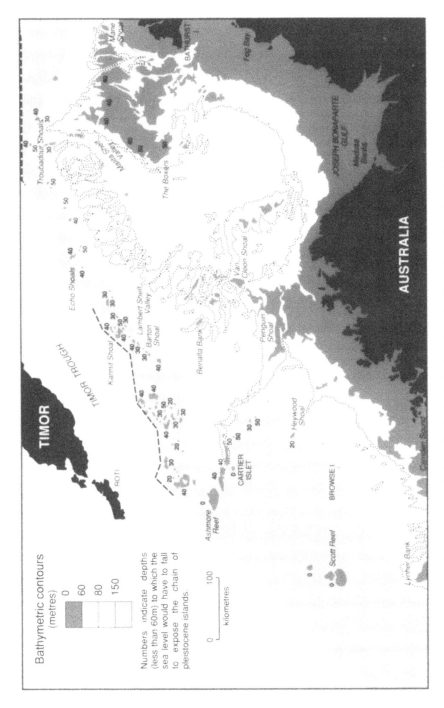

Bathymetric contours (metres)

- 0
- 60
- 80
- 150

Numbers indicate depths (less than 60m) to which the sea level would have to fall to expose the chain of pleistocene islands.

0   100

kilometres

TIMOR

ROTI

TIMOR TROUGH

Troubadout Shoals

Mane Shoals

BATHURST I

Fog Bay

Tassie Shoal

JOSEPH BONAPARTE GULF

Medial Bank

Echo Shoals

Karmt Shoal

Lambert Shelf

Barton Shoal

Benalla Bank

The Boxers

Van.

Cloon Shoal

AUSTRALIA

Penguin Shoal

Heywood Shoal

CARTIER ISLET

Ashmore Reef

BROWSE I

Scott Reef

Lynher Bank

Cassini Shoals

Map 4: Pleistocene map of northwestern Australia (to Australia–Indonesia seabed boundary). Based on AUSLIG transverse mercator projection

maritime skills, reached Australia, why do Australian Aborigines, in contrast with those in New Guinea (and Cape York), show such limited maritime capability? We can return to this matter later.

The Timor proposal seems to be capable of test by Australian scholars. This arises from the fact that at present sea levels some proposed major stepping stones lie above sea level. The biggest surface area is Ashmore Reef. Because it lay astride several possible routes, Cartier Island might be more interesting as a testing ground. And there are others, even including the outlier of Scott's Reef. Prehistorians are accustomed to claim that all the oldest sites lie underneath the sea. A thorough investigation of those areas presently above the surface and within Australian territory seems to be demanded.

In the meantime one final point might be raised, though very tentatively. Between, say, 30–25 000 BP, the 80 metre AUSLIG contour line would be highly relevant. This would yield large if broken land masses ringing Bonaparte Gulf. Population could grow in the whole island area and the population mass would simplify the transfer to the present Australian mainland in the final stages. Successful migration could have accelerated. Heretical as it may be, however, one is led to wonder whether the final sea lowering, far from aiding migration, may have introduced some obstacles to it in strictly maritime terms. Most of the island chain south-east of Timor rises out of water more than 150 metres deep and some of it from depths of several hundred metres. Many islands have extremely steep sides. A sea lowering to -130 metres bp would mean that arriving migrants would often have been presented with almost sheer 100 metre cliffs, unlike the conditions at -40 or -60 metres. This could have added 30–50 kilometres to the initial sea trip unless the migrants were targeted to points opposite East Timor.

This applies with even greater force to the Sulawesi–New Guinea route. In this case, the line of islands did not lie close offshore from the shelf. Inability to make landfall on one could have been disastrous. It is possible, then, that on this route successful migration depended around the climax not only on directional control but also on increased speed of passage — requiring more sophisticated craft than on the Timor route.

Leaving this tentative issue aside, directional control and sea distances do not exhaust the issues. Winds and currents were also important. Winds were crucial on long hauls; currents, especially tidal currents, have been regarded as important in narrow sea gaps. Unless the north-west monsoon altered significantly during the ice age, it blew directly from Timor to the island chain to the south east. On the Sulawesi–New Guinea route, it angled across the line of transfer. This added to the directional control requirements from Sulawesi but supported transfer from Timor. Ice age currents are even more problematical. Today, the southern equatorial current cuts southward through the island chain leading from Sulawesi, accentuating the effects of wind-drift and the need for directional control. In the case of Timor, any effects of such a current would be reduced by the great length of the island chain confronting migrants (with the exception of those from Roti and the extreme west of Timor). It has been suggested, in any event, that at certain times of the year (for perhaps two months preceding the onset of the full monsoon), a net surface drift from Timor to the Australian coast prevails. It appears that the general current conditions and this drift are likely to have been sustained in ice age conditions, given the absence of any net drift between

Australia and New Guinea — there was no effect from the physical joining of New Guinea and Australia (personal communication, Dr Wolanski, Institute of Maritime Science, Queensland).

Stepping stones in the pathways: possible time lags in migration

Sea distances (with wind and current problems) were not the only issues confronting the movement of human beings out of South-east Asia. There was also the possible dilatory influence of the land masses through which people passed. This is a matter that might escape the interest of non-Malthusians. One does not, however, need to be a Malthusian to appreciate that early humans might have accepted the benefits of resources as they passed by and spent time in waxing and multiplying. It is important to note that we are about equally ignorant of the actual presence of human beings in the Philippines, Sulawesi and Timor, so that there is little here to guide us. Moreover, we have to speculate about the population potential of the exposed Sunda Shelf in periods when substantial areas were exposed by seafalls to around −50 metres bp.

When seas fell to close to −40 metres bp humans could walk from Sumatra to Borneo; at −50 metres bp a similar walk directly north from Java was possible; and by −60 metres bp Borneo lay with almost direct access from Thailand and Vietnam (see NOAA maps 2 and 3, pages 19 and 20). The exploitation and occupation of the exposed Sunda Shelf was common to all early sources of ancestors of potential Aboriginal migrants in either the Gulf of Thailand or the Java Sea. From Java, however, two routes lay — to Borneo north or along the Lesser Sundas to Timor. The potential resources of the Lesser Sundas were considerably less, even though more readily acceptable, than those of Borneo. To those resources need to be added the population potential of former seabed on the Shelf.

Moreover, at Borneo there was another parting of the ways, one leading to Sulawesi, the other to the Philippines. Taking merely Borneo, Sulawesi and the Philippines into account, their resources vastly exceeded those of the Lesser Sundas. In terms of sea distances at −40 to −60 metres bp, Aborigines stood on the edge of Occam's razor in making the choice between the Philippines and Sulawesi (see NOAA maps 2 and 3, pages 19 and 20). It seems probable, therefore, that there could have been a much longer timelag in the initiation of migration beyond Java–Borneo than beyond Java–Lesser Sundas. Just how long this timelag might have been depends on production possibilities and rates of net reproduction. It is an essentially economic–demographic–ecological issue to which prehistorians might give some attention. It could have been a very long time relative to the decision-making in the Lesser Sundas, particularly if Timor travellers did not require much sailing as distinct from rafting skills.

The island chain south-east of Timor may have offered a rich environment for fish and birdlife. Many areas at −60 metres bp would probably have acquired vegetation within a century or so. It is possible that travellers along this route could also multiply. But any populations in this area must have been oriented towards the sea and indeed to movement between islands. Their incentive to be mobile by sea was very high.

On the other hand, as population buildup occurred in Borneo and Sulawesi, it might be hypothesised that the flow of migrants to New Guinea would be larger than through Timor to Australia. Nevertheless, at sea levels of the order of -65 metres bp, this probably larger human nucleus appears to have faced significantly greater risks in sea passage. We can only guess at the extent to which higher risks and a larger population base offset the probably lower risks and lower population base through Timor.

Birdsell's omission of a possible passage to New Guinea directly or indirectly from the Philippines seems curious. There are, indeed, two relatively long sea passages if one contemplates movement due south; and wind and current conditions exposed mariners moving south from the Philippines to high transfer costs (the risk, in the absence of directional controls, of being blown out into the Pacific Ocean). Given this, movement from Java to the Philippines may seem to have invited merely a return trip to Borneo. Nevertheless, the passage of some to the Philippines from Borneo may have been important. Only one short sea trip was required. Once there, very substantial production possibilities on land and sea were available. And it seems possible that, given the conditions of the Philippines, important opportunities and incentives to innovate in sea travel were presented. To consider this, we need to look more generally at innovation possibilities.

Maritime innovations

There is no meaningful theory of innovations. Nothing is known of very early watercraft. The rafts/canoes in southern Australia do not suggest themselves as means of transfer over 100 kilometres of sea along any South-east Asian island routes. Perhaps Aborigines lost the skills. Perhaps, however, they merely adapted techniques known at the time of the departure of their ancestors, using locally available materials. Thus Tasmanian efforts to tie layers of bark together, efficient for short trips but certain to be water-logged quickly (Jones, 1977), could either be local efforts or an echo of the use, in a similar way, of radically different materials in island South-east Asia. They contrast with the much more sophisticated New Guinea and Cape York craft (including various types of outrigger canoes) about which much has been written (Mulvaney and White, 1987; Walker and Sun Xiangjun, nd). The single-hull bark canoes used elsewhere in Australia do not commend themselves for sea transport. In the light of the following, it is intriguing that around the Kimberley coast and in the Gulf of Carpentaria we have today expert raft 'tide riders' using, with great skill, ostensibly highly primitive raft equipment (Flood, 1983).

Human beings did not need to encounter sea passages to come to terms with the capacity of timber to float. They must have observed floating timber in many areas of Eurasia. Nor did they need to design a *sailing* raft/canoe in order to contemplate the directional requirements of navigation. Prehistorians' efforts to trace through island South-east Asia to New Guinea the common linguistic roots of words for 'canoes' (Walker and Sun Xiangjun, nd) seem to deal with issues too recent to be relevant to the innovation of early modes of transport by water, though they may be highly relevant to an understanding of an acceleration of maritime technology and migration.

Since no ancient craft remain and nothing of the appropriate age is ever likely to be recovered, we have to speculate. This is clearly one case where the demand for something tangible to study is an obstacle to relevant hypotheses. Economic historians will be accustomed to Rostow's attempts to introduce the four Great Ratios of economic history. To those with some sense of humour, let me present another Great Ratio, this time for palaeoeconomic history: the tree : humans ratio, with a subset in the form of the giant-grass : humans ratio. In both cases, my favourite children's book would define them as huge, enormous and VERY LARGE. The fact that these ratios might not have been quite constant is irrelevant.

Trees and the logs that derive from them were offered everywhere to human beings. At the margins of any water body they demonstrated their ability to float and support other matter. In mainland and island South-east Asia, most of the giant grasses, the bamboos (Lessard and Chouinard, 1980), also proliferated far back in time. Much tougher for weather to destroy, bamboos nevertheless were exposed to two problems. The clumps in which they grew could be washed away by heavy rain scouring and they had a relatively short life expectancy. Typically they had one grand inflorescence and died as a clump. Moreover, the primitive tools of early humans could relatively easily cut them as straight, tapered stems. One did not need the hafted ground axe. And one person could handle them. Here are two types of objects that we can be confident were available in mass to early humans.

Various efforts have been made to suggest possible pre-Neolithic craft, tending to focus on a canoe, sailing raft or simplified outrigger (Lessard and Chouinard, 1980; Walker and Sun Xiangjun, nd). It seems more plausible that the earliest versions would be likely to be cruder and more general, and contain elements of all three as the most general and most readily assembled possibility, combining logs from trees and bamboos (Flood, 1983). Even a raft composed entirely of logs or bamboo can be stripped down to combine elements of all three more specialised craft.

The abundance of logs floating in the seas near and in island South-east Asia could probably be tested even from relatively recent literature. I have searched a little of this. In the late eighteenth century, D'Entrecasteaux, in search of the lost La Perouse, reported encountering trees in the ocean near the Admiralty Islands 'enough for a whole fleet' (de Rossell, 1800:132–140). If he was being literal, this meant many thousands. Forty years later, F. D. Bennett reported a 'froth' of logs, dead birds, fish etc. 'extending on either side [of the ship] as far as was visible with the naked eye'.[2] This was east of Halmahera. Bennett noted that many ships' captains claimed to have experienced similar phenomena.[3] Wilson on board *Gipsy* in 1842 reported at 0.32S 'Calm and light winds: immense trunks of trees are seen floating about washed from the shores of New Guinea' (unpublished journal reference, thanks to Nora Forster).

Given the life expectancy of trees, the number of limbs in their canopies, growth down to the seashore or along rivers and the frequent high winds and heavy rainfall of island South-east Asia (and the east coast of the mainland), and given the minimal human claims on timber, it seems inconceivable that there was not always a large supply of floating logs in the seas east of the Malay Peninsula. The same applies to bamboos.

To contemplate some primitive craft and experiment with it in still water is one thing; to do the same in surf, high winds and tidal rips another. Human beings could have made still water experiments on mainland South-east Asia. But were they ever able to experiment in relatively quiet waters closer to the first sea trip towards New Guinea/Australia?

Here we need to go back to sea depth contours. Prehistorians have not paid much attention to the seabed of the Sunda Shelf, preferring to think of it as, at certain times, simply exposed land for pedestrians. To repeat an earlier warning, given siltation and erosion in an area as tectonically active as island South-east Asia, one should not make too much of the specifics of the modern seabed.

The 60 metre depth contour in NOAA maps (maps 2 and 3, pp. 19 and 20) (with no seabed adjustment) shows four large bounded depressions once the seas had fallen by this amount — two off north-west Sumatra, below Bangkok, and two east of Djakarta. With a conservative adjustment for seabed uplift, it might be proposed that the 65–70 (or more) metre depth contour approximately indicates seabed exposure at −60 metres bp seafall. When the seas fell to around −90 metres bp, NOAA suggests two additional substantial depressions emerging out of the Gulf of Thailand. These latter two depressions are relevant in relation to exposed land surfaces only after about 25 000 BP. The other three potentially affect human behaviour at about 112 000, 64 000 and 35 000 BP.

In addition to these depressions, some probable drainage lines remaining today can be identified, though it is probable that the procedures adopted to establish these depth contour lines would miss those filled over the past 8–10 000 years by siltation. An additional feature of the Sunda seabed is that it tends to fall towards the south-east. Were seas to decline today, significantly more land would surface from Vietnam/Thailand and Borneo than from Malaya or Java.

Whatever its population potential, the Sunda Shelf was very much more than a pedestrian pathway. Were these depressions riverine valleys with ancient drainage systems, now concealed, running through them? Were there drainage systems that provided only overflow systems for lakes? Were there primeval now-silted river systems in the Gulf of Thailand and below the Java Sea that had large, relatively deep areas in these depressions where any primeval rivers spread out over large expanses? Were these depressions significantly deeper than they are today, having perhaps been silted significantly over the past millennia?

If these questions indicate the ignorance of a non-geographer, they also suggest that prehistorians may be missing a potential feast of research projects by not thoroughly investigating the Sunda seabed. Advice from the US Navy Oceanographic Service and from some oil companies in Bangkok suggests that the large depression north of Java was most probably a potential 'lake', surfacing as such at a seafall to about −60 metres bp. There is much greater uncertainty about the large depression below Bangkok and the two that appear at lower contours extending from the Gulf of Thailand. Here, resolution can probably be achieved only by seismic survey — or another ice age.

If the slope in the seabed persisted far back in time, people from Thailand/Malaya and Java would have been presented for thousands of years on several occasions with a large river valley, at least with an extension of the Chao Phraya or Menam River from Bangkok. In Java, one massive 'lake' and another smaller but very substantial one to the east would most probably have been presented on similar occasions for similar periods.

All explorers like naming objects. In these cases, I originally proposed that the two main potential 'lakes', as currently delineated, might appropriately be named Lake Migdol (below Bangkok) and Lake Baalzephon (off Java) (Exodus 14.2) on the grounds indicated in Exodus 14.21 (King James version). They might after all disappear with the wave of a hand! The novelty of the NOAA data and the difficulty of comparing their evidence with the Admiralty Charts prompt some caution in naming! The Admiralty Charts do, however, confirm the depression above East Java. It should also be noted that there are other subsea depressions of lesser size, and the following discussion does not depend on the named cases. However, the scale of these depressions would mean something of the first importance and some effort to test their existence would be warranted. With some trepidation, I suggest the names Lake Java and Lake Thailand. It might be noted that north-west near Sumatra another depression shows that might perhaps be a Lake Malaka.

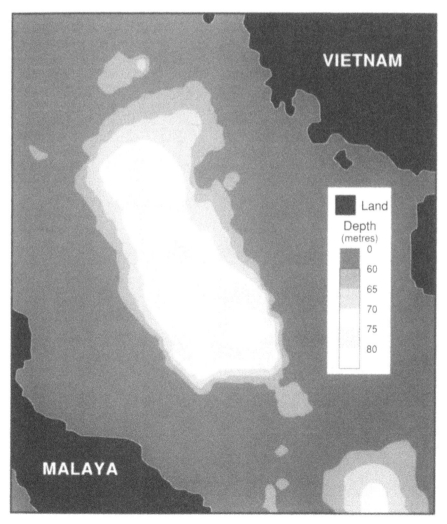

Map 5: Lake Thailand

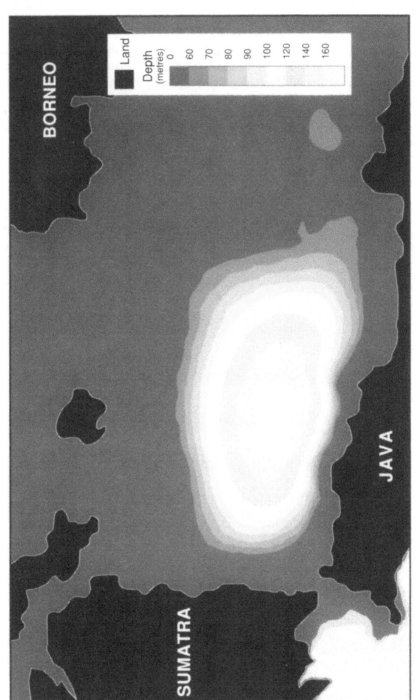

Map 6: Lake Java

Confining attention for purposes of simplicity to Lake Java (map 6, opposite) as an example, the following scenario is suggested. The lake in the exposed Sunda Shelf off Java would be fed with large volumes of fresh water, supplied by streams from Java. These streams would also feed in logs and bamboos (see my earlier comments on tree/human relativities). The lake might have become freshwater, the habitat for birdlife and freshwater fish, while the surrounding land would accumulate vegetation to attract animals. But even as a salt lake (with gradually reducing salinity), it and its surroundings would have presented a major focus for human beings on land and water. The same applies to the depression above East Java, though in this case the water flows would be primarily from Borneo.

Rather than early humans in island South-east Asia specifically inventing *de novo* a raft/canoe to sail the sea, it seems far more likely that they would have discovered by serendipity a variety of floating objects to cope with various tasks in lake areas. The area between Java and Borneo presents itself as an excellent location close to the maritime embarkation points. If, for example, the lake(s) existed for 1000 years before the sea reclaimed its own, forty generations of people had the opportunity to discover, exploit, adapt and extrapolate beyond their landbound limits. The higher the seabed rose as seas fell, the longer the lake(s) existed.

A single log rolls; stability can be achieved with two. Bamboos washed across a couple of logs form a platform on which one might sit, stand or place objects. Tie the bamboo and logs together with vine or rattan ropes and one can drag a raft through the water. Sit on the raft and paddle with feet or hands and it moves. A flat stick is better as a paddle. Only one person has to do it for others to copy. One might indeed say this is child's play. Alternatively, a bamboo clump, tangled in vines, has considerable supportive quality. Rearrange the vines, tie the bamboo tips together, and the essential triangular shape better suited for directional motion is presented. Separate the bamboo stems and a rectangular or triangular plane is presented, depending on how the natural taper of bamboos is used. Tie bamboo into bundles, interlock the bundles and one might have a craft suggestive of the more recent Tasmanian bundled bark craft.

Nature provided early humans with continuous instruction in geometry. Three basic plane shapes exist or are formed naturally by found timber objects — a single line with mass, a triangle and an oblong, the last fairly easily adjusted into a rectangle or square. These shapes did not need to be manufactured; the materials were ready to hand in profusion. With bamboos lashed across three logs, one could have the generic ancestor of the raft, the canoe and the outrigger. Such an object, including tangled vines, could have been delivered in rough form, perhaps frequently, to human beings after a downpour. The problem might, indeed, have consisted simply of working out what to do with it. A person of reasonable intelligence, with rational preferences favouring a given output with less rather than more effort — economic man — might not have taken very long to find some answers, and to improve on nature's offering. At the same time, the size of Lake Java would have required the development of craft to deal with at least choppy conditions if the lake were to be exploited — in other words there would have been a move a long way towards full maritime capability.

The preoccupation in the literature with sails, keels, outriggers and so on has independent merit in relation to later specialisations in maritime craft. At an earlier date, sails and directional equipment were probably crucial if one focuses on migration via Borneo, Sulawesi and New Guinea.[4] They are far less significant to any passage through Timor direct to Australia. If pre-Neolithic humans could use fire to burn holes through logs to achieve a lattice base with cross members, a very strong and highly seaworthy craft could have been generated, making possible the transfer of considerable numbers of people from Timor across 100 kilometres of sea around 60–70 000 years ago. But fire was not essential. Floating trees moving in sea currents did more than provide the potential to carry people. They delineated flow directions. This would be particularly the case in Timor during October– November, when there were likely to be relatively quiet seas and a net surface drift set lee on to Australia.

In all this speculation, two points are important. Human beings did, in fact, reach Australia and New Guinea at least 40 000 years ago. And in Australia, their recent descendants show little capacity for marine technology (Jones, 1977; Walker and Sun Xiangjun, nd). Logs float for a long time. According to modern safety standards, bamboo's characteristic skin and segmented compartments give it a seaworthy life of six months with continuous exposure to the sea (Lessard and Chouinard, 1980). Together or separately, these found materials could be exploited effectively without access to the ground-hafted axe that appears around 30 000 BP. Relatively simple ancestor craft of either bamboo or logs could have provided humans with the means to travel further than Timor (the longest leg to Timor at −60 metres bp was about 30 kilometres from Alor). They could easily have made the first passage (cf map 3, p. 20) from Borneo either to Sulawesi (about 50 kilometres at −60 metres bp) or to the Philippines (about 40 kilometres at −60 metres bp).

Beyond Sulawesi, however, the islands forming the chain to New Guinea were, apart from Ceram, relatively small and narrow, and aligned easterly. Directional control was far more important here than on the Timor run. The risks of missing landfall were very high. This, however, is not to imply rejection of the possibility of arrival in New Guinea via Borneo, Sulawesi and eastward, with less efficient craft in smaller numbers at an earlier stage.

The shape of Sulawesi, with its long peninsulas and deep bays, offered an opportunity and an incentive to achieve directional control. Prevalent wind directions there might have led to concentration on (rattan?) sails. But it is appropriate to draw attention to the forgotten leg to New Guinea, the possibility of transfer from Borneo to the Philippines and back through Borneo to Sulawesi. The island structure of the Philippines presented a persistent pull factor for would-be marin- ers. They tend to be ignored in a modern perspective because they are mostly too small for exploitation. But even at −40 metres bp, many became of significant size.

The first landfall in the Philippines was most probably the result of a walk up through Palawan to Busuanga Island and thence a short sea crossing to Mindoro or some very short sea trips up the Sulu Archipelago to Mindanao. At −60 metres bp Mindoro is joined to Luzon and thence continuous land to Leyte. Here was a vast safety net to catch early mariners blown eastward. Whatever casualties may have occurred, the risks of experimentation were greatly reduced and temptations to explore nearby islands considerable. One can only guess. But here appears to be an ideal location for people to be able and to want to learn about sails and stayboards. Such people could, indeed, have become the 'island hoppers' that Geoffrey

Blainey evoked (Blainey, 1985). They could have reached New Guinea, most safely via Borneo and Sulawesi. Once skilled, they could have arrived in New Guinea in larger numbers than those passing to Australia via Timor. But it seems likely that they would have been longer delayed and served to provide a later, accelerating flow of migrants to New Guinea and thence, perhaps, to Australia. But if these people ever went to Australia, why did their descendants forget so much of seacraft? The implication might be that these people did not really penetrate to Australia except, perhaps, to Cape York.

If this is so, it brings Timor into even greater focus as the main immediate ancestral source and perhaps the take-off point for a very large proportion of Aboriginal migrants to Australia. Successive sea lowerings to around −65 metres bp (and with some qualifications) the deeper climactic lowering of the sea centred for thousands of years around 17 000 BP — comparable with that at about 135 000 BP) would help to accelerate that flow. Supplementation by migration at an early stage with relatively primitive craft east from Sulawesi would have similar windows of migration opportunity. This would still allow penetration of the present Australia from both the north-west and north.

But unless any later Aborigines, having exploited more advanced craft and passed southward from New Guinea to the present Australian mainland, forgot or chose to abandon more developed maritime skills, those who settled the Australian mainland seem more likely to have arrived before the development of higher maritime skills or to have passed along routes not requiring advanced technology. New Guinea might then have been the staging point for the greater adventure, the conquest of the Pacific Ocean. In more parochial terms, it is also possible that later, more skilled arrivals drove some out of New Guinea onto the Australian mainland.

'Pull' factors

Before embarking on a larger canvas of possibilities, it is convenient to link directly the preceding discussion with one element of migration economics — the so-called 'pull' factor. Hunter gatherers may, indeed, have been perpetually inquisitive beings determined or willing to go where no person had been before. In travelling in island South-east Asia they could, for many of their sea trips, have seen their objective before departure. This also holds true from Timor.

It is possible that some travellers returned. Had they returned to Timor, they might have first reported an extensive fishing ground and, further to the east, a climate, vegetation and animals quite similar to those of Timor (though they might have encountered a few possibly dangerous animals; Allen et al., 1977). I would suggest that no such reports were necessary and that, even where land was invisible, human beings on Timor (and on successive islands east of Sulawesi) knew that land lay before them. They knew also that the land contained water, vegetation, bird and animal life. From Timor, in particular, they could almost chart the destination coast.

Lightning strikes and bushfires could have provided smoke observable from Timor at −60 metres bp along the enlarged Australian coastline or possibly even at −40 metres bp at the complex of land, particularly east of Troubadour Island.

There is Western Australian evidence (Deutch and Muir, 1980) of bushfire glow across flat terrain visible at a distance of 200 kilometres. Smoke is visible at a greater distance, particularly from an elevated position such as the coast of Timor. Where there is smoke there is not only fire but vegetation.

But there was, in addition, a continuous regular flow of advice from west New Guinea to Sulawesi and from north-west Australia to Timor. This was in the form of the seasonal migration of birds, one group from New Guinea to Sulawesi, the other from Australia to Timor. The migrations involved very large numbers of birds and meant inflow and outflow at relatively regular times annually, and in highly visible numbers. The birds from New Guinea to Sulawesi and from Australia to Timor included amongst others the brilliantly coloured 'dollarbird' (eaten in Indonesia today), which was a colourful and noisy messenger and direction finder. Where there are such birds there is fresh water; to a hunter gatherer one might reasonably expect fresh water to imply vegetation, fish and game in addition to the edible birds themselves (Morton and Brennan, nd; Nix, 1974). The island chain close to Timor suggests an area offering an extremely rich environment for seabirds, which perhaps moved in large numbers between Timor and the islands to the south-east. One does not therefore need to envisage a blind quest across the sea.

This matter might be advanced further if one could date the fossil flamingoes that have been found in central and north-east Australia (as, indeed, one might also date the climatic conditions of these areas). These were large migratory birds, brightly coloured, that could be expected to migrate between the exposed Sunda Shelf and Australia. Flying at all hours, day and night, in large numbers at relatively low elevation and uttering loud calls, they may have been excellent pathfinders. For several reasons, the fossil flamingoes may deserve more dating effort.

Notes

1 For example, the massive eruption of Krakatoa left part of the island remaining and a section of the seabed rose above sea level immediately adjacent to the original island. Again, two subsea 'lakes' in the Gulf of Carpentaria and Bass Strait are shown on modern maps. The Bass Strait 'lake' has been investigated by core samples and its presence established far back in time (Bowler and Jones, 1979).

2 *Narrative of a Whaling Voyage Round the Globe*, vol. 2, 1840, np, pp. 62–3: I have to thank Nora Forster for this reference.

3 Australian evidence is not irrelevant. When whites encountered the Murray River it was choked with timber debris and a very expensive clean-up campaign was required. Even current local evidence may be relevant. Thus Canberra's Lake Burley Griffin, which has a limited catchment area and comparatively few trees, requires a clean-up workforce of twenty to thirty men even though, in flood conditions, the dam gates are opened to dispose of floating debris. I have to thank David Pope's sharp eyes as he rides to work for this latter point.

4 Without citing extensive evidence, there is little doubt about islanders in South-east Asia being advanced in marine technology at an early stage (see, e.g., Bellwood, 1985; Gibbons and Clunie, 1986; Horridge, 1987; Kutzbach, 1981; Wasson, 1983). Island South-east Asia was an almost unique area in the world in which to develop sailing or rafting skills.

4

SCARCITY POSSIBILITIES IN ABORIGINAL MIGRATION

'Push' factors

If there were a specific 'pull' in terms of production possibilities to encourage potential migrants, were there also 'push' factors? Here we have to consider broader economic issues. In principle, these issues might be related in a relatively localised form to the Lesser Sundas or to the islands eastward from Sulawesi. Or one might look further afield. In both cases, we may partly depart from the culture-driven, non-Malthusian world conventionally perceived for the early hunter gatherer and consider possibilities which, if not necessarily fully Malthusian, nevertheless turn on possibilities of population/resource (or population/consumption) issues. In the one case, we might simply see populations expanding or resources dwindling in the Lesser Sundas or east of Borneo. Or we might consider possibilities of new entrants from further afield into these areas, driven themselves in part by population/consumption pressures. These new entrants might or might not have reached Australia/New Guinea. Their role could have been merely to 'shepherd', by physical conflict or resource competition, existing groups across the seas; and some of them, in turn, might have been similarly induced to depart. In either case, we need to consider the economic–demographic attitudes of prehistorians, not merely in Australia but also globally.

A first digression: palaeodemography

Demographic analysis is just a little bit more prominent (see, e.g., Hassan, 1981) than economic analysis in the toolkit of prehistorians. At about 120 000 years ago, the global perception is broadly of a tiny world population, subdivided into hunting-gathering bands of an average of forty or so persons, linked culturally into larger groups of about 500 persons. Thus, allowing for some cultural divergence, the world is seen as made up of a few thousand groups, each averaging perhaps around 500 strong. These groups are taken to have penetrated forest areas and occupied desert and sub-arctic regions beyond their favoured tropical and sub-tropical savanna and open woodland terrain by the end of the last interglacial. That they were in much of Africa, southern and northern Europe, India and China and had penetrated into sections of Siberia at one extreme and Java (at a very early stage and possibly after an earlier hominid) at the other seems established (Bellwood, 1985; Hassan, 1981). Only *Homo erectus* (or strictly, evidence of his society), has been identified in Burma, Thailand and Malaya. The presence of *Homo sapiens* in parts of island South-east Asia (Bellwood, 1985) implies a movement from India and/or China into mainland South-east Asia, and consequential coexistence, conflict and cohabitation there. Palaeodemographers propose that this tiny population grew until about 30 000 years ago at a rate a little above zero population growth. After about 30 000 BP population growth quickened and then accelerated in recent years with the development of agricultural and pastoral activity (Hassan, 1981).

Early population estimates are based largely on ideas about 'area carrying capacity' (Birdsell, 1972; Hassan, 1981). This is an animal analogue that rests on ideas of maximum population potential based on area biomass, essentially an externally imposed concept of natural science. This maximum potential is then adjusted downwards to allow for variance in supplies over time, for constraints imposed by strategic resources and for cultural ends that determine the process of population regulation. It is a remarkable concept that has little to do with contemporary human perceptions, preferences and decision-making and appears to disregard the varying degrees of resource competition that human beings faced from other creatures and in progressively expanding the tiny original human niche in the total ecological system. As a physical concept, it offers no real guide to human behaviour. Human beings, wandering over areas of variable dimension, leave, on this perspective, large quantities of 'unused' resources. There appear always to be other useable areas to be exploited. Normal food-gathering and migration are blurred into one process and the notion of scarcity is essentially irrelevant.

When one seeks to discover the empirical processes whereby numbers are derived, it emerges (Birdsell, 1972) that population estimates at about 120 000 years ago are based heavily on estimated densities of recent, supposedly very primitive, hunter gatherers located in 'disadvantageous' areas. A prominent area is in fact Australia, where densities estimated by Radcliffe-Brown in the 1920s are adopted (along with similarly dated estimates by Kroeber for some North American Indians). These estimates are supposed to be relevant to early man on the grounds that the possible but limited technological evolution of these groups is offset by the inhospitable environment (limited biomass). With these tiny populations, unused resources and more regions to wander in, motivation is reduced to almost anything except economics.

The fact that these old density estimates have been substantially revised is not wholly irrelevant. The reliance on old estimates in special areas leaves open the possibility of very large margins of error. Was Australia a 'poor' area 200 years ago compared to Europe during the 'ice age'? Were Australian production possibilities at any stage comparable to those of mainland and island South-east Asia? Given recent revisions of Australian densities, do we now make comparable upward revisions of world population? The answer to all these questions seems likely to be no.

But the basic approach is what seems open to fundamental doubt. Today's world contains vast unused resources because we lack the technology to exploit them, or choose not to. More directly, early populations were increasing, even if only slowly. If early humans were as inquisitive as suggested and sought out preferred areas, the question arises as to when and where they began to come into collision and competition with each other. In particular, how soon did distinct gathering groups in mainland South-east Asia become contiguous, with substantial numbers surrounding others? Once that began to happen, simplistic notions of continuous outward spread into adjoining regions cannot be sustained. It is manifestly unwise to apply to tiny groups the demographic relationships that have been developed for large numbers. This is what much of the existing palaeodemography does. Global populations may have grown extremely slowly because many small groups were non-viable while other groups achieved rapidly expanding populations. Did the latter occur in South-east Asia?

In the end, the issue of choice, of preference, by groups who as a matter of rational desire prefer not to have a chosen optimum disturbed is what is crucial. This optimum — not a maximum — is determined by such matters as production possibilities, technology, skill composition and tastes, with tastes including outputs of cultural concern in addition to mere food gathering. The human preferences of early hunter gatherers and the desired relationship between inputs and outputs need to be taken as heavily conditioned by competitors. Early humans were not at the top of the scientists' food chain; they were often part of it.

The following simple diagrams may help to relate the area carrying capacity concept to that of an economist's optimum. In figure 1a (p. 38), the various lines are successive 'scientific' reductions from some maximum potential based on biomass. In figure 1b (p. 38), let us assume some fixed ratio between dependants and workforce so that an optimal labour input implies an optimal population. The vertical axis could be taken to measure an economist's input and output in energy terms. The horizontal axis measures an economist's labour supply. The shapes of the energy input/output functions would be fluctuations around the horizontal in the case of 'carrying capacity' as in figure 1a. Economists would expect them to be curved, with the growth of energy inputs tending to increase and that of outputs to slacken after some volume of activity. There is no identifiable optimum in the natural science case except by arbitrary external decision. There is one at OD labour in the economists' system. A crude maximum is determined by the maximum distance between the two curves. This maximum can be adjusted to a more distinct 'optimum' concept by altering either or both curves (say OB to OC) to allow for preferences for leisure, loss of efficiency from tending children, degradation of some resource supplies (in e.g., ice age conditions) etc. An optimal labour is then less at OE.

The essential point is that such an economists' optimum is a matter of human (in this case, group) choice and its disturbance may be resisted. Prehistorians tend to think that if some major exogenous disturbance occurred, early hunter gatherers always had something else to fall back on. It is suggested here that they had

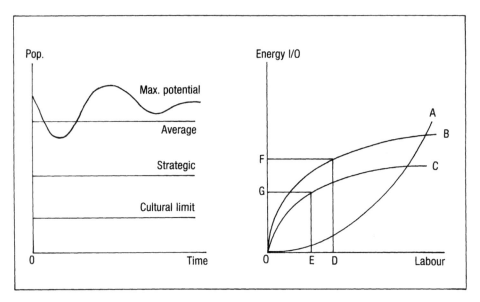

Figure 1a: Area carrying capacity, population and biomass

Figure 1b: Area carrying capacity, population and energy input

options that could include, at least for some, a search for some response to preserve their prefered mode of operation. Alternatively, exogenous disturbances might have been of such magnitude as to induce, even compel, major reallocations of workforce that depended on geographical shifts. These disturbances need not be disadvantageous; it is possible, and indeed likely, that some ice age changes were, at times, beneficial in the sense of improving production possibilities and population potential. Migration was not, then, merely an extension of nomadic practices but in certain circumstances could induce at least some of any group to hive off and move away. This could be total withdrawal from an area (as seems to have happened in the Thar Desert of north-west India; Misra and Rajaguri, 1986; Singh, 1971; Singh *et al.*, 1974; Wasson *et al.*, 1983), or merely a small trickle of separation and relocation of segments of groups. Either adjustment could mean joining or conflicting with other groups in preferred areas; in either case, another equilibrium would be disturbed. Is it possible that during ice age fluctuations some such trickling adjustment/reallocation occurred that impinged not only directly but also indirectly on the occupants of island South-east Asia? And did its volume change over time?

A second digression: aggregate and relative productivity changes

Archaeologists are so preoccupied with the analysis of stone tools as an indicator of technological change that they may be missing a different and possibly more significant source of technological development. This is in the human use of human beings, particularly in the changing allocation of the workforce. Ostensibly, significant changes in toolkits in terms of ground tools (especially hafted ground axes) are identified around about 30 000 BP. Is it possible to suggest the likelihood of earlier readjustments of a different sort? And more particularly, might they be related to migration?

The simple population optimum concept suggested above could be disturbed by changes in either aggregate or relative productivity within any group. Another source of change particularly relevant here is alteration in either direction affecting net reproduction rates through changes in age-specific fertility or death rates. These two possibilities may be, and are likely to be, interrelated. They are what concern the rest of the discussion. The less technically inclined may be prepared to take the following few pages on trust and move to the migration scenarios. In doing so, they should be aware that these scenarios depend on two basic propositions: change may be induced because total productivity increases in some area or because relative productivity of different outputs may change. That is all that is at stake.

An allocative diagram

Traditionally, hunter gatherers may be assumed to have sought a variety of land-based goods in savanna-woodland, in forests, at the seashore and in rivers or lakes. Let us assume, for simplicity's sake, that they gather baskets of 'land goods' and baskets of 'seafoods'. In addition, it is assumed that they are indifferent about the various mixes of these goods but that they will not be satisfied unless they have some limitingly low quantity from each basket. In figure 2 (p. 40), in the upper right quadrant, we can then insert a series of indifference curves, each one representing equally satisfying combinations, and successive curves representing higher levels of satisfaction. No curves go to the axes because some quantities of each basket are necessary. I_1 and I_2 then represent two such indifference curves. The diagonal lines G_1 and G_2 are 'price' ratios, or the rate at which individuals in any group will swap one type of commodity for the other.

In the bottom left-hand quadrant, the line L_1 indicates various allocations possible out of a total workforce of OL_1. In the top left-hand quadrant, OF_1 is some given production function for seafood collection and, in the lower right-hand quadrant, the land gathering production function OV is shown. These two functions follow the conventional shape implying, after some point, decelerating yields.

The base position of the group is taken to be the allocation of OD_1 of labour to seafood and OC_1 to land food gathering, yielding OB_1 of seafoods and OE_1 of land goods. This places them in an optimal position on the indifference curve I_1 at X. Let us assume that some ice age exogenous disturbance occurs that reduces the yield of seafoods per unit of labour input and the production function falls to OF_2. The group does not immediately react to this and persists with the original distribution of the workforce. They will continue to collect OE_1 of land goods but only OB_3 of seafoods. This is not an optimal position in the new conditions and it would be possible to improve matters by redistributing more labour at OD_2 to seafoods and less land labour at OE_2 to land gathering. They will regain an

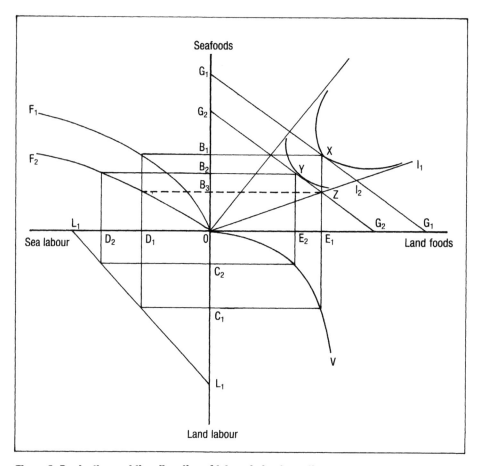

Figure 2: Production and the allocation of labour in hunter gatherer groups

optimum at Y on the indifference curve I_2. This is an improvement on the interim Z point but distinctly inferior to the earlier optimum at X.

One can reverse the procedure by assuming that the base seafood production function was OF_2 and an improvement in conditions lifts it to OF_1. Equally, one can substitute any chosen components of the various outputs of hunter gatherers for those nominated. It should be stressed that this has nothing necessarily to do with any crude maximising assumption. Thus leisure could be placed on either axis (as could other satisfactions in war, ritual, socialising etc.), or one could assume that points X and Y are optimal, conditional upon these other satisfactions.

If tasks were gender-related, with fishing done by men and land food gathering by women, a longterm demographic 'solution' might be sought in the preservation of male children and the killing of female infants. In the first case outlined, a crisis point would in any case be reached if OF_2 fell to such a point that quite inadequate volumes of seafoods were collected or if its shape changed so that declining returns began significantly before the fish catch OB_2 was attained. Population restraint may then be quite inadequate. Tastes might be altered or new locations sought (technological change is deliberately omitted despite this being a logical possibility). In the first instance, the group could move away from coastal resources and concentrate on land gathering. In the second case it could move to seek a better seaside resort. But even before such a crisis point, the consciousness of reduced satisfaction would prompt the group to make some marginal adjustment towards changing tastes, or some marginal relocation, or both.

It is equally possible, within the limits of the diagram and of the historical circumstances, that both yields could rise substantially to such an extent that population constraints are lifted or age-specific fertility and death rates reduced. A growth in population of any group could lead to a socially unmanageable magnitude, prompting splintering.

Both aggregate and relative yields may have been affected in ice age conditions at different times and in different places. Equally, indeed, yields may have fluctuated up and down and moved in directions seemingly contrary to ice age expectations. The dimension and direction of these changes and fluctuations are the crucial issue in the economics and demography of ice age migration.

5

SOME POSSIBLE MIGRATION SCENARIOS

A variety of ice age models has been attempted in non-economic areas. Climatologists, meteorologists, oceanographers, biogeographers, earth scientists, geneticists and others have made massive attempts to try to stimulate a variety of issues during the ice age, either globally or for some major area of the world (e.g. Bryson and Swain, 1981; Bryson and Murray, 1977; Cline, 1981; Gates, 1976; Kutzbach, 1981; Peterson *et al.*, 1979; Walker and Sun Xiangjun, nd; Williamson and Barry, 1974). Unfortunately, little of this bears on island or mainland South-east Asia. Moreover, most of it is directed towards the climax conditions of about 17 000 BP and has only marginal bearing on much of the period relevant to the specific human adaptation over time that took the form of migration into island South-east Asia and to Australia/New Guinea. Certainly, there is no economics in any of the available modelling.

A first basic condition for any palaeoeconomic history is that so far there is no evidence within Australia of markedly different types of human beings (granted the distinction between some gracile and robust people). On the other hand, only a very tiny fraction (perhaps 0.00002%) of ever-dying persons in Australia have been identified (Pardoe, 1988) and a much smaller fraction (perhaps 0.0000003%) actually studied. Nevertheless, this constraint is accepted. So far as 'push' factors go, one must look for processes that, in effect, extruded essentially similar people out of mainland into island South-east Asia and on to Australia. Secondly, so far as the model goes, possible distinct regions might be defined in terms of (a) islands east of Bali and Borneo, (b) islands to the west of the Malay Peninsula, (c) mainland South-east Asia, (d) China, perhaps divided into north and south China, and (e) India. (Biogeographers will be infuriated with this cavalier inattention to micro-variations.)

Thirdly, so far as specification of periods within the ice age goes, we might adopt the Chappell and Shackleton oxygen isotope indicators of sea level variations as broad demarcators (see graph 1, p. 15). However, it is important to be prepared to qualify this acceptance. There are many intriguing time-lags in the influence of exogenous variables in ice age conditions. Eurocentric perceptions of the progression of the ice age suggest a sequence of glaciation, reduced temperatures, increased aridity, vegetational changes and sea level variations. Sea level variations may be far from being the most responsive to the waxing and waning of glaciers. Conventionally, water is locked up in growing glaciers and not returned to the oceans. But vast quantities of water are held in and under land masses, in inland lakes, in forests and even in animals. There may, then, be a significant time lag between the waxing and waning of glaciers and the falling and recovery of sea levels. Similarly, the speed of vegetational adjustments may vary greatly. Nevertheless, sea level variations are a useful and relatively simple proxy for the major ice age ups and downs.

Finally, it would be seriously misleading to treat the ice age as merely a progression towards increasingly difficult conditions. The sea level indicators show marked fluctuations. But, in addition, human beings have a remarkable ability to adapt and innovate and it is possible that exogenous stress may lead to improved circumstances through human response (Boserup, 1965). It is possible that human behaviour foreshortened some of the time-lags that one can now identify and may even have obliterated them.

If climate, vegetation and sea conditions, and land structures at the closing stages of the last interglacial were, in fact, reasonably similar to those of today (allowing for recent deforestation and so on), it seems most plausible that the main candidates for leadership in the vanguard of groups mobile towards island Southeast Asia came from the area of the present Cambodia, Laos, Thailand and Burma (I am not concerned with more distant origins). This mobility might, indeed, have been a combination of overall improvement in periods of glaciation in some parts of these areas and declining seafood yields in others; and with actual reversal in the periods when glaciation waned. The issue of the make-up of the vanguard is important to any 'push' hypothesis. It is highly unlikely that long distance sea travel was possible until very recently, or that some conquering horde trampled their predecessors underfoot in the race to Australia.

It seems doubtful whether genetic research is likely to uncover this vanguard. Genes cannot be passed with their donors motionless (except briefly). It is essential to try to reconstruct the movement of actual people. In the absence of dateable archaeological evidence before 40 000 BP in Java and Borneo and until much later between these locations and New Guinea, any effort at reconstruction at the moment lies at the door of biogeographers, climatologists and oceanographers. Their efforts might be helped by some ideas of economics. In the meantime, three scenarios may be presented on the staging of generations towards Australia/New Guinea.

Scenario I: Wallacean life-styles

Once human beings developed minimal craft sufficient to attain Sulawesi on the one side and the Lesser Sundas as far as Timor on the other, they had achieved more than merely maritime technology. Prehistorians make much of the so-called 'Wallace Line' which roughly demarcates Eurasian animals from those of Australia/New Guinea (Bellwood, 1985). Comparatively little attention is paid to the fact that, west of the Wallace Line, human beings had been subject to relatively intense competition in the food chain and were, indeed, part of the food chain. East of Bali and Borneo, human beings could live, for the first time in their history, without fear of predators (apart from sharks and crocodiles) or even of substantial competition. This is not to imply that radically fewer deaths occurred, though this is not impossible. What is perhaps most significant is that human beings could order their daily lives without much concern for physical security or concern over competitive disorganisation of their activities. For the first time in human history, human beings were, in fact, at the top of the food chain. This was the beginning of an Australian lifestyle.

What this might have meant for productivity, age-specific death rates and linked fertility and, perhaps above all, for the gradual ability of humans to manage and adapt their environment (as Aborigines in Australia so markedly did) is something that should be explored in detail. Biogeographers debate vigorously over the climatic effects of the ice age (and its fluctuations) on mainland and island South-east Asia (we will return to this). It seems agreed that temperatures were little affected and that aridity east of the Wallace Line did not vary much (Bellwood, 1985). The Lesser Sundas, in particular, were almost entirely open-woodland areas (Allen *et al.*, 1988; Bellwood, 1985) with substantial seasonal rainfall — the archetype desiderata of hunter gatherers. They were surrounded by seas that fell and rose. On the relatively steep sides of all the Lesser Sundas, any variation in sea harvests due to the death of coral reefs was likely to occur by exposure as the sea fell or by drowning as the sea rose, though some reefs could keep pace with sea rises. Fluctuations in ice age conditions may, then, have made a quite limited difference to productivity on the sea edge relative to the land, though seafalls could have created somewhat less attractive conditions than sea rises.

With at least adequate conditions for hunting and gathering, and no constraining influences from predators, it seems possible that age-specific death rates might well have fallen significantly. This would have had a feedback on age-specific fertility rates and hence on potential net reproduction rates. Limitation on island size would have restricted population mass until Timor was reached. But in Timor a sufficient nucleus was achievable for a conscious decision to allow or encourage splinter groups to make the jump to north-west Australia at appropriate times during the ice age. This seems a more distinctly 'plannable' decision than the one required to migrate from the islands east of Sulawesi. The most appropriate times would seem likely at somewhere around 65 000 BP, 35 000 BP and then for perhaps 15 000 years, centred on about 17 000 years ago, but broader possibilities have been indicated earlier. Thereafter, as human beings became 'residential', with settled agriculture, the impetus to migrate may have been spent. Alternatively, at these times, the exposure of the Sunda Shelf lessened conflict over access to the Lesser Sundas and allowed the relatively peaceable build-up of early populations.

Scenario II: mainland climate, vegetation and the seas

Throughout 115 000 to about 8000 BP, human beings could always walk down the Malay Peninsula to Bali. With minimal watercraft, they could reach Timor with relative ease. This continuity of access contrasts sharply with the ability to reach

Borneo and hence Sulawesi and the Philippines. These more northerly passages required either relatively advanced marine technology or a substantial seafall. Over the period when we can be reasonably confident that this technology did not exist, human passage to Borneo and beyond was barred during roughly 127–114 000, 109–93 000, 87–77 000, 72 000, 60–57 000 and 54–47 000 BP (the 'dating' is from the sea depth graph and is not intended literally). In other words, unbroken access to Bali to 47 000 BP contrasts with intermittent access to Borneo. The significance of these intermittent episodes provides part of the foundation for Scenario III. In the meantime, a second scenario attempts to link mainland South-east Asia and the southern spine of the Indonesian Islands as a more or less (potentially) continuous process.

This second scenario focuses on the question whether any 'decision' of advance guards of human beings to migrate was accelerated by persons following in their footsteps into the Lesser Sundas or Sulawesi. We know that *Homo erectus* left evidence of his presence before the last ice age in Burma, Thailand and Malaya (Hassan, 1981). Given the established presence of *Homo sapiens* just to the west of Burma, it seems unlikely that these more modern humans did not occupy the very extensive savanna and monsoonal woodlands of Burma, Laos, Thailand and Cambodia at a very early stage. It should be clear that this is merely a reasonable inference; we do not, in fact, know. In the last resort, the reasoning is circular: Aborigines arrived in Australia over 40 000 years ago; they must have passed through island South-east Asia; therefore *Homo sapiens* must have been established in mainland South-east Asia well before the Aborigines arrived here. The option is not plausible: a long march from China (or a long sea trip until much later).

The role of China is a source of considerable debate (e.g. Bellwood, 1985; Flood, 1983; Kirk and Szathmary, 1985). It seems clear that northern and central China, at various times during the ice age, were subject to variable desert conditions as indicated by loess deposits (Derbyshire, 1987; Kukla, 1987; Street and Grove, 1979; Wasson *et al.*, 1983; Whitmore, 1987). These areas escaped extensive glacier development but were probably deeply affected by the derived consequences of glaciation. But, for reasons taken up later, direct intervention by people from China during this period prior to, say, 30 000 years ago, seems likely to be very limited. Once they developed the ability to travel significant distances by sea, they could have passed from Taiwan to the Philippines and thence further south. In this event, their role seems more likely to have been to alter the later genetic make-up of the islands and to contribute to the conquest of the Pacific just as, earlier, they most probably influenced the genetic make-up of mainland South-east Asia. Their significance in directly settling the Americas appears as much more substantial than in the occupation of Australia.

Certainly, if once established in mainland South-east Asia by or during the last interglacial, *Homo sapiens* had a very large and favourable area over which to hunt and gather. Once we enter the last ice age the impact on this habitat is subject to considerable debate. One might, perhaps, begin with the view that populations in the savanna and open woodlands on the mainland experienced, however slowly, a rising *trend* population (possibilities of fluctuation arise in the third scenario). With no ecological changes, one might expect a viable population base at or near the beginning of the last ice age to grow on grounds of adequate resource supplies, technological developments, accumulation of know-how in learning-by-doing, and in reallocations and reskilling of the workforce. Improving per capita consumption would tend to reduce age-specific death rates with a feedback to increased birth rates.

The implied population growth could then have led gradually to increasing group size, unmanageable groups and splintering. Such splintering meant reloca-tion, either through long-distance movement down the Malay Peninsula into Sumatra and Java or by short-distance 'shuffling' migration, herding competing groups south and east. Sea levels were no bar as far as Bali.

But a prime determinant of such a potential trend growth of population was resource supply or, more generally, ecological conditions. Eurocentric and climac-tic views of the ice age present a picture of profound ecological changes elsewhere. Did these occur in mainland South-east Asia? Opinions differ markedly. Walker (personal communication) tends to opt (on evidence in Yunnan Province) for minimal change, Flenley (personal communication) believes (from Sumatra) that there is some evidence of expansion and retreat of rainforests, Bellwood (1985) appears to accept considerable reduction in rainfall in Malaysia and Bowler (in Mulvaney and White, 1987) argues explicitly for the period to about 55 000 BP as one of increased aridity in Australia that would be mirrored at least in part in Asia.

If we can hypothesise with the majority opinion that there was some tendency for rainforests to retreat and savanna and open woodland to extend during periods of increasing (northern) glaciation, we might infer phases of increased output and population potential, with migration consequences indicated. However, if increased northern glaciation actually improved human ecology in mainland South-east Asia, one would expect relaxation of glaciation to force a retreat in prime habitat. It does not follow that migration tendencies were relaxed. On the contrary, periods of reduced northern glaciation might be seen as ones of stress in which migration actually intensified as people attempted to find substitute locations.

End to end, such ecological fluctuations could then have generated a persistent trickling to Java throughout the major fluctuations of the ice age. Fluctuations in conditions could then be added to the periods of comparative stability, when trend population increases would be expected to stimulate a similar trickling flow.

This scenario suggests then, subject to Scenario III, the changing conditions necessary for a tendency to a continuous movement towards Java and Timor. Unless this movement were typically by long-distance migration, it implies the herding of a vanguard towards Australia. As population in Java increased, even long-distance migration would tend to yield the same result, though some groups might be leap-frogged. The implication would be that the relatively early settlers would have been pushed towards Australia. Another implication would be that the process is likely to have generated conflict, and probably increasing conflict as populations grew.

Scenario III: seabed exposure

Accepting at face value the graph of sea level changes, for purposes of approxima-tion, Borneo was accessible by land (from Sumatra) over major periods during 113–108 000, 90–87 000, 76–62 000 and 57–48 000 BP, in addition to during the long climactic sea lowering. There were, then, several long periods when population movements towards Bali and Timor were partially diverted at least to the extent that a supplementary outlet for migrants was offered. On much briefer and fewer occasions at about 112 000, 64 000 and 35 000 BP, most of the Sunda Shelf lay exposed. Depending on the extent of seabed uplift, these occasions may have extended for a few thousand years on each occasion.

Substantial seafalls and rises during these three occasions presented radical changes in terms of resources, population, technology and migration. Commentary here may risk interpreting and extrapolating the modern seabed using undue detail. This is deliberate in that the prevalent tendency in most prehistory literature, namely to exploit only one or two sea depth contours, obfuscates the issues. It is an easy rule of thumb to calculate the rate of seabed exposure on the assumption of a featureless incline plane. On this basis, the sea appears to recede everywhere at an alarming rate, with visible impact within a few years. This is wrong, just as it has already been seen to be wrong in relation to the Australian Shelf. Just as migration potential from Timor has been misinterpreted, so the issues confronting different peoples on the Sunda Shelf were highly variable.

Seafalls to about −20 metres bp probably meant relatively little disturbance. Along the coastlines of the Gulf of Thailand and northern Java, relatively narrow strips of exposed seabed emerged, except in a few special areas around Bangkok and the Mekong River mouth. Some limited sections of the Malay coast extended a little more than elsewhere.

It is worth pausing at this point to note the very narrow strip of exposed seabed along the eastern Vietnamese coast. It might be anticipated that this strip quite quickly (within 100 years or so?) became a mangrove tangle. Throughout the rest of the ice age, including its climax, no significant widening of this very narrow strip occurred. This would suggest a very limited opportunity for possible Chinese migrants to move south along the exposed bed. Chinese influence over the past 100 000 years through this mode of land passage does not seem likely to have been major. After perhaps 30 000 or so BP, people in China may have developed adequate watercraft to move by sea south of Taiwan but if this is the case their primary contribution then was to alter the genetic and cultural make-up of the islands, possibly also introducing new tool technology (influences that could be expected to increase as maritime technology developed). The genetic influence corresponds to their probable genetic contribution, much earlier, through trickling migration overland, to people in mainland South-east Asia.

By −30 metres and still more so by −40 metres bp, the sea association with the north Java coast had changed relatively little. But major alterations had occurred at the head of the Gulf of Thailand and along the eastern coast of the Gulf. These seafall phases would have presented severe problems of stress for any people living in southern Thailand, Cambodia and Vietnam. These were the groups most exposed to pressure to relocate. But once the seas fell to −60 or −65 metres bp, radically different prospects emerged. Allowing even a very slight seabed uplift, essentially the whole Sunda Shelf was uncovered, the exposed seabed roughly doubling the land expanse of mainland South-east Asia. An approximation to the outcome might be indicated by reference to the 70 metres sea depth contours.

Vegetation development, the growing presence of animals and birds, Lake Java and the extension of river drainage south of Borneo seem likely to have presented the opportunity for very substantial productivity and population increase on the

Java seabed. In the Gulf of Thailand, it is possible that a similar 'lake' developed which would have quickly become a freshwater lake. Alternatively, the extension southward of the Chao Phraya or Menam led a great river system through a very large gentle 'valley' and one would expect other river channels to develop from the east Malay coast.

The evaluation of this whole exposed seabed as a potential habitat for human beings seems to be a prime research task of biogeographers and others. My own brief forays make it clear that oil companies already hold important information that would contribute to the eventual answer. For present purposes, what is proposed here is that, after initial stress problems, the seabed offered opportunities for significant population growth, regardless of penetration to Borneo or beyond Java. As already discussed, it probably provided the occasion for emergent watercraft. While shelf exposure may have reduced the pressure to migrate across the sea, it did present the opportunity to learn how to do so.

Any investigation would serve to do more than merely identify the production possibilities and population potential. In relation to migration, the effect of the return of the seas depended on the extent of Shelf exploitation. The return was rapid. It did more than alter production possibilities. It enforced withdrawal and a retreat to the islands and mainland. Retreat meant collision between groups — on Borneo, on the mainland and in Java and Sumatra. Though we cannot yet guess at the magnitudes involved, here was the occasion for a build-up of population pressure and intensified inducements to migration.

The direction of this retreat is vital. If it was mainly to Borneo, the migration set was to Sulawesi/New Guinea and Philippines. If the greater part of the retreat was to the mainland and Java, the dominant migration pressure was towards Timor and Australia. Depending on the presence of people, the likely times of this intensified pressure were around 110–109 000, 63–62 000 and 32–30 000 BP.

Although we cannot reconstruct the ecology of the exposed Shelf, there are some reasons for believing that the strongest thrust of the retreat would lead to migration more towards Timor. As any retreat was occurring, particularly on the first two occasions, it seems plausible that the greatest population numbers would have been on the mainland and in Java. At the same time as mainland coastal dwellers were confronted with those retreating off the Shelf, the mainland savanna and open woodland dwellers may have been facing stress from the return of the rainforests. Relocation in the face of these different stress and conflict conditions would occur as access to Borneo was being closed off, resuming the longterm route via the Lesser Sundas.

6

A SYNTHESIS

W here there are no hard facts there can be no hard conclusions. It should be stressed that the following conclusions do not reject the notion of early human beings as 'inquisitive wanderers'. This speculative discussion suggests:

(a) Contrary to prevalent understanding, it seems likely that Australia received substantial migrant flows from Timor at a relatively early stage and more persistently than by other routes. Flows via New Guinea may have become more prominent with the development of directional skills in sailing.

(b) Though accidents may have occurred, there seem to be few grounds for perceiving Aboriginal migration to be the result of casual accidents.

(c) There seem to be several reasons for believing it likely that there were pressures potentially leading to a more or less persistent and rising flow of migration to Australia at least from around 65 000 BP and possibly earlier, even though there may have been some interruptions to this flow.

(d) Means to travel by sea from Timor did not depend on very advanced maritime technology.

(e) With quite minimal watercraft, lowering sea levels (and hence reduced sea distances) were not as generally dominant an issue in opening opportunities for transfer as has often been suggested; on the other hand, the facility to travel directly from Timor to Australia was determined by comparatively small sea level changes and by the shape of the Australian Shelf.

(f) Opportunity and motive to develop appropriate sea craft to travel to and beyond Timor, to Sulawesi and the Philippines, appear to have arisen north of Java particularly, and possibly in the Gulf of Thailand at special occasions. Within the limits of present dating of Aboriginal presence, the most acutely important occasion seems probably to have been around 65 000 BP, though earlier development is not inconceivable.

(g) There appear to have been significant 'pull' factors towards Australia, making it possible to perceive migration as a conscious decision in the expectation of recognised production possibilities at the area of disembarkation.

(h) Problems of scarcity and population pressure appear likely candidates to explain the migration process, and increasingly so until the last great seafall towards the climax of the ice age (which might have actually relaxed pressures to migrate).

(i) Motives to migrate appear likely to have varied considerably according to time and place. There is no necessary conflict between Malthusian and non-Malthusian considerations. The two sets can be fused into a more complete explanatory process, with the Malthusian issues of scarcity becoming increasingly important and, on a few special occasions, overwhelming.

(j) It seems unlikely that migration occurred wholly in the absence of conflict.

(k) Prehistorians may find it profitable to pay greater attention to demography and economics in order to advance their discipline.

(l) Reconstruction of the ecology of the exposed Sunda and Sahul Shelves and a more thorough investigation of their current contours and subsea drainage seem vital. The alternative is, of course, to await the next ice age, when a more sensible prehistory may be written. But, in the meantime, existing islands south-east of Timor demand thorough scientific investigation. It is no longer possible to claim that all early Aboriginal sites must now lie beneath the sea.

PART II

DEVELOPMENT, STRUCTURE AND FUNCTION OF ABORIGINAL ECONOMY

7

INTRODUCTION

E conomy is not a compartment of social activity but a process of choice. It is concerned with issues of accommodating to problems of scarcity: subject to some scarcity constraint(s), what goods and services and how much of each are to be produced, how far different wants may be satisfied, the methods of allocating resources, the adoption of different modes of production, the establishment of systems of exchange and the distribution of benefits between different individuals and groups. These choices do not occur in a social vacuum — a large variety of aspects of social behaviour impinge more or less strongly on the process. Indeed, there is an interaction between economics and other social considerations. The value systems of any society, the institutions through which choice operates, systems of property rights, the methods of enforcing agreements or contracts and the relationships between individuals and larger groups all underlie choice. In considering the development, structure and function of Aboriginal economy, it is essential to approach the subject as a process of choice within this larger interactive context.

Economists have tended until recently to ignore these underlying issues and to focus unduly on market activity as an abstraction. In principle, allocation, exchange and distribution are then seen as achieved either by the market or, as an alternative, by some form of direction. But is there an alternative mode of solving economic problems? By contrast, anthropologists have tended to be preoccupied with these other aspects of 'primitive' society and, again until recently, treated economics as a distinct 'material' compartment of society. Fortunately, there has been a recent tendency to convergence between economics and anthropology, and economic decision-making has come to be seen as part of an integrated and interactive totality. This convergence is the more important in that some economists have come to recognise processes of choice that occur outside the conventionally defined market and to acknowledge the significance of production, consumption and sharing arrangements within households. In other words, consumption is no longer perceived simply as consumption by and for atomistic individuals; production is not confined to inputs and outputs in a market; and sharing is not defined primarily by reference to market concepts of prices, income and wealth. Within these households, production, consumption and sharing decisions do not depend on clearly recognised price signals as they are supposed to do in the market. There seem, then, to be alternatives to markets or central direction.

This convergence is vital in that Aboriginal society depended only marginally on exchange and trade. It was composed of groups of varying size. Basically, the small hunting and gathering bands might be seen as quasi-households, producing not for exchange but for their own satisfactions. These dominated Aboriginal economy on a day-to-day basis. At the time of European settlement in Australia, these small groups had reasonably distinctive property rights in land and other assets (including rights in ritual). But they also coalesced in a variety of ways. They recognised larger kinship relations, vital to many of their social and economic practices and these larger kin groups, in turn, acknowledged property, ritual and other rights. From time to time, the bands came together physically in larger associations for special purposes. To a limited degree, they traded within and beyond these kin groups; and there were episodes of conflict between them. Any attempt to comprehend Aboriginal economy depends on incorporating many aspects of these larger associations, in terms both of the occasions of physical association and the persisting implications of Aboriginal recognition of the interrelationships between individuals, bands and larger groups, and of their connections with the land in which they lived. These provide the foundations for alternative methods of allocative and consumption decision-making.

It is difficult enough for an outsider today to comprehend adequately the modus operandi of another modern society or economy. Wrapped in profound attitudes to land, myth, ritual, complex kin relationships and other institutional and value systems, only dimly perceived today, traditional Aboriginal economy is obscured by many characteristics that challenge the modern imagination. Nevertheless, one can be over-awed by these problems. It is essential to focus on the fact that, essentially, the Aboriginal and modern economic problems were identical in form. It was the mode of choosing that was distinctive. Once we recognise this, it is possible at least to direct discussion of the ways types of choices were articulated even if we cannot fully grasp the reasons why choices were made in the manner adopted. Moreover, we need to be concerned with issues of long-term stability rather than merely short-term equilibrium. In much of this chapter we will be concerned with implications of relationships rather than reasons for the existence of particular attitudes, institutions or behaviour patterns.

There is, however, another matter. It is undoubtedly important to try to grasp as far as we can the structure and function of Aboriginal economy at the time of first European settlement and to look at issues of static relationships. But it is also essential to ask whether Aboriginal economy was simply static or whether it was, in 1788, in a process of evolution and development. Within the timespan of 50 000 or more years, Aboriginal economy must have been subject to development and change; it may have displayed growth characteristics in the modern sense of increased output per unit of input or increased consumption per head.

One might argue that change over such a timespan would be imperceptibly slow, making its identification largely pointless. Change and growth in the rest of the world appear, however, to have been the product of slow evolution and sudden spurts. Did Aborigines have a similar experience? One might expect, for example, the structure and function of Aboriginal economy at the time of the very first settlements to be significantly different from that when the continent was largely filled in. The effort required to grapple with that transformation is comparable in principle to the task of understanding the progression from the first European settlement in Australia to the substantially completed occupation of the continent. Was Aboriginal occupation a slow or rapid process? How did they accommodate to the different ecological areas that were encountered? Did they merely make minor adaptations to known technology or were there massive changes in tastes, technology, methods of production and allocation of labour? Did the population shrink with production setbacks and expand to absorb increased productivity or were per capita gains achieved, particularly with the aid of population control?

Moreover, one needs to consider the extent to which change was due to exogenous or endogenous factors. So much of modern European economic history is based on the premise of endogeneity that one can too readily lose sight of the significance of exogenous influences (as, indeed Europeans and others have come to realise for themselves). To Aborigines over the past 50 000 years, exogenous influences were often drastic. Did these enforce rapid change? Was the change that ensued essentially an adaptive response as, for example, we perceive animals adapting to ecological change? Or did the response contain innovative elements? And were there innovations regardless of exogenous pressures? Since one issue in this book is the substantial displacement of an Aboriginal by a European economy, there is a special interest in whether the rate of such changes may have increased in the period prior to first settlement.

In expressing questions in this form, we are bordering on investigation of motivation. Put baldly, we may be interested in whether Aborigines behaved rationally or not — rationally in the sense of pursuing a consciously preferred outcome of activity. To many anthropologists, this will be seen as looking at Aboriginal economic behaviour through the eyes of so-called 'economic man'. This perception is a misunderstanding. In considering Aboriginal behaviour, so far as we can understand it, we are concerned with implications, not motives. It is important to try to assess, at least in general terms, whether Aboriginal economic behaviour implied rationality in the sense given. This is not to impose concepts of maximisation (that few economists, in any event, impose on modern economic behaviour). Aborigines may be seen, for example, to prefer more leisure or more ritualistic activity to more consumption goods. They may be seen as being satisfied with a limited range of ends. Neither perception entails the conclusion that they behaved 'irrationally'.

Aboriginal economy in Australia was established over thousands of years by successfully arriving immigrants from island South-east Asia and by their locally born descendants. Though some efforts have been made to model the possible relationship between immigration and local net natural increase and the possible time taken to occupy the whole Australian continent, there are no data on which we might base any such modelling. The discussion in Part I has suggested several scenarios that might point to some fluctuation in migration flows and to circumstances that might suggest a rising flow of migration. If we accept prevalent views of very low rates of net natural increase amongst hunter gatherers, it would follow that population build-up to occupy the entire Australian continent even within a timespan of several millennia is explicable primarily by immigration inflow. Radical change in net reproduction rates of those successfully transferring to Australia would require major social adjustment, including substantial alterations in division of labour and resource exploitation.

These alternative explanations have important implications for our perceptions of Aboriginal demography and social organisation at the time of European settlement. They also have considerable significance for the dynamics of Aboriginal economy over the past 50 000 years and for any appraisal of its structure and function. A population build-up dominantly through migration meant a continuous learning-by-doing of newcomers in responding to Australian ecology in its novelty and its changes. Population growth essentially by net natural increase of a small number of ever-arriving migrants would mean primary emphasis on the intergenerational transfer of ecological understanding and a socially managed gradual adaptation to change in the environment. A predominantly migrant source of population expansion would imply the likelihood of a more rapid transmission of technological change from mainland and island South-east Asia to Australia. It would also suggest the probability of increasing conflict at arrival points between earlier and later arrivals, at least as the continent began to 'fill up'. It may be possible to follow up some of these and other implications, to test in Australia and in South-east Asia which is the more likely explanation.

In any event, it is not plausible to approach the study of Aboriginal economy in Australia in terms of a static structure and function. However slow change may have been, there can be little doubt that the economy at the end of the eighteenth century was the product of development, expansion, change and innovation. It seems almost certain that change in some large areas of the continent may have been at certain times quite radical and fairly rapid; in other parts, change may have been more drawn-out but even more radical. Thus the rise of the seas after 17 000 BP and perhaps particularly after about 8000 BP must have led to relocation and concentration, and possibly to adaptation of consumption patterns and technology. On the other hand, contrasts in water supply conditions in central Australia, for example, between around 40–25 000 BP and after 25 000 BP seem likely to point to a slow but eventually drastic transformation in economic behaviour.

The elements of dynamism in the Aboriginal economy in more recent millennia are indicated also by regional differences in consumption patterns, production structure, division of labour and other characteristics. By whatever routes Aborigines eventually occupied all areas of the Australian mainland and Tasmania, they must have adapted to changing production possibilities to lead to these regional differences. Cross-sectional contrast was necessarily the product of temporal change and development and this change, not stasis, is a central question in Aboriginal economic history.

In strategic terms, this dynamism might be summed up in the proposition that Aborigines evolved in Australia from hunter gatherers to resource managers and 'improvers'. They were not alone in this; Amerindians displayed similar development. The so-called 'failure' of Aborigines to become 'farmers' is debated at length in the literature and weighed heavily against them in the eventual European occupation of the continent. It seems generally agreed that Aborigines achieved a large-scale alteration in the Australian environment through burning and it is possible that this evolved from at least 30 000 BP. The ecological and economic implications of this use of fire is a prominent issue below. But areal burning was not the only form of resource management and change; much more intricate processes have to be considered, reaching a possible technological peak in the 'eel farming' of Western Victoria during the past few thousand years.

To focus only on ecology and resource management in discussing Aboriginal economic history would be seriously misleading. Until very recently, this focus was the norm in the literature of prehistory and anthropology. Extremely valuable empirical studies have been made of Aboriginal food gathering and its technology. These have been taken to encompass Aboriginal economy, treated as a separate compartment of Aboriginal society and culture — and defined as 'material' as distinct from 'non-material' culture. This distinction is now, fortunately, being blurred. Many aspects of Aboriginal social structure and function are beginning to be brought into consideration as affecting and derived from economic behaviour, including inter-group associations, property rights in land, marriage customs, property in ritual and so on (an excellent example is in Jones, 1980).

These extensions are peculiarly important in any discussion of Aboriginal economy. In the absence of any clearly defined market, individual property rights or central direction with communal property, and with little in the way of government or overt laws, Aborigines nevertheless achieved an orderly system of economic decision-making. Much of this order is explicable through aspects of Aboriginal society not overtly concerned with food gathering. Continuous sustained activity, in daily association, was conducted in small groups and there is no evidence that this ever changed in principle over time. How decisions were ordered in such groups and how and why they interrelated with larger population nuclei are important matters for economists to try to understand.

It is not implied that Aboriginal bands equate directly with modern households. What is important is that, like modern households, Aboriginal bands had an array of ends that extended far beyond simple productive activity in food gathering and tool making. Like modern households, Aboriginal bands had ends including the satisfaction of food consumption, leisure, education, learning-by-doing, ritual and religion, order, reproduction, investment, warfare and so on. It was the attempt to achieve modes of satisfying these competing demands that made up the problem of the Aboriginal economy, as it does the modern household. Hunting and gathering was only a small part of the total behaviour in which economic considerations were relevant.

Sahlins (1972) has been influential in encouraging anthropologists to believe in the affluence of hunter gatherers. Even if his arguments were accepted — and there seem a good many reasons to question them — in terms of simple dietary tests, it does not follow that Aborigines had an easy and undemanding set of economic problems (that is, alternative decisions between which, for some reasons of scarcity, they had to choose). The satisfaction of the array of ends suggested above required much more than hunting and gathering. In the best of conditions, hunter gatherers had one scarce resource and this, it is suggested may be a valuable way of considering Aboriginal economy. This resource was time (Becker, 1965). To satisfy their varied ends, did Aborigines make time budgeting a significant matter? It is a question that Sahlins would answer in the negative. Well, let us see.

8

THE PROCESS OF EARLY SETTLEMENT

A mere 25 years ago, the common assumption was that Aborigines had settled Australia during only the past 10 000 years or so and that they naturally congregated on coastal areas, spread more thinly along inland riverine locations and dispersed sparsely over the arid interior. Until much more recently, it was universally accepted that the Aboriginal population of Australia as a whole had reached only 300 000 or so at the time of European settlement. Though there is still debate and doubt about the size of the immediate precontact population, this picture of Aboriginal occupation has been radically revised, particularly as a result of prehistorians' efforts since about 1965.

Map 7 (p. 58) summarises present understanding of the range of dated locations, as currently estimated, of Aboriginal settlement prior to 10 000 BP. The map does not report all finds and dates, merely the oldest reasonably firmly established 'dates', according to radio-carbon dating methods, at each major location. Even now, three important reservations must be made. First, new finds must be expected, possibly altering the implied perspective. Second, radio-carbon dating is limited to identifying 'dates' up to about 40 000 BP, with rapidly increasing orders of error as that length of time is approached. Improved techniques may extend times further back. Thirdly, some sites are known to contain material at present undateable or difficult to determine, with the probability of more ancient material remains, so that understatements may occur for this reason also.

So far as this summary presentation goes, two points are reasonably clear. First, so far as the present area of Australia is concerned, the oldest sites (approximately 40 000 BP) lie in the southern part of the mainland, near Perth, Melbourne and in western New South Wales. Secondly, all major environmental areas were occupied by Aborigines well before the climax of the ice age at about 17 000 BP. These include settlements in the now arid centre of Australia where sites have been dated at earlier than 20 000 BP.

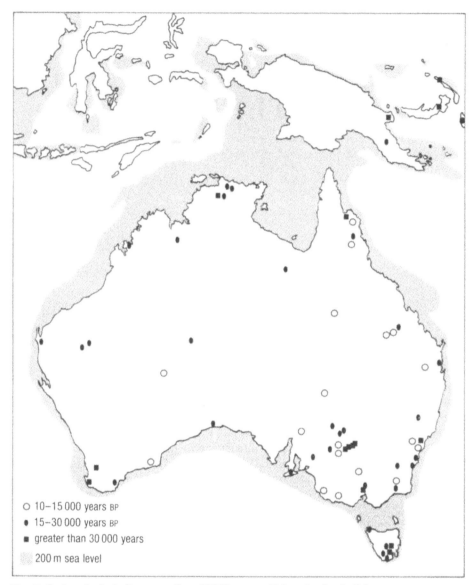

Map 7: Archaeological sites more than 10 000 years old (greater Australia)

Reproduced with the kind permission of Prof. D. J. Mulvaney. Original map drawn by Joan Goodrum.

One might, perhaps, be a little cautious about this present-day geographical perspective. Over the period during which one might say the whole of the present Australia held Aboriginal sites, from a minimum of 40 000 to around 15 000 BP, the continental area was radically different from that of today. New Guinea and

Tasmania were joined physically with the present Australian continent in one land mass over most of the 100 000 years before about 8000 BP. All coastlines extended considerably beyond their present limits but the total land extensions due to lowering of sea levels varied considerably over time and were subject to quite large fluctuations even before the final lowering and return of the seas. Maps 8a and 8b (pp. 59 and 60) show, from NOAA tape data (NOAA Bathymetric Tapes, 1988), the coarsely defined coastal configurations as represented by sea depth contours at 40, 65, and 130 metres. The last takes into account the extreme climactic lowering of the seas and the others demarcate important levels prior to about 20 000 BP and during sea resurgence after 17 000 BP. Readers may make their own approximate adjustments for seabed uplift in response to sea level falls. It might be noted that some shortcomings of the NOAA tapes were shown in the preceding chapter in relation to the coast of northwestern Australia; no comparable shortcomings appear to arise elsewhere (though there are micro-problems).

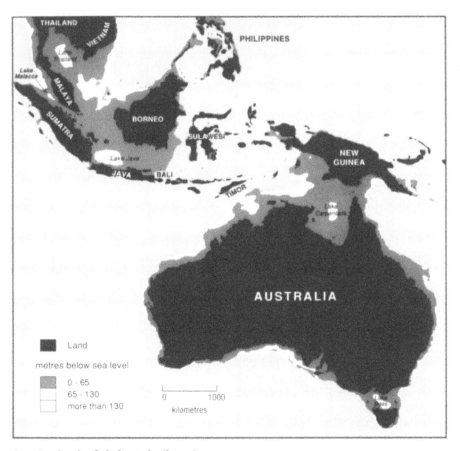

Map 8a: Sunda–Sahul sea depth contours

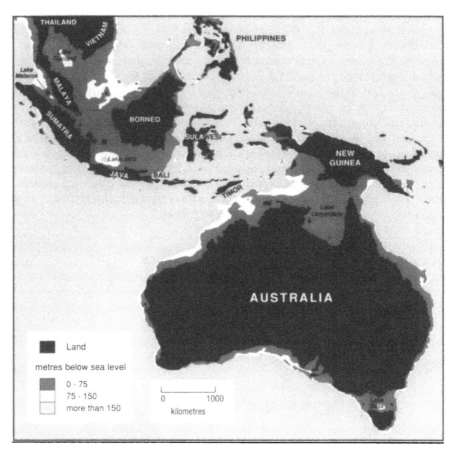

Map 8b: Sunda–Sahul sea depth contours

Looked at with this larger and changing geographical perspective, it is appropriate to bring into account the very early settlement dates in New Guinea. We seem
to have both the north and south of the enlarged continental mass occupied by, at
the latest, 40 000 BP, and a penetration throughout the total landmass by about
20 000 BP. This penetration included settlement of the relatively frigid Tasmania
by about 30 000 BP and the arid centre of the continent by 20–25 000 BP. Many
original settlements around Australia may now lie under the sea. Present evidence
seems to suggest Aborigines' remarkable capacity to locate right across the
continental mass at least during the 20 000 years after 40 000 BP. It would be more
interesting, if one could, to try to estimate the sequence of occupation of sites over
long periods and to attempt to hazard informed guesses about variations in
populations at these sites. Prehistorians have tended to focus on the oldest 'dates'
rather than the temporal sequence of early settlement. It might be suggested that
the latter is the more important to work towards. No doubt the task is hard. If the

objective is feasible, it would be desirable to have more efforts directed towards the scale of occupation of each site over time rather than to be so preoccupied with the first settlements. In fact, we need both.

Several theories have been developed to account for the process of Aboriginal settlement. Bowdler (Butlin, 1983) proposes that, as fisher-people of island South-east Asia, Aborigines arriving predominantly from New Guinea made their way over several millennia around the Australian coast from the north and only later moved to occupy the inland riverine areas, particularly up the Murray–Darling river systems. Birdsell (Allen *et al.*, 1972) believed that Aborigines radiated relatively quickly (during perhaps a couple of thousand years) across the continent from a focal point based in Arnhem Land. Horton (1981) suggests that Aborigines followed supplies of available water that, in turn, provided essential support to the megafauna that Aborigines first encountered and that flourished until about the climax of the ice age. Horton also makes a prime point of radiation from Arnhem Land. But he proposes that, as the megafauna died out with the drying of the Australian continent (perhaps also from over-hunting by Aborigines), so the Aborigines withdrew to a coastal concentration.

It is doubtful whether we yet have enough evidence to place any great reliance on any of these theories. Bowdler's approach appears to assume that Aborigines had a minimal capacity to adapt their tastes, to innovate or to respond to alternative production possibilities (ecological conditions). Ecology and habit appear to dominate. Birdsell seems to accept a highly flexible response of Aborigines to alternative production possibilities and also to the social and economic consequences of increased rates of net natural increase (required to populate the continent quickly). Horton follows Birdsell with the one qualification of dependence on water.

Some of the problems with these approaches can be explored by reference to figure 2 (p. 40).

With the possible exception of movements into Sumatra and Borneo, the transfer of human beings into island South-east Asia placed them in an environment in which land areas were limited and sea resources prominent. It is often proposed, indeed, that early humans were largely coastal dwellers. The grounds for this proposition are far from clear. Sea association seems likely, in any event, to have changed with the exposure of the Sunda Shelf. Certainly, once human beings moved into the Lesser Sundas and beyond, or from Sulawesi until they reached New Guinea/Australia, sea harvests must have been dominant in their production and consumption patterns. One cannot, however, jump from this to the conclusion that migrants towards the Sahul Shelf placed a low value on products from the land. Supply conditions imposed a constraint on their preferences and production practices presumably evolved around the sea.

In figure 3 (p. 62), in the top right-hand quadrant, we have the line Csa representing a severe constraint on the satisfaction of consumption, truncating the effective range of the indifference curves Isa in island South-east Asian conditions. The top left-hand quadrant shows Pssa, the seafood production function of island South-east Asia, representing advantageous sea harvesting conditions. In the bottom right-hand quadrant we have the nominal simulation of a production function in island land-gathering activities shown as Plsa. Limited land resources imply a severe restriction on total output potential and the early onset of

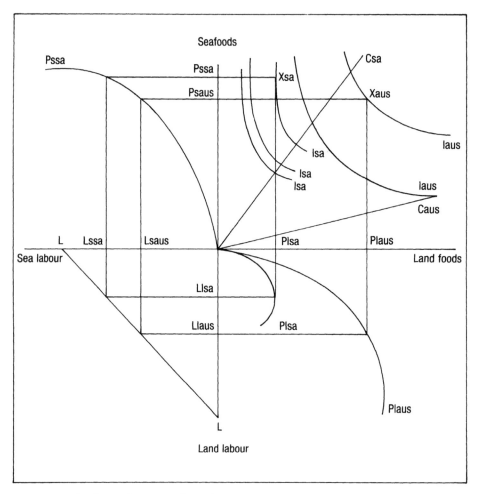

Figure 3: Production and consumption patterns

diminishing returns. With total labour supplies at L, migrants in passage allocate Lssa of labour to seafood harvests and the limited volume of Plsa to land harvesting. They settle at a preferred position, determined by their tastes and supply constraints at Xsa in the right-hand quadrant as a nominal island 'optimum'. At this point, they consume large quantities of seafood at Pssa and limited volumes of land goods at Plsa.

On arrival in Australia/New Guinea, land supply constraints are greatly relaxed. For simplicity, it is assumed that the sea harvesting production function remains unchanged but we now include Plaus, a greatly improved land productivity potential in Australia/New Guinea conditions relative to the small land areas of island South-east Asia. The formal theory of flexible response would imply a radical reallocation of labour resources. It might be noted, however, that figure 3 incorporates in the top right-hand quadrant the line Caus representing a consumption constraint indicating for Australia/New Guinea a limitingly low level of the fish foods without which Aborigines would be dissatisfied. But, given this attachment to fish, Aboriginal redeployment of labour, in a highly flexible scenario, would yield labour allotted to land gathering greatly increased to Plaus and a somewhat reduced sea-gathering workforce at Lsaus in the new continental circumstances. The resulting formal 'equilibrium' would place them at Xaus in the upper right-hand quadrant, in a position much preferred to Xsa, at which they had been held in the islands.

Habit and tradition may have died hard. Arriving migrants may have continued to believe that land production conditions were as in the islands or that they could not adapt. It is on this, essentially, that Bowdler must rely. Aborigines certainly encountered many strange animals, including the possibly dangerous Australian tiger and local grazing megafauna. But there were many animals and birds with which they were familiar. Whether we can project back the modern similarity of vegetation in South-east Asia and Australia is uncertain but Golson (Mulvaney and Golson, 1971) has shown a remarkable presence of South-east Asian plants across northern Australia. It seems unlikely that Aborigines did not respond to these new production possibilities. All or only some may have done so. In either case, it seems plausible to believe that the most likely outcome of arrival was a greater exploitation of land resources.

To move towards the Birdsell–Horton scenarios of early inland penetration depends, basically, on assuming either that Aborigines were willing to forsake fish foods for land animals and plants or that interior water systems (not merely, as Horton proposes, access to drinking water) were available that provided an alternative source of fish foods. Some technological adaptation would be implied to the extent that river and lake fishing differ from sea harvesting. Provided these adaptations were not major, it does not require the literal dependence on behaviour indicated in figure 3 (opposite) to make the reasonable inference that inland penetration would have occurred at an early stage. This does not readily accommodate to Birdsell's more or less random penetration nor, for that matter, to Horton's focus on drinking water for megafauna. These latter may have been important and perhaps Aborigines hunted them to the point of overkill. But what becomes crucial is whether, along with available land resources, interior water resources offered Aborigines an effective alternative to persisting with an attachment to the coastline. In Sumatra, Borneo and Sulawesi, mobile human beings had faced the same choice. What then were the climatic and river–lake conditions of interior Australia?

One important feature arose from the extended seabed throughout most of the time between 90–10 000 BP. This was the emergence of two large lakes, one in the Gulf of Carpentaria (Tolcher, 1986), the other in Bass Strait (Blum, 1988). Lakes Bass and Carpentaria between them provided a large resource potential, with their brackish water sustaining masses of fish and fowl and their surrounds providing vegetation for human beings and animals. It is intriguing that two large lakes, emerging from the Sahul Shelf, should match two on the Sunda Shelf. It is possible that these two pairs of lakes provided the conditions for massive transfers of birds between the two shelves. Reverting to the approach in Part I, the flights of birds observable from Timor could be tracked most immediately to Lake Carpentaria and subsequently to Lake Bass. Here was the potential for a massive pull factor across the top end of the present Australian continent and down from New Guinea.

If such a path (particularly across the top end) were chosen, what lay between the newly surfaced land masses west and south-west of Darwin and Lake Carpentaria? A little of the shape of climatic conditions within Australia is beginning to emerge but it is doubtful whether very firm statements can as yet be made. Bowler (Bowler, 1978; Bowler and Jones, 1979; Mulvaney and White, 1987) has suggested a tripartite division of the past 120 000 years: (a) broadly to about 60 000 BP, climate not greatly dissimilar to that of today; (b) a gradual drying and cooling after 60 000 BP, both changes accelerating rapidly after 20 000 BP reaching famine conditions in much of Australia for a few thousand years centred on 17 000 BP; and (c) increased precipitation and warming to about 8000 BP and the establishment thereafter of present-day conditions. Within these long periods there were reversals of trend and micro-regional contrasts. Efforts through CLIMANZ (1983) have extended some of the detail of the more recent experience, though conclusions are fairly opaque for periods before 20 000 BP.

In the period to 60 000 BP and indeed for a very considerable time thereafter, a characteristic of prime importance is the nature of water regimes from Lake Eyre and Lake Frome in south-central Australia to the headwaters of the Diamantina and Georgina channels (Mulvaney and White, 1987; cf map 8). It is relevant to a consideration of these regimes that until 50–60 000 years ago the Darling and Murray Rivers, with their various tributaries, appear to have been much broader streams than they are today, with a large array of related lakes. The modern narrow channels and dry lakes do not merely fail to indicate prior conditions; they imply that, even though the present climate corresponds broadly to that during 120–60 000 BP, an enduring change, a diminution, occurred in water regimes in eastern Australia in the course of moving to the ice age climax. Similarly, Lakes Eyre and Frome were, 120 000 years ago, parts of a very much larger central lake system and their reduced form might be dated from around 30 000 BP. Until some time towards 30 000 BP, substantial flows of fresh water were fed into these large central lake systems through the rivers flowing (as they now rarely do) from the Channel Country south of the Gulf of Carpentaria (Mulvaney and White, 1987; NOAA, 1988; Nanson and Young, 1988; Nanson and Young, 1988; Thome and Raymond, 1989). Aborigines arriving and moving between, say about 50–30 000 BP did not have to reach Lake Carpentaria to find attractive production potential. They could almost certainly have done so there, but in addition it appears likely that they could also have followed the pleistocene river channels, the habitat of birds and fish, down to the Lake Eyre–Lake Frome complex. It seems improbable that they would have suffered food shortages on the way; and for those attached to fish this part of their menu would most probably have remained intact while being amplified by other items.

Though conditions may have deteriorated after 60 000 BP, it may be doubted whether they uniformly, persistently and drastically deteriorated until about 30 000 BP. A similar gradual deterioration followed in the Murray–Darling systems. After 30 000 BP the deterioration in the interior might have been partly ameliorated for Aborigines, as hunters, because fauna (particularly megafauna) came to concentrate around dwindling water resources. But that was, if at all, a short-term benefit as the climax of the ice age approached. The extreme aridity after 20 000 BP forced

Aborigines out of the interior into the better watered and stocked margins of the continent. It seems more plausible that it was over this later period that Aborigines were induced to seek the security of coast and estuaries. Similarly, the formation of glaciers on the south-east highlands limited the flow of snow-fed streams and a contraction of habitat followed in the Murray–Murrumbidgee basin, where possibly a similar withdrawal to the margins followed.

These scenarios are not suggested as the only ones. It is unlikely that all groups behaved in identical ways. Some may have moved progressively around the coast and others inland during the years say 60–30 000 BP. Basically, they are suggested as filling the continent from many directions. Those that may have followed the tracks through the centre were the ones most exposed to subsequent adaptation increasingly after 30 000 BP; but even on the Murray and Darling extensive adaptation was demanded as aridity and cold increased to the ice age climax.

How far Aborigines succeeded in adapting to these massive changes still remains to be delineated. Decades of patient research and the accumulation of understanding are required before much can be said with any conviction. The available dating makes it clear that considerable adaptation to these exogenous changes was achieved, disposing of any view of Aborigines as unadaptive and non-innovative. As the ice age ended and the present interglacial began from 8–10 000 years ago, Aborigines were able to form the social and economic system and population dispersion that confronted European settlers in 1788. By implication, the past 8–10 000 years were another phase of change and development to achieve this precontact system. It is convenient to jump to precontact conditions before returning to consider some aspects of the likely expansion, change and growth that accompanied the few thousand years before European arrival.

In doing so, however, the following discussion on variety in Aboriginal economy at 1788 can be read with two issues in mind. The immediate objective is to qualify any later generalisations. The second issue is that the emergence and clarity of cross-section difference by region were the outcomes of changes over an extended period. On the simplest construct of a common cultural origin or on the looser assumption of origins in island South-east Asia, patterns of production and consumption, specifics of technology, tastes, marriage arrangements and so on must have altered in order to achieve this variety. In other words, there is a clear implication of dynamism — over whatever period — in Aboriginal society and economy. Aborigines must have been responsive to change and differences in ecology, must have adapted and, in the end, must have achieved considerable innovation in order to establish continent-wide diversity.

9

VARIETY IN THE PRECONTACT ABORIGINAL ECONOMY

Various attempts have been made to portray or reconstruct the immediate precontact distribution of Aborigines across Australia, whether in terms of tribal boundaries, social-linguistic divisions or other modes of differentiation. One of the more recent attempts by Peterson (1976) provides a convenient reference in terms of language, culture and ecology. Peterson presents sixteen distinct areas (cf the much larger number of tribal divisions by Tindale) and for present purposes these provide complications enough to point summarily to diversity and variety in Aboriginal economic activity, and in social form and structure relevant to economic decision-making. These and other contrasts have led many recent writers to deny that 'Aboriginal economy' can be treated as a general concept. This rejection needs to be encountered head on.

For those preoccupied with the specifics of ecology or of particular responses of Aborigines to challenges of different production possibilities and technology, the contrasts between areas loom large (Lawrence, 1968). The differences are important and some appreciation of them is a necessary qualification to any generalisations that follow. But it is essential to appreciate that these illustrations are drawn from older literature that treats economics as a particular compartment, a 'material' segment of a total culture. As already discussed above, economics is properly looked at as a process of choosing. Nevertheless, the older literature is very valuable for its empirical content. Whether perceived as hunter gatherers or as resource managers, Aborigines in Peterson's sixteen-fold division can be looked at in a variety of ways: in terms of tastes and consumption patterns, productive activity and production methods, technology, modes of distribution and exchange, and band size; or more indirectly through issues such as marital and reproductive processes, kinship systems, ritual, myth, ceremony, mode of government and so on.

All that is intended here is to give a few hints about this diversity in certain respects (Lawrence, 1968; Mulvaney and Golson, 1971). Aborigines prefer foods from the sea or land; did they prefer animal or plant foods? In general we can only infer preferences from consumption patterns and these, in turn, are influenced by production possibilities. The focus of hunter-gatherer activity on the small band, which was both the producing and the consuming unit, reinforces this confusion. Given the close association of each band with particular areas and the totems and rituals related to each group, there were some specific, ritualistically-imposed constraints specific to each area. But other groups imposed more obscure constraints, such as the relatively recent Tasmanian limitation on the consumption of scale fish (which was consumed by earlier Tasmanians). Interesting as these limitations are, however, they are less significant than the variety of consumption patterns across the continent: the dominance of seafood consumption in some areas, for example, or the exploitation of grains in others, or of cycads or yams elsewhere.

Much of this differentiation can be seen as closely linked to ecology or production possibilities. Root crops were scarcer in the arid interior and grains were more important; cycads spread across northern Australia and down the east coast; seafoods in considerable variety were more abundant in northern Australia; waterfowl were seasonally more available in south-eastern and northern Australia; freshwater fish depended necessarily on inland water sources; the concentration of animals was strongly influenced by supplies of drinking water and grasslands or open woodlands.

Though regional variety followed, the dependence of consumption patterns on ecology or production possibilities was far from complete (Lawrence, 1968). Apart from the fact that Aborigines in different areas did not consume all the variety of foods available to them, there appear to have been quite strong preferences affecting their behaviour and actual productive activity to satisfy their tastes. Thus Aborigines on eastern Cape York appear to have followed a strongly seasonal pattern of movement but one which placed slighter reliance on land resources. Immediately adjoining them, on the west of the Cape, the bands appear to have been relatively stationary for perhaps six months, located on or near the seashore, and then to have moved almost wholly inland to exploit land resources for the other half of the year. In the Botany Bay area, there appear to have been frequent small relocations, with groups rarely moving over very long distances and remaining closely related to estuaries.

Band size varied greatly. Though band size is frequently represented at about forty or so, there appear to have been considerable deviations from this mean. Moreover the frequency of grouping of bands appears to have varied significantly. So in the arid interior a band might frequently consist of one man and his wives and children, while in richer environments — for example, western Victoria — routine associations of several families appear to have been common. It is possible that the peak of such regular associations was reached in association with almost residential eel-farming in the Western District of Victoria (Lourandos, 1980). Similarly, in the interior, small groups appear to have come together less frequently than was the case in richer environments, and very large gatherings over limited periods appear to have depended on the seasonal availability of rich harvests in one or a small range of particular foods — bogong moths in the eastern highlands (Flood, 1983); eels in western Victoria (Lourandos, 1980), and so on.

Hunting and fishing technology was similarly varied. Stone axes and adzes may have been needed to build the more advanced watercraft of Cape York, or even the simpler but ingenious double raft of the Kimberleys coast, or the single-hulled bark canoes in the south. But it was human intelligence and muscle that generated the complex and varied stone fish traps of the inland rivers and the coast, and skilled fingers that produced from varied materials the variety of nets used for fishing, bird hunting and animal catching. The purposeful use of fire appears to be common throughout Australia (as it was in North America) but even here difference is concealed beneath generality: the times of the year for firing, the scale of area to be burned, the mode of control and other characteristics of 'fire-stick farming' were all strongly influenced by Aboriginal appreciation of the particular circumstances, peculiar to each location, in which fire was used to burn over woodland, to expose or capture a harvest or to generate or regenerate pastures for grazing animals. An obvious contrast is the ability of Aborigines to burn over yam fields to expose the crop but their apparent inability to use fire in this direct manner to burn over areas from which grains were harvested (though fire was used in burning part of 'stooks').

Storage or a limited ability to store foodstuffs is represented as a major problem for Aborigines. Storage questions might arise in the transport of food or water for short periods, mechanisms for transporting collected goods, longer term storage of such food as grains, and the preservation of meat and other perishables.

Water carriers were developed in a large variety of moulds — from human skulls to wooden implements and the complete skins of animals. Similarly, collected goods could be transported in wooden instruments, including spear throwers, and in net bags and other devices. In many areas Aborigines are shown as placing a high value on very fresh foodstuffs; in others, particularly in the interior, sun-drying of meat, particularly fish, was practised. There were, however, other modes of storage that did not require particular containers or treatment of foods. Thus yams could be preserved *in situ* by controlled harvesting; grass seeds kept fresh by stooking; and, perhaps above all, food could be retained at hand by ensuring the presence of 'meat on the hoof' — live animals attracted to grazing on pastures created deliberately by the areal firing of woodlands.

Land was fundamental to Aboriginal culture. Having said this, the concern here is with land as a basic means of production. Wrapped as it is in concepts of kin and familial relations, of myth and ritual, it would be rash for an outsider to try to penetrate far into the varieties of land areas and landed property. In some cases, it appears that some individual property rights in land or in some specific resource did exist. Instances have been identified in northern Australia. But basic common property rights in land appear to have been related to the band. Sometimes such areas were clearly demarcated while in others a good deal of boundary obscurity appears to have existed. In south-west Western Australia, a clearly defined family range appears to have existed within a larger boundary across which different groups might flow (Mulvaney and Golson, 1971). With larger ceremonial gatherings, property rights appear to have attached to larger groupings, as in the case of the moth festivals in the south-east highlands, while in others ceremonial occasions appear to have moved, in times of affluence, to particular band areas. Yet again, on the Darling River, there appear to have been occasions of temporary transfer of rights between different groups, exchanging river for inland locations and vice versa.

Interlocking with concepts of landed property were kinship systems. These affected the locations within which individuals were associated, rights to or expectation of some access to other land resources in times of stress or for social and ceremonial or trade purposes, descent and inheritance, and marital arrangements. Kinship is a peculiarly arcane subject, with a vast and often conflicting literature. Its complexity for present purposes is greatly increased to the extent that much writing relates to surviving remnants, chiefly in northern Australia, amongst whom traditional practices have very probably broken down, at least partially. It is improbable that any observers in the nineteenth century were ever able to acquire sufficient insight into Aboriginal culture for their observations to have much depth. It seems clear, however, that any property rights, including rights of access to resources or women, differed greatly in different regions. One might construct complex grid systems of degrees of relationships, operating either matrilineally or patrilineally. Within such a grid (Berndt and Tonkinson, 1988), Aboriginal society appears to have run the full gamut of close genetic association, relatively loose association and, at the extreme, strict recognition of 'kin' association, with groups having no explicit genetic connection. Within this variety, descent and inheritance might come through maternal or paternal lines, in part affecting the authority of either women or men in Aboriginal affairs.

Polygyny was widespread throughout Australia. Essentially, this meant the marriage of several females to one tribal group or elder. Wives might also accrue through inheritance following the death of a male. Wives were, it is now suggested, bestowed through kinship rules, helping to cement kin relationships. However, there appears to have been considerable variety in the number of wives of a group elder and similar variety in the access of younger men to marital status. There is modern indication of a relatively wide dispersion around the mean of the number of wives per man in northern Australia. Information relating to more arid areas suggests the high frequency of groups composed of a single male with several wives and no other married males (Lawrence, 1968). Historical data for Victoria appear to imply the presence of polygyny but with fewer wives per man and a more general distribution of married females (Blum, 1988). Procedures also varied greatly in terms of the bestowal of females, frequently following male determination but in some cases, such as in parts of the Kimberleys, where females had a strong voice in their unions, subject to kinship rules. Throughout Australia, property rights in women appear to have been very important and, kinship considerations apart, these property rights are important issues for economists to consider. It is also of some moment to appraise the implications of greater or lesser access by young males to women and the variable degrees of dependence on the part of younger males that followed. This dependence was not necessarily a simple deterministic matter. Young males, at least in some areas, could transfer between groups (subject to kinship rules) and this confuses any simple generalisation. It also raises the question of order and modes of control.

It is commonly represented that government was weak in Aboriginal society. In the sense of a strong hierarchy, formal rules and prescriptive penalties, together with organised enforcement systems dealing with large numbers of groups, this is undoubtedly true. Thus Dawson's (1880) misconceptions about Aboriginal 'chiefs' have long been discarded. Nevertheless, within bands and the relatively small tribal groupings in Australia, elders had a strong presence. Order and rule were important even in diurnal gathering and hunting activities, whether these were carried out in common or by individuals. At this level, there appears to have been great variety in the role of women versus men. Even at the level of larger groupings, women were often more important in the role of elders than were men. In an essentially non-literate society, the process of living in common provided a flow of information in both daily and larger assemblies. This information was not necessarily accurate or judicially evaluated (as indicated in, for example, pay-back killings). But group and tribal law could be sternly enforced, with the extreme of severe injury or death for alleged wrongdoers. Almost inevitably, in the absence of codification and given the existence of variable rules of conduct, it is only reasonable to assume a considerable variety in the process of order and justice.

10

THE NATURE AND
FUNCTION OF
ABORIGINAL ECONOMY

W e need to depart from a simple focus on either hunting and gathering, or even on Aborigines as resource managers, though the contrast between these two characterisations is essential in leading us into a consideration of dynamic and not merely static issues. Any general approach necessarily cuts across the detail and variety hinted at above. We do need to try to understand the nature and function of Aboriginal economy as a set of static relationships. But we need also to consider the possibility that, at the time of first European settlement, Aboriginal economy was developing rather than static. Moreover, it is important to bear in mind that even an apparently traditional and static economy contains dynamic elements.

A considerable number of characteristics of Aboriginal society need to be taken into account:

- varied ends of order, security, insurance, communication, capital formation and maintenance (both human and physical), food, clothing, dwellings, leisure, ritual, ceremonial etc.;
- omnivorous diet;
- limited inter-group trade or exchange within bands;
- more or less non-residential productive activity;
- diurnal operation in small groups;
- a marked, if not exclusive, division of labour by gender;
- ordered learning-by-doing or 'education';
- limited and generally non-durable physical capital;
- limited storage capacity;
- land and resource management;
- communal sharing rules;
- communal property rights in land by small groups;
- the practice of polygyny (implying concentrated property rights in women);
- property rights in ritual;

- population control;
- complex kin relations;
- formal non-literacy;
- limited formal government.

This lengthy set of characteristics implies a complex matrix with many relationships that give us more than enough to juggle with. To make matters more difficult, there appears to have been no unique relationship between any of the variables listed. This follows in a general way from the hints of variety in Aboriginal economy already made in the preceding section. We cannot be expected to do justice to them in the limited scope available here. All that is intended is to discuss some of the interrelationships that appear crucial to the structure and function of Aboriginal economy. In this limited discussion, it is important to stress that the *focus is on economic implications and not necessarily on motivation*. Economists' approaches along this route are often misunderstood. It is not implied that Aborigines consciously behaved in a so-called 'rational' economic way. What is important is to try to discover whether, regardless of overt motivation, the outcomes were more or less consistent with this concept of rationality.

Standards of commodity consumption: the 'first affluent society?'

The first item in the list of characteristics above does not imply that Aborigines had infinite wants. Marshall Sahlins (1972) proposed, instead, that Aborigines specifically sought a low standard of living in terms of food, shelter and clothing. He was attempting to combat both modern notions of scarcity derived from the notion of the infinite wants of human beings and also an older view that hunter gatherers were exposed to continuous risks of starvation and to the need to work long hours each day to procure adequate supplies. Sahlins argued, in contrast, that hunter gatherers had an objectively low standard of living with which they were satisfied and that they could attain this standard, subject to migratory activity, with comparative ease, working quite limited hours each day. Moreover, with limited storage capability, this meant that their daily supplies were typically fresh (Hart and Pilling, 1960; Higgs, 1975). With reasonable if unequal sharing rules, this activity supplied adequate nutrition for all members of each group. Given limited demands for clothing, housing or other physical capital, hunter gatherers were 'the original affluent society'.

Sahlins' perspective is based on both recent ethnographic studies and the nineteenth century reports of observers, particularly in relation to Australian Aborigines. Explorers making very early contact with Aborigines reported repeatedly that they hunted and gathered for few hours (the statements appear to range from 4 to 6 hours per day) and, frequently, that they appeared to have plenty of food in their camps (Giles, 1889; Grey, 1841; Kirk, 1986; Sturt, 1849). Amongst other sources, Sahlins cites the findings of the 1948 American–Australian Scientific Expedition to Arnhem Land, which are similar to the nineteenth century observations; and finds these in conformity with McCarthy and McArthur (1960) in northern Australia. Aborigines appeared to spend a great deal of their time gossiping, playing or sleeping. Earlier commentators in the nineteenth century also placed great emphasis on the apparent extent of leisure time. Sahlins' conclusion: the failure of Aborigines to develop an advanced culture was due to idleness.

The assumption underlying this inference and the view of Aboriginal society as 'affluent' within the condition of limited ends is recent, and nineteenth century reports assume that Aboriginal society was reasonably comparable, in the locations and at the times reported, to its precontact form and function. This implies that population densities, marital and reproductive practices, access to natural resources, self-reliance on food supplies wholly acquired by each group, division of labour, systems of order, use of precontact technology, control of land and, perhaps above all, morale had remained more or less intact, or at any rate were not so severely disrupted as to induce a major change in Aboriginal work practices.

It is more than a little doubtful whether one can accept any of these implications; if so, one is led to question the general perception. This is not necessarily to imply that precontact Aborigines had low nutritional standards relative to European settlers or explorers in Australia in the early years of Australian settlement. On the contrary, because Aborigines had adopted an omnivorous diet drawn from an environment that they understood intimately, it is almost certain that for the first 50 years or so of European occupation, Aborigines other than those directly constrained and degraded by Europeans had significantly higher nutritional standards than the European settlers. For reasons discussed below, it is possible — I believe likely — that in areas not occupied by Europeans Aboriginal standards in eastern Australia were higher at about 1820–40 than they had been in 1788 (see discussion below). This is not to imply that Aboriginal standards were high throughout the year or in every year. It is generally recognised that seasonal factors, particularly in winter, created shortages, and that periodic droughts or floods, the former sometimes of long duration, could lead to severe difficulties.

A few nineteenth century reporters (Curr, 1886; Smyth, 1878) were perceptive enough to think it likely that Aboriginal modes of behaviour and particularly their work practices had been altered since European contact. Brough Smyth cites some commentators explicitly in these terms in relation to Victoria and elsewhere; Robinson's Journal (Presland, 1977) is replete with descriptions of disorganisation in the 1840s; Radcliffe-Brown (1930) acknowledges massive population disturbances by the 1830s, and so on. But at these dates it is important to appreciate that standards were not particularly high for Europeans. If, indeed, precontact Aborigines regularly achieved the food intake proposed by modern investigators, they must have had a far superior diet to that of the European settlers. If this is so, why did their population not explode? Was population control so effective?

Competing ends in Aboriginal society

In evaluating Aboriginal behaviour and perhaps more particularly the reports of observers over the past 200 years, the relationship between production and consumption needs careful clarification. As quasi-households, hunting and gathering bands predominantly consumed their own output. In order to understand the variety of ends to be satisfied in Aboriginal society, it is convenient to rank the extent to which the production and consumption processes were separable. Put in another way, what time lapse occurred between production and consumption? In some cases, this time interval was substantial; at the other extreme, production and consumption were instantaneous. Until one recognises this, the variety of satisfactions sought and the question of time-budgeting to satisfy competing ends by Aborigines will not be revealed.

It is easy to follow the Sahlins representation (which rests heavily on the conventional notion of economic activity as a separate compartment of social behaviour) of time spent in hunting and gathering and much of the balance in 'idleness' — that is, various recreational activities including the extreme of going to sleep after sufficient hunting or gathering. The notion that Aborigines, being easily well fed for at least most of the year, could then indulge in festivals, ceremonial and rituals seems a seriously misleading perspective. These activities were highly prized. The crucial question is whether these other ends had significant bearing on the functioning of the Aboriginal economic system. The fact that their immediate implications were overtly social ignores a central issue that social and economic behaviour needs to be seen as integrated and interactive.

In male hunting or fishing and in much of female gathering of vegetable products, the time lapse is reasonably clear. Several hours spent in these activities, usually though not always during the day, were followed by transport back to camp, preparation of food, cooking and finally consumption. It might be noted that these activities were not always confined to daylight hours and there is frequent reference to, for example, night-time fishing (Collins, nd). In these latter examples, Aborigines operated as 'shift workers' and it is not surprising that, at times, a good deal of daylight might be spent in sleeping. But in any event a clear distinction between production and consumption of many consumer goods existed. This distinction might have been reinforced by Aborigines' apparent strong preference (Hart and Pilling, 1960; Meehan, 1975) for fresh products and their tendency to produce in any day only the consumption goods required for that day's catering.

Production did indeed often require transport back to camp and hence the allocation of time for this transport process and the demand for transport services. In terms of a simplified division of labour, men demanded the transport services of women to deliver vegetables and women demanded male transport services to carry back animals. At the camp, food required some preparation, a fire to be built and a cooking process to follow. An implicit demand for and allocation of time to these activities followed, predominantly demanded by males of women. Sharing of food once cooked also entailed labour and time input into its distribution to subgroups and individuals, frequently a male function.

However, we need to go far beyond these ends or these time intervals between production and consumption. Within the context of consumption goods, there was often a short interval between production and consumption. The collection of, for example, berries, fruits or nuts might lead to some immediate consumption by gatherers, with only part of the output returned to the campsite. Similarly hunters appear to have consumed part of their catch at kill locations (Smyth, 1878). But commodities were not all simply consumption goods. In Aboriginal society, the distinction between capital and consumption goods is blurred. There was a demand for clothing, bedding, stone tools and a myriad of wooden or fibre implements, as well as the capital items needed for long- and short-stay dwellings, stone fish traps, eel canals, canoes or rafts. These needed to be produced, repaired or replaced from time to time. All represented a demand to be satisfied and required the allocation of labour time. In some cases there appears to have been demand for sustained specialised services, as in painting, special ceremonial objects and so on. In these cases, consumption extended over relatively long periods as the services of durable items — capital — were used up.

This is still far from exhausting the satisfactions sought by Aborigines and it is necessary to move beyond commodity production to services of a more general sort. Here we may confront a total confusion of production and consumption. This confusion may have led earlier observers to misinterpret much of Aboriginal activity and, in the extreme, to see highly prized efforts as merely games, leisure or, in the last resort, 'idleness'.

As Possner has suggested, communication of information was crucial to illiterate 'primitive' societies. Information might be communicated in terms of apparently indolent discussion, debate or squabbles around a camp fire. But the crucial question is, what was being communicated? Was it a discussion of marital infidelity? If so, how important was it to marriage partners and the whole band that this be constrained? Did it threaten order and stability and hence the functioning of the economy? What was the demand for order and for the enforcement of justice? Was the discussion a review of the day's productive activity and the forecasting of the need to relocate to maintain productivity? How significant was the demand for production forecasts? These are merely two illustrations of the persistent demand for information, the satisfaction of which might require a considerable amount of time not readily captured by external observers. The amount of time might be extended insofar as particular formalities might need to be observed in transmitting information.

A similar process related to the demand for education. Though on-the-job training was almost certainly important, there were gradations in ages where this type of training was limited or impossible. Time allotted to initiation ceremonies apart, the oversight of children's play around a camp site was important. This play might merely be casual; even then some demand existed for care and oversight. But it might also be highly motivated in the case of games of skill, agility, and endurance. The fact that adults did not necessarily participate directly should not obscure their demand for care and, in the last resort, education and training.

The extreme condition of blurring between production and consumption lay in the participatory dancing and singing around a campsite by a small band or in a larger gathering. These could have been merely the expression of a demand for entertainment that the group could satisfy only by its own efforts and time. They could also be — and often clearly were — attempts to satisfy demands to sustain the traditions and myths of the group (which was in turn a demand for the preservation of identity and cohesion). This was far from merely leisure-time activity; it was an expression of deep social purpose. But whether as entertainment or attempts to sustain group identity or relationships, these activities were designed to satisfy demands that required allocation of time. In the process, they preserved identity, order and consequently economic efficiency and equity.

The production both of goods and of these varied services was part of the total economic activity of the band or larger group. To the services referred to, one might add war and defence, marriage and death ceremonies, all of which demanded the diversion of Aboriginal resources. The more complex the culture, the more these services appear to have been prized and the more they were elaborated into time-consuming activities. That they had other implications than merely economic may, through the extent to which they were prized, make it the more important to recognise their economic significance and not only their broader cultural features.

Aboriginal production functions and the residual

In 'explaining' the conditions of production, one way in which economists proceed is to identify a production function and the inputs that go into generating output. The simplest general form is the Cobb–Douglas production function, where output is treated as a function of capital and labour, each weighted by its marginal product. In relation to the Aboriginal economy, this has limited relevance, first because Aborigines generally, except in some special conditions, employed comparatively little capital and the primary inputs were land and labour. Secondly, economists have found in relation to modern economies that, having identified the contributions of labour and capital, there is a large unexplained element, the residual. This is composed of a large variety of items, including education, learning by doing, quality of inputs and other issues. In Aboriginal society, matters such as the intimate and detailed knowledge of resources, the variance in supplies seasonally and between different years; the limitations on exploitation and the opportunities for management; basic attitudes towards land; and the sense of 'belonging' were fundamental. In conventional modern terminology, learning and understanding the potential of land resources and commitments to constraint on exploitation were of overwhelming importance in the Aboriginal economy.

In effect, the 'residual' becomes the dominant consideration. Though one may discuss ecology as an important consideration, it was the human attitude to these resources and the land from which they derived that was fundamental. It would be unimaginable that one could look, for example, to changes in land areas and levels of workforce as the prime explanations of Aboriginal commodity output. This is not to say that variations in these simple inputs were irrelevant. What is suggested is that we need to focus on the 'residual' in discussing Aboriginal output and most importantly to explore a variety of interrelationships outside of but affecting inputs of land, labour and capital in order to understand the structure and function of Aboriginal economy. It is on this foundation that the rest of this section rests. Some matters discussed are comparatively conventional but others lie far away from the conventional approach of economists.

Gathering bands and division of labour

Whatever the per capita achievement may have been, precontact Aborigines clearly depended on small groups that were mobile in varying degrees, and they exploited an ordered division of labour to achieve their hunting and gathering output. The general convention is that men hunted and women gathered, though many qualifications to this pattern are recognised. These qualifications appear to be of considerable importance. Certain styles of hunting, by tracking and chasing larger animals or by tree climbing and chopping, depended on the relatively unencumbered movement of relevant humans, with a high degree of individual effort. Capture of smaller animals was not nearly so prescriptive and allowed participation by less freely moving individuals and by hunters working in common. Gathering allowed maximum potential to encumbered members of the group, whether it was for plants, seafoods or eggs, and was achievable either by individuals or in groups.

Elementary considerations of the theory of comparative advantage would point to the logic of the general understanding of gender division of labour: women carrying or caring for children were under the greatest physical constraint. This joint product of females, yielding human capital and food, also encouraged them to work in slower-moving groups to accommodate to the limitations of and share the tasks in caring for children. Equally, it did not constrain them from joining males in fishing from land (cf. the distinction between line fishing on the one hand and spear or boat fishing on the other), from the capture of river fish by methods other than swimming, or from participation in limited-area communal hunting of small animals. With these gender constraints during child-bearing years, women could not expect to attain individual hunting skills in respect of larger fast-moving animals, so that even after child-bearing years they would remain at a comparative disadvantage. Leaving any broader cultural considerations aside, it was efficient, therefore, to make a significant gender differentiation in upbringing and training and confirm a broad life-time array of comparative advantage and disadvantage.

The fact that men, not possessing these constraints, *could* gather is irrelevant. They might, indeed, have done so when the yield from hunting was so low that their marginal product in hunting fell below that in gathering. Even this has to be qualified by the relatively high risk — high degree of uncertainty of success — of hunting. In addition, preferences of the group might have pointed to this male specialisation in areas of particularly low hunting yield because of the strong demands for *some* hunting products whether for food or to supply clothing or other consumption or capital input items. In these conditions, the expected consequence would, theoretically, be reduced group size and a sex imbalance with relatively few males and more females. This seems to have been a common condition in central Australia. In areas of greater abundance of both hunting and gathering products — western Victoria is an excellent example — larger group size and a greater equality of numbers of each sex with a marked gender division of labour appears to be consistent with expectations.

Individual production and economies of scale

Harvesting of individual items in general depended essentially on individual hunting or gathering activity. Within these limits and given existing technology, there was limited opportunity for increased productivity through joint efforts, apart from the indirect benefit of any communal child care. Productivity could vary with the ability to achieve detailed understanding of the available resources and their variance in a group's area, and this might follow from different types of common behaviour to be discussed later. For the moment, however, it is important to note the opportunities for and implications of activity in common in a different context.

Clearly, in many areas, joint activities were undertaken within small hunting and gathering bands and on a much larger scale on special occasions of tribal gatherings. In many of these joint processes men, women and children often acted in unison; in others, men acted jointly. Basically, the issue is whether Aborigines, acting in common, could achieve economies of scale.

On occasions of tribal groupings, very large numbers of men (said at times to be several hundred in Queensland), together with dogs, took part in great kangaroo hunting drives. Efficiency derived from the ability to contain animal movements, more quickly capture wounded animals, share in transportation back to camp and so on. Similarly, in periods of eel migration in western Victoria, both men and women were able to capture a higher proportion of migrating eels through the presence of greater numbers of predatory humans.

But there were many circumstances related to the exploitation of capital. The most remarkable was the development of massive networks of eel canals directing and restricting the movement of eels but also ensuring that a higher proportion of eels survived to achieve their end in human stomachs. The eel canals, reminiscent of possible horticultural channels in New Guinea, entailed a great deal of communal effort. This was required first to construct the system but also and very importantly to maintain it intact. The provision of this extensive asset not only increased the yield per person but also enhanced the supply. Closely related to these were extensive stone fish traps, where rocks, often too large to be handled by individual men, were placed in river systems or coastal locations. This joint effort with carefully chosen placement provided circumstances in which, as river or tidal levels fell, fish remained, particularly in the rivers, trapped but alive *and stored* ready for easy capture.

Less dramatic but nevertheless significant was the varied use of nets and moveable 'fences' used to capture fish, birds or animals. Again one needs to note that it was not merely used in common but also communally constructed and maintained. It seems probable that many nets were the product of both sexes, jointly generating equipment that might at times be many metres long. Because they were often damaged by fleeing animals or flying birds or were exposed to the debris carried by river or estuarine flow, inspection and maintenance were major and continuing requirements for the group as a whole.

As productive equipment, their use depended on effort in common. Nets stretched between trees across narrow river valleys were exploited by parties of men, some startling birds to fly towards the nets with others high in trees making noises like hawks to induce birds to fly low. Cooperation of this style could greatly enlarge capture rates. Modern notions that Aborigines, lacking guns, could not match modern kill rates are misconceptions. Similar joint efforts using brush net-fences to surround animals or to place nets across travel lines are another example of highly productive joint action in which, in this case, women and children appear often to have joined as pursuers rather than killers of game.

But the most pervasive process of action in common was in the use of fire (Gudeman, 1986; Hallam, 1985; Jones, 1980), applied in most areas of Australia. Fire was often used in association with net fences to enhance capture rates. The use of fire had implications other than those discussed here and it will be necessary to return to it. But fire was used with limited areal burning both to capture game or to expose other foods, including eggs, slow-moving creatures and yam fields. It provided a short-term abundance, it simplified all gathering tasks and it removed snakes and other dangerous creatures. Given the nature of many Australian shrubs and grasses, it reduced physical injury and allowed unimpeded movement, further enhancing productivity. This latter factor seems to have been peculiarly prominent in western Cape York, as one factor in explaining the tendency to focus on the seashore for half the year and land resources for the balance. Above all, however, the use of fire depended on control to prevent more than a given limited area being burnt or even to ensure that special objects within the fired area were protected. That control depended on group, not individual, effort. Failure of control could lead to destructive damage. At the extreme, this failure could damage neighbours' resources, creating inter-group or inter-tribal tensions.

There were, then, within any given group, many opportunities for economies of scale in specific enterprises and sometimes economies of scale for the group as a whole in a wide range of activities. These opportunities posed a considerable variety of choices in production planning for Aborigines. There was, however, an additional major problem of choosing. This was in the migratory pattern that each group displayed.

Seasonality and variance in production

However much the resources may have been managed, there was, in every area of Australia, considerable variance in supplies. This variance arose on a seasonal basis throughout the year; and it was also due to climatic conditions yielding floods or droughts, with effects extending beyond the year and beyond the limits of specific groups or tribes. The extreme of this variance is indicated in nineteenth and twentieth century evidence (likely to have been relevant to immediate precontact conditions) of prolonged Australia-wide droughts with a periodicity at about 40 years.

Let us concentrate on 'normal' seasonal movements. It is not sufficient to say, as much of the older and even some recent literature does, that Aborigines responded to the 'rhythms' of the seasons. (I ignore Elkins' extreme view (Mulvaney and White, 1987) that Aborigines were merely parasitical on nature!). There is a high degree of irregularity in these so-called rhythms. What is implied is a good deal of uncertainty and the need for information and protection. Notions of 'traditional behaviour' will not take us very far. Indeed, in this context, it is the variance in Aboriginal behaviour, not any standardised migratory pattern, that implies a basic rationality and, indeed, a high order of intelligent management. Will some alternative location yield higher productivity, not merely in one type of goods but in the mix preferred by any group? What are the costs of transfer? What is the optimal extent to which any area should be 'cropped' of its resources? Is there advantage in opportunistic responses to sudden micro-variations in climate? How are these variations to be identified? Is any action feasible that would make an area of exploitation more attractive at some future date? Who determines the responses?

It is not suggested that Aborigines made conscious cost–benefit calculations yielding a strictly optimal decision. Ecologists have attempted to develop theories of transfer for migratory animals, based on relative marginal productivity in alternative locations and on the costs of transfer. Curiously, they hesitate to apply these theories (all of which are conventional and simple economic theorems) to so-called primitive hunter gatherers (Smith, 1983). Yet to make these theorems relevant does not require any further assumption than that Aborigines generally behaved as if they were motivated in these ways. To accommodate to Aboriginal practice, it would be appropriate to assess the net transfer costs for travel to an alternative area and the transport costs of harvests to camp within any given area relative to these costs in the alternative location. Aborigines may, in fact, have recognised other cultural stimuli that happened to be consistent with optimal seasonal behaviour. To suggest this, however, flies against our knowledge of Aborigines' very obvious mastery of the details of their ecology. Given that detailed understanding and the knowledge of their dependence on the long-term viability of different locations, it seems implausible that Aborigines had not worked out the broad essentials of these theorems, or something closely akin to them.

It is consistent with this that Aborigines widely differentiated between the durability of dwellings in areas where substantial amounts of time were spent and of those used when they were travelling; such differentiation meant that the costs of transfer were reduced. Similarly, belongings were frequently left at points of use. So we have extensive scatters of implements left in association with large middens; historical evidence of implements routinely left behind at more perma-nent locations. Similarly, there is evidence of individuals keeping each other informed by smoke signals of the supply conditions in different areas around a gathering range. Both uncertainty about resource prospects and the costs of transfer were thereby limited. Clearly, intimate knowledge acquired over many generations would simplify any 'calculus' but the fact that Aborigines had learned, from long tradition, to behave in a broadly seasonal manner does not mean that they were caught in an unchanging web of 'traditional practice'.

What does seem likely, in contrast with the much-abused notion of modern 'economic man', is that Aborigines appear to have been concerned with long-term viability and with a degree of resource management that would ensure their ability to return to any locations, not merely to 'mine' one and leave it. Substantial seasonal changes clearly imposed some degree of movement. After some period of exploitation of a given area, marginal costs would be expected to rise either because seasonal crops were being exhausted or because increasing distances to base camp imposed rising transport costs. Resource management could ameliorate that pressure, reduce uncertainties, or accelerate decline in supply conditions, but it could not eliminate them.

In any seasonal gathering pattern, it appears reasonably clear that Aborigines chose to emphasise resources with greater rather than less seasonal abundance. There has been in the older literature a tendency to emphasise the opportunistic and omnivorous elements in Aboriginal consumption. This emphasis does have a value. It seems improbable that Aboriginal women typically gathered with a single crop in mind or that men went solely to hunt a particular type of animal. The netting of ducks in season, the transfer to small wallabies in others, the collection of yams at some times or the digging of fern roots at others all imply more than opportunism or merely ecological conditioning. Higher yield goods in season were preferred. But in such a conscious choice — an obviously rational one — other supplies that happened to come (and often could be expected to come) their way were sensibly caught in their harvest. Though they might emphasise a seasonally strategic good, they were not single-product producers. Areal firing, in particular, was commonly designed to deliver a variety of products.

Order and property rights

This question is not dealt with clearly in the available literature, yet it is a crucial one. In the absence of strong government or a market, one needs to search for some other decision-making mechanism, particularly in the allocation of the workforce. Again the answer in terms of 'traditional' behaviour, important as tradition may have been, does not seem adequate. It is represented, for example, that some young men could actually leave a given group and, within kin constraints, join another. Degrees of freedom on that scale imply a decision-making process for different subgroups to allocate their time between different tasks individually, to take or not take part in communal activity or to relocate individually on a smaller scale. The indicated opportunities for individual consumption also imply a degree of conflict between individual and group interest.

A group could not survive unless interdependence of its members was recognised as a fundamental characteristic. It would have been impossible if many individuals could choose on a daily basis to pursue their own specific productive activity and hence produce a consumption output to suit their personal preferences. One factor that underlay the ordered activity of the group was its limited size and communal existence. It has been suggested that, in the absence of literacy, the costs of communication were high for primitive societies. Small size and communal living made it possible for everyone to know a great deal about each other, for opinions to be exchanged readily, for the day's activities to be debated. Reference has already been made to women 'gossiping' in groups, about frequent 'squabbles' breaking out and so on. What the literature does not indicate is the content of the 'gossip' and 'squabbles', except in relation to extreme circumstances where punishment was meted out to some wrong-doer. These verbal activities contrast with Sahlins' contemporary picture of the idleness and outright somnolence of recent Aboriginal groups. It seems plausible that there were indeed debates about productive activity (and individual views and preferences) that must have figured prominently in the group's concerns and that debates often yielded resolutions about immediate future courses of action. It is likely that these resolutions would not merely be about production as such but also about the satisfaction of consumption preferences. In many respects, the two were interchangeable concepts. Nevertheless, what sanctions constrained any individual or subgroup to depart from some (hypothetical) consensus? Physical punishment was possible, particularly for women. But could this merely lead to disintegration?

Such verbal exchanges as occurred at campsites reinforced another characteristic that tended to enforce a basic conformity to a group resolution. This was the need for individual as well as group insurance. The less affluent any group was, or the more exposed it was to risk and uncertainty in the maintenance of supplies, the greater the need for insurance. One might expect, then, a graduation in the extent to which insurance was necessary. Insurance could be achieved partly (but not necessarily fully) by the acceptance of interdependence of each member of the group. To break away or even to diverge from a 'production plan' would court the risk of interruption of supplies.

The need for insurance operated on a much larger scale than that of the group. In this context, extended kin relationships provided a larger system of insurance in the event of more serious threats to supplies. Kinship systems figure prominently in anthropological literature and properly so, if only from this perspective. Kinship relationships were cemented in a large variety of ways: in ritual, ceremony, exchange of goods and, perhaps above all, exchange of women. These exchanges provided amongst other things for the expectation of mutual support in time of need. Because ritual, ceremony and kin obligations were so prominent, each individual in a group was caught in a complex net that constrained independent deviant behaviour.

But Aboriginal groups did not lack a system of hierarchy and authority. Here the underlying issue appears to have been inequality in property rights, partly between individuals, partly between the sexes and partly between the generations. These elements of inequality might directly underwrite a system of order. The hope or expectation of access to them served as an incentive to those seeking to acquire property rights. All these conditions acted to impose a substantial degree of order in decision-making and, in the last resort, the implementation of sanctions. In a modern society, the functioning of the market depends crucially on property rights and it is not surprising that these, in a different form and a different manner, played a major role in the effective functioning of the Aboriginal economy.

Rose (1987) is one of the most vigorous exponents of the argument that property rights in women were basic to Aboriginal order. Women provided vital property instruments to cement ties between groups. But within the smaller bands the common adoption of polygyny provided a solid foundation for the exercise of order by elders. In the process, a hierarchical structure was established amongst women as well. It seems probable that a subsidiary hierarchy may also have been developed among younger men.

Land, kinship and cross-transfers of women by marriage made up an interlocking system that underpinned much of Aboriginal culture (Gudeman, 1986). Acceptance of all the associated ritual and ceremony was fundamental to the stability and functioning of Aboriginal society. 'Belonging to land' went far beyond modern notions of residence and nationalism but this concept needs to be seen as part of Aboriginal recognition of their deep and intimate dependence on land and their need to understand fully its potential resources. 'Belonging to land' also meant that land belonged to each group or band. In choosing wives or having wives bestowed upon them, men received women from other groups as determined by complex grid patterns of kin relationships, and the relevant females became part of the husband's gathering band and belonged to that land area. The insurance implications of this interchange of females have already been discussed.

Typically, most females were acquired as wives by older men, the elder or elders. This did not exclude marriage for younger men, an issue to be taken up shortly. Indeed, the distribution of wives and the degree of concentration of 'ownership' could vary significantly between groups. Group elders might be seen, stylistically, as possessing several wives with a great age range from old age to virtual infancy. Indeed, depending on succession and inheritance, an elder might have a wife significantly older than himself.

The possession of a woman was a valuable asset. She produced and cared for children. And she provided the bulk of the most secure sources of food. She prepared much of the food eaten, cooked and sewed, wove bags and nets and often built the transitory shelters. She participated in a vital way in many joint activities. She even participated in battles. She provided sexual enjoyment. Given the separation of the sexes at camps, one might, perhaps, question whether she was allowed to provide much continuing companionship. Excluded from the possession of weapons, she was, at least in the last resort, physically subject to male authority (exceptions might arise in cases where women were actually the effective elders of a group). Women were also progressively the possessors of their own ritual and lore, contributing directly to cultural stability and hence to the economic viability of the group. As they aged from childhood, women acquired increasing command, through learning-by-doing and through direct instruction, of the detailed knowledge of the ecology and its resource management as well as the ritual on which the security of group supplies depended.

Young men had, then, several reasons to lust after women. In this stylistic representation, the attachment of females in varying age ranges to an elder male provided him with a hierarchy of skills, child-bearing opportunities and constraints. It was also a means of focusing through older women information about the attitudes and the knowledge of each of the wives and their dependants. It provided a system of ensuring the handing down of the cultural traditions and stock of understanding of areal resources and management related to females. It does not follow that male elders merely dominated. Polygyny of this form may also have given older males some additional ability to control population size. Women, on the other hand, had considerable bargaining power and one may well wonder whether there were occasions when a senior wife acted or was forced to act as a shop steward! But the ultimate threat of physical dominance by males tended strongly to yield an essentially male chain of authority.

Sexual issues apart, there appear to be several reasons for expecting the establishment of authority in a broad female hierarchy by age. Once past child-bearing years, an older woman was no longer constrained with infants and was a more flexible instrument of production. She had acquired a high degree of skill in and understanding of productive processes, and could be expected to exercise oversight of female groups, to be prominent in training new recruits to the workforce, to be exploited to assess the merits of alternative gathering areas where special and reliable understanding might be necessary, and in other ways to feed in the essential information to the varied output decisions that needed to be made. In addition, women had their own rituals and ceremonies. As effective owners of this female ritual and capable of its controlled transfer to younger females, older women were a prime source of tribal and band traditions and practices, helping further to bind Aboriginal society and hence Aboriginal economy together. Moreover, it should be recognised that a claim of authority downwards could serve as a chain of information upwards.

Theoretically, one might expect such a concentration of ownership of women to be at its greatest in areas of greatest scarcity of resources and where maximum order was necessary in both hunting and gathering to ensure adequate supplies. Some relaxation of these conditions would tend to encourage the enlargement of the band size and with it a reduction in the degree of concentration in the 'ownership' of females. That is, the more married males in a group, the somewhat greater dispersion there was in the degree of concentration of property. The question of access of younger men to females became then a significant issue in sustaining the ordered operation of any band where this matter arose.

Younger males, members of a band, might trespass or seek to trespass on an elder's property. Here the significance of band size, communal dwelling and the process of communication of information become important. Trespass would be difficult without relatively early exposure in conditions where women worked and slept reasonably closely together. Discussions around a campsite would be a ready means of public identification of culprits. Rose suggests that there was no invariant response. Some trespass could be tolerated. Persistent behaviour might lead to penalties either within the band or at tribal gatherings. In the last resort, identified culprits could be punished by beating, spearing, being driven out of a band or killed. As in land ownership, there was not necessarily a precise boundary line, just as in any stable system of order there is an uncertain line between tolerance and harshness. Economists might suggest this as tending to 'optimal' behaviour.

Younger men might obtain wives as bequests from dead relatives, the inheritance process passing through an identifiable system of relationship and thereby sometimes yielding to a man a wife older than himself. But the more important sequence was bestowal achieved by the attainment of appropriate status and by performance. Here, elders had another powerful property instrument to reinforce their authority, property in ritual. Young males had to pass through initiation ceremonies and other rites, with ritualistic understanding transmitted by elders. But they would normally expect to wait a considerable number of years before some of them could expect to marry. The more daring could, perhaps, raid another group and steal a wife. This might bring threats or acts of retaliation on their own band and might be less than beneficial. Performance and recognition within the group could, for a limited proportion of males, achieve bestowal. Such bestowal could often be of an infant girl, imposing a long period of orderly behaviour on the man to achieve his eventual goal. These requirements sustained the authority of elders in decision-making processes and could be at least part of the explanation for successful hunters ostentatiously surrendering the prime parts of their catches. To that extent, not only was production incentive offered but sharing rules were underwritten.

Consumption behaviour

As producers, small Aboriginal groups were also consumers of their own production (there are separate issues arising in respect to the limited trade carried on at large tribal gatherings). It is customary to emphasise consumption in common and goods being delivered back to an evening camp for preparation. Implicitly, at this point, the central issue appears then to be the sharing rules adopted in the absence of a formal market and of rates of exchange between different goods. If nothing else, the substantial if qualified division of labour required some sharing or implicit exchange relationship between different producers.

It seems clear that there were sharing rules at such campsites. Observers

(Smyth, 1878) report the frequent arrangements whereby successful hunters received the less substantial part of the capture; and of ordered division according to relationship, sex and age, with women being delivered the (allegedly) least acceptable part of the harvest. One might hesitate to judge too firmly whether European observers could adequately evaluate Aboriginal preferences. Nevertheless, it is difficult to cast much doubt on this widespread conception.

But there are at least two other considerations that might be major issues determining the satisfaction of preferences by individual members of any group. One was that not all foods were eaten in common round a camp. The second is that production choices had important implications for consumer satisfaction and the two need to be seen as interactive.

There is ample evidence of individual consumption. This is not surprising if only because hunters and gatherers expended considerable energy in their harvesting activities. Some commentators refer in passing to hunters eating 'leaves' while hunting; others to one or two hunters eating part of a catch before returning it to camp. Both men and women are indicated as eating manna gum during the day's work and consuming berries and wild fruit during picking. There are innocent statements about Aborigines obtaining grubs from trees and roots and 'with great enjoyment and much laughter' eating them *on the spot*.

However significant these (and possible unknown) examples may have been, it is clear that Aborigines could and did respond at least partly in a strictly individual and not merely communal manner in sharing total harvests. But there was another more important route whereby the satisfaction of particular wants might be determined. This was through productive activity and the allocation of time to different possible pursuits. The discussion above relating to productive activity can be read as bearing on consumption patterns and preferences. To a large degree, the two were inseparable. In other words, labour allocation between alternative activities lay at the base of the process of satisfying alternative consumption demands.

Exchange and trade

Given the concentration of activity within small bands, their separation from others for long periods, limited storage capacity for foodstuffs and a broad similarity of supply conditions, the opportunity for sufficient differences in comparative advantage to generate trade flows was limited. Nevertheless, this basic explanation of trade appears to have been directly relevant in some degree. Most notably, the arrival of trepang fishermen from Sulawesi created a special condition on the northern shoreline of Australia. This was exceptional and recent. It led to new products, new inputs (the dingo) and new ideas that might percolate throughout Australia. More generally, we do not know when immigration ceased (or if it ever did) so that there may have been a continuous source of inflow of migrant capital with changing technology and new ways of doing old things. This may be part of the explanation for technological changes that can be observed over many millennia and may bear on the growth processes to be discussed below.

There were, however, special resource supply conditions in particular areas yielding valued objects that were traded over long distances. Thus axe heads from

Gippsland were traded far into Australia. Such processes appear to have been of long standing, in that comparable equipment throughout large parts of Western Australia can have come only from locations now submerged under the sea.

There were less overt trading relations. Allen's description of subgroups on the Darling exchanging river for interior land locations for periods within the year is an ingenious method whereby people were moved to goods rather than the reverse. The network of kinship systems and limitations on marriage might be thought of, in this context, as imposing a prohibitive tax on domestic transactions and hence the generation of 'trade' in women. At larger gatherings, in which again people moved to goods rather than vice versa, trade in women was only part of a complex exchange in which ceremonial and ritual were shared, along with the seasonal rich supplies that were a condition of these assemblies.

At the other extreme of these overt exchanges, there was the process of 'silent' trade identified by Stanner. Here goods were left to be collected by some subsequent visitor and some return commodity put in place without the traders coming face to face. This trade illustrates one character of Aboriginal trade that has received some prominence, the concept that exchange was not normally 'equal' but rather that some transfers were clearly of goods or services not obviously required by something of comparable value. The extreme appears to be where transactions were one-sided. This is a suspect concept. The exchange of goods or services of unequal value might be read as an unequal trade balance and hence either the repayment of a past debt or the acceptance of a future one. In other words, a capital transfer was involved, with a debt to be paid and collected. If that assumption underlay Aboriginal trade, as anthropologists often suggest, then one needs to be cautious of thinking in terms of unequal trade. The building up of a debt, the arrangement for insurance, the expectation of some future, perhaps long-delayed, return makes it difficult to think of Aborigines accepting unequal trade exchanges.

In these conditions, it is hard to assess how important trade and exchange were in the Aboriginal economy. Most of it was probably concentrated at particular times of the year, with small bands being essentially self-contained (under 'normal' circumstances). Nevertheless, insofar as cases of transfer of people to resources rather than goods to people have been identified, there remains the question whether a different articulation of trading relations may have existed, making trade more significant and widespread than has been suggested.

11

DYNAMIC ELEMENTS IN
THE ABORIGINAL
ECONOMY

So far, emphasis has been placed on some of the major aspects of so-called 'traditional' behaviour. There are many qualifications and some other matters that might have been discussed. In the available space it is necessary to concentrate on a different issue, the dynamic elements in Aboriginal economy. Some fall within the limits of what might be regarded as a 'static' economy (and there is a fine dividing line between what one might mean by 'static' and 'dynamic'); others would suggest the possibility of change in one or all of three senses — structural change; increase in real income per head; increase in aggregate output and population (including increased densities per land unit).

Intergenerational transfers

Intergenerational transfer of knowledge depends on increasing the understanding of new recruits in generational terms, so maintaining human capital intact requires some dynamic action. An existing generation must run faster so that, relative to it, a succeeding generation can stand still. This encompasses more than just the productive activities of hunting and gathering or even of resource management. The intergenerational transfer of ritual and myth, both lore and law, is vital. These are important issues that Possner's otherwise very valuable contribution omits.

If the maintenance of human capital is a matter that needs to be added to concepts of hunting and gathering, so does learning by doing for an existing generation. This learning by doing may be important in seasonal adaptations, and even in moving between well known areas; seasonal characteristics change and with them the specifics of production possibilities. This matter is important enough and has attracted some attempts at formalisation. But there are others that are closely related. Longer term exogenous or endogenous changes require adaptation and a new learning; the transmission of techniques and information between smaller and larger groups introduces potential novelty that needs to be understood — or, if appropriate, discarded. Climatic changes, the exhaustion by overkill of some food resources, the introduction of new hunting methods illustrated by the arrival of the dingo or the introduction of eel canals indicate each type of *new* educational requirement. Moreover learning challenges were not merely physical and technological; at every step, ritual and ceremony were integral parts of the absorption of desired behaviour.

To 'traditional' hunting and gathering objectives, we need to add, then, education, training and learning or relearning as a basic end of Aboriginal activity. These may have been intermediate inputs into the productive process or final ends in the preservation of group or tribal tradition. This distinction is in fact obscure to the extent that the transmission of understanding and tradition sustained the functioning (morale?) of Aboriginal society. The ends involved may have been achieved as on-the-job training, merely ancillary to normal diurnal or even ceremonial activity, or they may have been achieved by the commitment of specific labour or time inputs. If the latter, they imposed demands for extra time budgeting; and even as ancillary activities it is likely that they extended the time used by primary hunters and gatherers to secure their output objectives.

To the extent that division of labour at least frequently separated the sexes as adults and training was required both in diurnal activity and in tribal or group tradition, the question that immediately arises is the potential source of the range of education/training required. Women, specialised in gathering techniques, could scarcely teach young males the rudiments of hunting, nor could men teach girls the tasks of gathering. Even without extreme divisions of labour, the question of gender skills and property rights in understanding is likely to have led to the need to allocate time to the various educational requirements.

It is consistent with this approach that initiation ceremonies occupy such a large role in the literature — ceremonies that applied to both boys and girls. These can be too easily regarded as ceremonial and ritual, as ends in themselves. Even as such, they transferred understanding — property rights — of elders to their successors and maintained the social fabric and hence the efficient functioning of the group. But there are indications of additional time budgeting. Thus Brough Smyth (1878) reports the presence of old men specifically instructing boys on a regular basis. But it bears repetition that, much more generally, there is the record of what has been seen by Europeans as merely leisure time activities — during which adults appear at ease — in which children participate in games of skill and agility. What appears to be adult leisure is important as educational time and an important end to be satisfied. Reputedly games of a form of 'football' (Brough Smyth), organised throwing of small spears or boomerangs, climbing and wrestling could all transmit skills; and adult oversight of these activities could appear to be indolence. At a more philosophical level — but nevertheless relevant also to economic behaviour — there were reprimands or advice in respect of such issues as not damaging or even marking the land unless for some specific purpose. The ultimate in such instruction occurred during large gatherings when all age groups could witness in a variety of ways some of the fundamental institutional values of a tribe.

This matter of education and learning or relearning is introduced in order to stress that, at the most elementary and traditional level, there were dynamic elements in Aboriginal society. These were not the only dynamic issues and we can turn from them to questions of expansion, growth and structural change.

Expansion, growth and structural change

These are matters of prime importance if one is interested in whether Aboriginal society and economy were merely 'traditional' (stationary) or in a process of change at the time of European settlement. Here we cannot look only at cross-sectional relationships at 1788 but need to consider likely changes over some period prior to European arrival. In doing so, it is important to bear in mind that, prior to the eighteenth century, change, expansion and growth in what we now think of as the developed economies were extremely slow relative to the pace of today. We need to adopt a comparable perspective and perhaps even a longer one in dealing with the Aboriginal economy.

Structural change connotes an alteration in the composition of output, consumption and the workforce, and in this case it is important to specify the range and variety of production possibilities. Expansion means an increase in aggregate output, the numbers in the workforce, the total volume of 'supplies' (aggregate ecological 'improvement') or the total land. Growth relates to an increase in output per unit of population, workforce, land or physical capital, or some other source of increased consumption per head (greater efficiency in consumption itself).

In the light of the collision of cultures that occurred in Australia after 1788, it is interesting to consider the fact that a mere 17 000 years ago most of Europe and particularly Britain were overlain with massive glaciers. Population must almost certainly have been minimal. By contrast, Aborigines in Australia had a land area significantly larger than today and had had the opportunity for development, free of glacial extremes, for several millennia before 17 000 BP. Across the Pacific, and particularly in South America and Mexico, a very complex, urbanised, quite highly developed and integrated society had been established (or waxed and waned) during, at most, the past 20–30 000 years (Sturt, 1849). From this perspective it is, perhaps, not surprising that Sahlins stresses the 'failure' of Australian Aborigines to develop an 'advanced' culture. In terms of Western Europe, development appears to have been concentrated during the past 4–8000 years, even though one might extend horticultural and some grazing and farming development earlier. By 500 years ago, Western Europeans had achieved global mobility. It is perhaps reasonable to adopt a time perspective for change in Aboriginal economy over a span of the order of 4–8000 years.

Exogenous factors

Seas reached their present levels, according to graph 1 (p. 15), at about 6000 BP. They may have been rising throughout the preceding 11 000 years but most importantly, between about 11 000 and 6000 BP, sea levels had risen through critically important points between −60 metres bp and current levels. One should beware of treating this graph literally. For what it is worth, it might be taken to suggest a number of significantly different regional effects over this latter period.

Possibly at around about 9000 BP Lakes Bass and Carpentaria could have been invaded by the sea, thus altering their hitherto brackish character and the resources associated with them. By perhaps something like 8000 BP, Tasmania and New Guinea were physically separated from Australia and it seems likely that any Aborigines occupying the exposed seabed areas off north-west Australia were being forced inland to the present Australian continent. Later still, perhaps around 7000 BP, Aborigines were in retreat from what are now the eastern limits of the Great Barrier Reef off Queensland. Within a further thousand years, the present geographical limits of mainland Australia were defined.

These changes brought massive disturbances and readjustments more rapid than anything that had occurred during the preceding ice age. Insofar as withdrawing populations moved towards any established inland people, one would expect a general tendency towards conflict and an increased concentration of population. One may, then, need to read any recent archaeological record carefully to avoid a misinterpretation of such concentration. Increased concentration over these millennia did not necessarily mean increased population, despite higher population densities. But not all these changes were disadvantageous, at least when one allows ecological readaptation over a span of a few hundred years. Thus the recovering of the Barrier Reef seabed during perhaps the 1000 years or so after around 8000 BP would encourage a rapid coral regrowth and the generation of masses of marine life on a far richer scale than was likely to have been the case when Aborigines relied on relatively steeply shelving coasts and deep water. It is possible, indeed, that for Queensland in particular the return of the seas over these 1000 odd years was dominantly beneficial for aggregate productivity. Short-term distress may have been concentrated at sea margins in relation to land resources. On the other hand, in Bass Strait, related to an area far smaller than Queensland, the impact was probably largely disadvantageous because of lowered relative or aggregate productivity.

Changes on the present Australian land mass appear as similarly diverse. Former glaciation that had induced the retreat of rainforests meant that its reversal at 17–12 000 years ago led to the return of rainforests that were not particularly advantageous to hunter gatherers. Thus in south-west Tasmania or on the Atherton Tableland in Queensland, the past 12 000 years may have seen the recovery of dense forests and a reduction in production potential. It is probable that this experience was replicated along the coast in Queensland and in part of coastal New South Wales.

Different changes, also disadvantaging Aborigines, occurred in central Australia. One hypothesis is that the extreme of the ice age pushed monsoonal conditions southwards in Australia, improving production potential in the centre. Relaxation of ice age conditions tended to dry out the centre of Australia, extending the area of low rainfall as heavy monsoon conditions moved north. At the same time, the redefinition of monsoonal conditions in Australia meant the gradual restoration of flood rains into the Darling tributaries, just as the disappearance of glaciation on the Eastern Highlands restored flow to the Murray–Murrumbidgee. In eastern Australia, more advantageous conditions, as we know them today, took shape over the past 10 000 years and possibly particularly over the past 6000.

CLIMANZ has attempted to speculate about these and other changes

(CLIMANZ, 1983). The essential implication appears to be that productivity in northern and eastern Australia improved over the few thousand years before Europeans settled Australia. In an enlarging dry centre, conditions deteriorated. What the net effect on Aboriginal productivity and population potential was is a matter of guesswork. It seems almost certain that the changes imposed major adaptations on Aborigines in terms of production and consumption patterns. However, there were other more nearly if not wholly endogenous changes that may have yielded population expansion or growth in per capita productivity.

Technological changes

Archaeologists cannot agree about whether the many changes evident in Aboriginal stone tool-kits over the past 5000 or so years were the results of imported technology or were made independent of the outside world. Certainly there appear to have been substantial changes over this time (Flood, 1983; Mulvaney and White, 1987). Stone tools became smaller, finer and possible more precise. In some cases, it appears hard to determine whether some of these changes were the result of fashion rather than the search for improved efficiency. It seems unlikely, however, that the exploitation of fine stone spear tips did not improve killing efficiency — whether hunting for animals or fish — as opposed to dominantly wooden or thick-tipped spears. Possibly of acute significance was the development of hafting of axes with resin glues and, above all, the hafted fine stone chisel or adze. With this implement Aborigines were in a position to develop a large variety of finely shaped wooden tools and implements on which, in the last resort, their efficiency depended. The adze seems to be a product predominantly of the past 4000 years. With this, the hollowing of logs, the shaping of spear-throwers, the construction of shields, the removal of bark for canoes, housing or artistic products, including all forms of carving, to name a few, became much more efficient. Perhaps of equal significance, the maintenance (resharpening, reshaping) of wooden implements was greatly facilitated. One might suggest, indeed, that stone age people looked to stone tools predominantly to produce wooden equipment.

These technological changes bore, with no visible differentiation, on hunting and gathering alike. Implements to hunt, fish, dig and gather were equally improved. Potential productivity change could then be expected to go beyond increased efficiency of individual activity in these various areas. To the extent that tasks requiring effort by individuals were more efficiently performed, one might expect that more time was available for activities in common. In other words, the potential for undertaking large digging operations in the construction of big cooking ovens, in creating elevated sites near food resources and, in the last resort, in undertaking massive projects in the extensive channel works of eel canals became more feasible as wooden implements could be made, repaired or resharpened with less effort. One of the striking changes associated with eel canals was the tendency of Aborigines to establish essentially residential locations with durable houses.

Perhaps even more generally, it became more feasible to undertake routine tasks in which economies of scale through joint activity led to increased output per unit of input. The stone adze chisel appears, therefore, as possibly crucial in releasing Aborigines from a commitment to time in individual activity and enabling increased activity in joint hunting drives, in larger ceremonial gatherings and in a more detailed understanding and ability to manage rather than merely exploit the resources at their disposal. It enhanced indirectly opportunities for more attention to ceremonial activity, the coherence and stability of their society, and hence their economic efficiency.

Another major change during the past 4000 years was clearly an import. This was the dingo. There is still considerable debate about the precise time of immigration of the dingo but the consensus appears to place it within this timespan. The dingo enabled a great increase in hunting efficiency, whether for large kangaroos or smaller animals, and it appears to have spread rapidly throughout the whole of Australia. By implication, its direct effect was on male efficiency but it should also be seen as contributing to the productivity of much activity in common wherever hunting was involved. By helping to discount the risks of male enterprises, the dingo might then be seen as freeing male time for male ritual and male dominance. In turn, these non-commodity activities helped to preserve social control and the effectiveness of order in allocating the workforce, adding further, if indirectly, to economic efficiency.

Resource management and productivity increase

We have no effective knowledge of when early human beings began to change from literal hunters and gatherers to become managers and 'improvers' of the resources on which they depended. Horticulture may have developed outside Australia some tens of thousands of years ago. Organised agrarian and pastoral activity may be limited to the past 10 000 or so years. Within Australia, Aborigines were for long perceived as 'failing' to become farmers and it was on this perception that Aboriginal land rights were rejected by the British government, the original settlers and subsequent generations in Australia. (Ironically, many European farmers subsequently 'failed' in their efforts to come to terms with Australian environmental conditions, and over large areas their activities not merely altered the environment but degraded, in the long run, the productivity of Australian land.)

Non-residential Aborigines might have remained on small areas, mining and exhausting their resources to such an extent that they would be unusable for long periods. Aborigines did not do so and that very fact implies a process of deliberate resource management. Migration on a seasonal basis — that is, returning annually (or more frequently) to parts of their hunting and gathering areas — indicates a form of resource management. Equally, however, this behaviour could be represented as no more than rational decision-making in the treatment of any location, moving when productivity, adjusted for transfer and transport costs, fell below that at some alternative site. On this perspective it left the ecology or resource flow unaltered in the long run. But it also avoided long-term resource depletion. Spiritual attachment to the land, the sense of bonding with land, the protective myths and ritual, and attitudes that land ownership meant, in part, the right to share resources with others might be seen as modes of achieving, in the absence of market signals or governing directions, techniques of order in land/labour combinations that ensured an approximation to this style of rational behaviour or long-term resource management.

There is a growing literature discussing 'resource management' along these lines

(Broome, 1982; Harris, 1980; Jones, 1980; Mulvaney and Golson, 1971; Brough Smyth, 1878; Walker, 1972; Williams, 1987; Williams and Hunn, 1982). Much of this presentation of the structure and function of Aboriginal economy is based directly or indirectly on this literature. Here, however, the focus is on efforts not merely to sustain *by conscious action on supply sources* the long-term resource supplies from given areas or locations, nor only to stabilise potential output and its seasonal yield but, in the last resort, to increase the aggregate flow of product potential from given areas.

Basically, agrarian activity evolved outside Australia around the processes of digging/ploughing, fertilising, planting, cultivating and harvesting. In island South-east Asia and New Guinea, a prior important process was slashing and burning a forest area for purposes of planting on a short-term basis. Aborigines have been said not even to have followed the New Guinea example of short-term horticulture, still less to have followed the European agrarian path. The European development was, to a very large extent, barred in Australia by the absence of indigenous four-legged animals that could be used for draught purposes. We do not know whether we can reasonably 'criticise' Aborigines for failing to follow the New Guinea example. Aborigines used fire for burning (we will return to this) but, over the past 5–8000 years, they used it at a time when the Australian climate was set towards its present character. Burning achieved in the main open woodland and grassland, not a brief farming window before the rainforest closed back in again. Rainfall was either monsoonal floods or intermittent and uncertain. The long-term outcome of burning was pasture not agricultural plots.

Accepting the technical sequence of extra-Australian agrarian activity, Aborigines might be seen as having approached farming activity in a variety of ways. Some acts may have been unaware; others quite purposive. Thus the extensive digging of yam fields was comparable to cultivation in turning over and aerating soil; yams may have grown better afterwards. Similarly, digging for fern roots may have assisted ferns to grow. Less obviously deliberate as a sequence, the mere intervention of humans in gathering seeds tended, subject to harvesting constraints, to liberate many plants from overcrowding and competition for soil nutrients. This may have been particularly important in relation to cycads. It may also have applied to the stooking of wild millet, where human exploitation removed the mass but ensured replacement of some seeds in appropriate areas. Evidence relating to yams suggests steps towards purposive action. Taboos on digging flowering yams might be further evidence of this. More deliberately, the replanting of the tops of yams suggests some perception of plant reproduction. Similarly, myths relating to the planting of baobab trees also suggest conscious action.

There are other allusive actions. The deliberate singeing of the tips of blackboy shrubs may have been accidental association. Whether singed by the sun or by humans with firesticks, the plants were then receptors of moths whose eggs yielded large grubs in the roots of plants so affected. Though cause and effect may have been wrongly connected, there can be little doubt but that action of this type implied a minute and attentive interest in ecological conditions. There can, however, be little doubt about the purposive action that Robinson recorded and Lourandos has emphasised in the construction of eel canals to encourage a population increase in eels and to simplify their capture. The sheer scale of the eel canals in western Victoria, probably the result of activity over the past few thousand years, is indicative of the ability of Aborigines, in appropriate circumstances, to act deliberately on a large scale to enhance resource potential.

The most pervasive and complex behaviour was, however, in the use of fire. Fire may have been used many millennia ago. We have no idea whether its use was purposive. There can be little doubt that over the past 5–8000 years, the use of fire to influence the environment was deliberate. It was not merely to create conditions for joint hunting and gathering that would yield a quick harvest. Fire had and was intended to have a major influence on the natural environment throughout Australia.

It might be noted that a similar use of fire has been recognised in the case of the Amerindians (Williams and Hunn, 1982). Here, however, planned burning appears as a much less risky and a more controllable operation. Burning in north America in very early spring allowed surface material to be removed at a time when the branches of highly combustible trees were still ice-covered and inert, and when subsurface soil was also frozen, protecting the growing tips of many plants. Subject to careful seasonal use, fire was a relatively safe instrument of ecological adaptation to use in North America.

In Australian conditions, the risks were much higher for climatic reasons. Control of the use of fire in relation to terrain, wind and temperature conditions and by the assembly of substantial numbers of people was fundamental in Australia. But once control was achieved and the risks ameliorated if not eliminated, fire could be used for areal burning with less limitation by exogenous seasonal conditions than was the case in North America. The implications were such that they fully justify Rhys Jones's (Allen *et al.*, 1977) use of the term 'fire-stick farming'. It seems most probable that, over several millennia, fire-stick farming drastically altered the Australian environment and was a major factor in creating the open woodland and grasslands that Europeans first encountered. Ironically, Aboriginal use of fire paved the way for their displacement by Europeans in creating 'natural pastures' to which the Europeans fell heir.

Fire-stick farming had many implications. Applied to many small areas, it provided at any given time a patchwork system of ecological adaptation and regeneration. Sequential burning of different areas meant that much of the Australian continent was progressively adapted over a very long period. We are not concerned here with the consequence already discussed of the immediate killing, disturbing or revealing of an animal and vegetable harvest but rather with the long-term adaptation and improvement of productivity that followed.

Some Australian plants require fire to release seeds for germination. Many have growing tips below the soil surface and even when completely burnt above ground will respond with new growth. Others are highly fire resistant and fire may serve to burn off predatory insects, diseased foliage and dead branches. Controlled firing thinned out vegetation, reducing excess competition and promoting the survival of the fittest, in true Darwinian manner. It encouraged the emergence of relatively open woodland mixed with grasses, selectively accommodated to repeated burning. This was the environment that Europeans encountered at first settlement, the product of several thousands of years of Aboriginal intervention and change. Fire-induced change meant that it was eminently adapted to hunting and gathering — and also to the introduction, with minimal technology, of European livestock.

Fire also returned nutrients to the soil. This fact, combined with the differential growth rates of plants, encouraged grassland development as a first response. Fire-stick farming was, then, a prominent element in controlled pastoralism by Aborigines. Different types of grazing animals could be attracted to areas as it suited Aborigines and these animals could be induced to shift to new locations to suit other combinations of Aboriginal resources at different seasonal times. Equally, such pasture improvement could be concentrated in micro-areas where Aborigines wished to gather for reasons other than the capture of grazing animals, in particular near water. It seems improbable that this did not yield a significant increase in both vegetable and animal supply as compared with the situation that would have existed in the absence of firing.

The use of fire in this way included elements of seeding, fertilising, thinning and cultivating, as well as the selective encouragement of particular plants and animals. It depended on Aboriginal awareness of appropriate seasonal conditions, the frequency with which any area could be burned and the associations of different flora and fauna in particular conditions. It also depended on control. All this meant purposive action to alter and improve production potential. An essential consequence was that it allowed Aborigines an enlarged choice in terms of social behaviour. Gradually improving productivity might be taken out in preferences other than food. More time could be allotted to 'cultural' ends and in the articulation of a richer and more varied culture. Alternatively, population could expand to accommodate to increased food supplies and the reduced demands on time to sustain food production. Over the past 25–30 000 years, the basic exogenous changes, particularly in climatic conditions, appear to have been such as to concentrate a great deal of this improved potential over the past 6–8000 years.

Of course, the choice was not simply between population increase or a richer culture. Aborigines might have optimised their chances by choosing some combination of the two broad options. But it does seem plausible to suggest that a major opportunity for population increase emerged over this period. It is possible that the timespan was more limited. Once the present shore of the Australian continent emerged about 8000 years ago, there remained a considerable period for the ecological conditions existing in 1788 to take shape. Aborigines were required to make major adaptations, regionally, in terms of productive activity and of consumption patterns. Resource management depended on an acute awareness of ecology through long-term learning by doing and this could only be established as an accepted 'best practice' over a very long period. It is possible then that Aborigines at the time of European settlement either had comparatively recently experienced major population and cultural change or were in the process of doing so. If only for this reason, one cannot simply conclude that the Aborigines observed by Europeans were then simply practising long established and unchanging 'traditional' modes of behaviour as a static society established over many millennia.

PART III

DISEASE, ECONOMICS AND DEMOGRAPHY

12

INTRODUCTION

As a case example of the depopulation of indigenous societies by European settlement, Australia stands in succession to the far more substantial one of North America and large parts of South America. In all cases, however, the scale of this depopulation has been disregarded because of long-held views of the very sparse use of natural resources by hunter gatherers. This, in turn, appears to be deeply rooted in the non-Malthusian view of hunter-gatherer economies. If scarcity was not a significant problem, hunter gatherers must have used resources very lightly and hence populations cannot have been large enough to stress natural resources. In the United States, population estimates by Kroeber and somewhat more generally by Mooney during the 1920s set the precontact Amerindian populations at very low levels — for the United States and Canada at approximately a million persons. Following this tradition, the long-held view of precontact Aboriginal numbers in Australia at 250–300 000 (but possibly more) derives from Radcliffe-Brown in an official estimate published in 1930.

Both sets of low numbers have been challenged relatively recently. In the United States, the main original challenger was Dobyns during the 1960s, followed by Zubrowe (1990: 754–65). Dobyns' revisions suggested precontact American numbers at 10–15 times the Mooney–Kroeber estimates and Dobyns has expanded this re-estimation to propose very large pre-Columbian populations (100–130 millions) for the whole American hemisphere. These revisions imply massive depopulation and widespread destruction of indigenous populations in the New World and, as European settlement occurred, the transfer of very large resources from these indigenous populations to the benefit first of the settlers and secondly to resident Europeans.

In the Australian case, the first substantial questioning was made by Lourandos for the particular area of Western Victoria. Lourandos' argument was based on the evidence of massive earth works for eel farming, associated with stone dwellings and substantially 'village' residence by the local Aborigines. Just before Lourandos' publication, archaeologists were displaying some unease with the traditional estimates and Rhys Jones attempted, from archaeological evidence, to re-estimate Tasmanian populations. He raised the traditional numbers of about 3000 precontact to only about 5000 — still a low number and below early nineteenth century official estimates at a time when significant depopulation had already occurred on the island.

In my book *Our Original Aggression* (1983), I attempted a slightly wider reconsideration to cover New South Wales and Victoria and from that made some rough extrapolations to the whole of Australia. This yielded the suggestion that Australian precontact Aboriginal populations might need to be thought of as in the order of five times the Radcliffe-Brown estimates, with population bounds of 1–1 500 000 persons in 1788. My 'guesstimations' suggested a population for New South Wales and Victoria alone at about the same level that Radcliffe-Brown had proposed for Australia as a whole. The present uncertainty about these estimates is indicated in the fact that the bicentennial publication, *Australians: Historical Statistics* contains two completely conflicting estimates of Aboriginal populations, while the companion volume *Australians to 1788* includes a third and different number as a professional (archaeological and anthropological) re-valuation by Mulvaney and White, proposing a precontact population of about 700 000.

The Radcliffe-Brown number of 250–300 000 had very comfortable implications, even granted his qualification 'and possibly more'. A large number of Aborigines survive in Australia and though they have been pushed aside by colonists, it may have seemed that no drastic damage had been done by taking their resources. But precontact populations of 700 000, 1 or 1.5 millions imply massive depopulation and widespread destruction of indigenous societies and economies.

The point is made to indicate the importance of the numbers game. The process of depopulation and resource displacement is a matter for the next chapter. What we are concerned with in this chapter is: how can we re-estimate precontact Aboriginal numbers? Were the hunter gatherers pressing so very lightly on the available resources that colonists might virtually disregard their presence, claiming that they had established no effective claim to the territory of Australia? If they did press so lightly, how did they manage it? Birth control and infanticide? Intertribal battles? Technical incompetence with poor diet and starvation? Disease? If there were, say, a million precontact Aborigines, the discussion of their economy in the preceding chapter becomes more interesting and relevant. But could they still have a high standard of food consumption with that level of population? If so, was their population expanding or was it subject to some checks, even if less severe ones than any required to yield an approximation to Radcliffe-Brown's estimates?

I do not believe that we are likely, in the foreseeable future, to make any re-estimation based on archaeological evidence (except in such cases as Western Victorian eel farming). This is not necessarily because of disciplinary shortcomings but to a large extent because Aborigines today stand as a barrier to modern scientific investigations. One option is the procedure adopted in *Our Original Aggression* (1983), which is to take early, reasonably well founded numbers for various areas and, with available historical evidence, project these numbers back to 1788. This implies adopting a system of population dynamics. We take assumed population structures at 1788, subject the population to known historical shocks and estimate the degree of consequential population loss. To the extent to which we can chain these shocks together to derive an aggregate percentage depopulation we can reverse the projections and extrapolate backwards from given early estimates. Unlike history, models can run backwards!

There is no suggestion that we can derive other than approximations by this procedure and we must be content with upper and lower bounds in the result. From a pedagogic point of view this requires, however, that we deal with some colonial history (even if only in sketchy terms) in order to achieve the estimated rates of depopulation. In part, then, we have to take into account, summarily, part of the discussion of the next chapter in order to set up likely numbers of precontact Aborigines. If this means some degree of repetition, it is unavoidable.

Summarily, Aborigines were subject to three major types of disturbance after 1788. These were disease episodes, the withdrawal of resources, and killing. In the American case, the prime depopulating mechanism was introduced diseases, above all smallpox, delivered from time to time by incoming colonists or invaders. There are some instances in North America where transmission or attempts at transmission may have been deliberate. Notwithstanding Hollywood's efforts to display the deaths of Amerindians around waggon trains and despite the historical record of Indian wars, disease appears to stand out as the prime agent. Killing and resource taking occurred as the last stage. Neither in Australia nor in North America were indigenous people integrated in colonial societies, even though they were often used for various purposes. In the North American case, the relatively short Atlantic sea trip meant the comparatively easy delivery of diseases to which the Amerindians were not accustomed. As exposed populations, the consequence was that they died in large numbers. Australian Aborigines were protected from diseases introduced by the colonists because of the long sea voyage, even if only from South Africa. At the same time, local Aborigines were geographically quite closely associated with the Indonesian islands. A vital question then arises. Were they so unaccustomed to the diseases that were prominent in depopulating North America? Were Australian Aborigines exposed populations to the same degree as the Amerindians? Had they acquired significant immunity? In the process of acquiring that hypothetical immunity, had they been provided with a mechanism for checking the expansion of their population?

A note on Radcliffe-Brown's numbers

Let us first of all dispose of Radcliffe-Brown's procedures. There are several points to be made. First, his was a careful and conservative attempt by a skilled anthropologist to estimate as he put it the 'original' Aboriginal population of Australia, but in doing so he specifically labelled it (in italics) as 'the *minimum* that we can reasonably estimate' (Radcliffe-Brown, 1930: 696). Subsequent readers have ignored this heavy qualification. Secondly, he began with an area in Western Australia that he had studied closely, and reached his own conclusions on 'carrying capacity', essentially an animal analogue, and estimated tribe size. That area, which did not present high advantage to Aborigines, served as a reference point where historical numbers were lacking, even when he was dealing with manifestly superior resource conditions. Again, this was his conservatism. Thirdly, in choosing estimates available in the historical record, he invariably and explicitly opted for the lowest. The words 'conservatively low', the 'lowest possible' and 'an irreducible minimum' are bunched tightly in a publication of a little over eight pages. All this has been subsequently ignored. Fourthly, the estimates are made location by location throughout Australia, taking numbers at the time of first contact with colonists. In fact, this means numbers are adopted as 'original' when in fact they are for dates scattered over a period from 1788 to the 1920s! This gives a special piquancy to the fifth point that he acknowledged for Victoria: the chosen numbers (in the early 1840s) were subsequent to smallpox epidemics with which, he acknowledged, he could not deal.

In general, there are some marked inconsistencies in population densities for different parts of Australia that are not easily acceptable. But it needs to be remembered that Radcliffe-Brown was viewing Australia from the perspective from which modern anthropology began, the Aborigines of north-western Australia. These were far from possessing the best resources in Australia, yet their experience, after colonial contact, is projected throughout Australia. It also needs to be recognised that Radcliffe-Brown was more than doubling the received official estimate (125 000) that had previously been published in the *Commonwealth Year Book of Australia*. His 'lowest possible' figures were a major challenge to the official perspective. In addition, his warnings about his conservatism were totally disregarded, an inattention to words that is curious in a scientific profession. In reality, he was advising readers to look for much larger numbers for strictly precontact populations. It is, perhaps, unfortunate that he muddied the waters by presenting locality estimates that were spread over a long period of time, with little relevance to 1788. The question remains, can we do any better?

13

THE PROBLEM OF AN EXPOSED POPULATION

Historically, we can recognise a series of post-1788 incidents affecting Australian Aborigines up to 1850. These were:

- smallpox epidemics in 1789 and about 1828;
- venereal disease, particularly gonorrhea, recognised by 1789 at Botany Bay and probably carried by sealers around the coast by 1800;
- a sequence of introduced diseases: influenza in 1820, whooping cough in 1828, influenza and measles in 1840 but also, probably persistently, pneumonia and tuberculosis from 1788;
- colonial removal of Aboriginal resources in a minor way from 1788, becoming widespread between 1815 and 1850; and
- killing of Aborigines by colonists, intermittently from 1788 but on an increasing scale from 1815.

Killing has become something of a research industry. Amerindian and South American experience suggests strongly that disease was the prime killer. Clearly, that was in conditions of an exposed population lacking immunological defences. Before we can begin to assess the impact of disease on Aborigines, we have to face up to the question: were Australian Aborigines lacking immune defences? Had they been exposed to some and perhaps all colonially introduced diseases before 1788? If so, had they been exposed frequently? The question of frequency is important in that immune defences can disappear as infants are produced (for smallpox) or even after a lapse of time for adults for other diseases. Little immunity is likely, in any event, to have been developed for diseases such as influenza or tuberculosis.

These questions bring us particularly to northern visitors to Australia, the so-called Macassan trepang fishermen. These fishermen came from Sulawesi for purposes of catching and curing trepang along the north Australian coast, and subsequently exporting the product primarily to China. They came with the north-west monsoon (December) and left with the onset of the south-east trades (around April). It may not have been much before 1700 that an established trepang trade between Macassar and China developed so that it is possible that regular annual visits did not begin until the eighteenth century. Nevertheless, these visits were clearly in train some time before 1788. There is evidence of Indonesian presence on the north Australian coast several centuries earlier, reflecting the high compe-tence of Indonesians in ship building and sailing at a very early date. Equally, the arrival of the dingo in Australia, now dated at no less than 2–3000 years ago, implies some interaction between the northern islands and Australian Aborigines over long periods. The rising of the seas after the end of the ice age had not left Aborigines completely isolated from the outside world. But it was not until the eighteenth century that frequent contact appears to have occurred.

That contact brought regular visits, possibly some trade, certainly some vocabu-lary and some human associations. But it also meant that northern Australian Aborigines could be subject to disease transmission carried by the visiting fishermen. Did this mean that Aborigines were, then, not an exposed population by 1788? Did it mean, in other words, that they had been infected by imported diseases and hence may have developed some immunological defences? If so, what might those diseases have been? And, further, could these diseases have been spread throughout Australia relatively frequently, creating a widely dispersed protected population?

In the light of post-1788 history, the disease most relevant was smallpox. This disease is asserted on medical evidence to have been present in south-east Australia in 1789 and about 1828, and in localities at which it was observed to have produced massive mortality. Moreover it was the disease most strongly implicated in the depopulation of the indigenous residents of the Americas. Other diseases may have played a part in both the Americas and Australia and may also have been delivered by Macassan visitors to Australia. In what follows, attention is concen-trated on smallpox.

In pursuing the question of smallpox, it is important to appreciate a few characteristics of the disease. In endemic conditions, smallpox is primarily a disease of childhood. Survival from infection almost invariably meant lifetime immunity, so that where smallpox had established itself in a community there was, typically, a mass of adults immune by prior infection and a slowly increasing body of infants all of whom, substantially, were exposed. Evidence of prior infection was readily identified by a characteristic pitting of the face, particularly around the nasal area. Once the numbers of such exposed populations increased sufficiently, it was possible and likely for limited epidemics to occur, affecting the young and others who for some reason had escaped early age infection. On European evidence, these smaller epidemics happened throughout the eighteenth century at intervals averaging about a decade. Those children who had attained 5 to 15 years of age had a very high chance of survival (and subsequent immunity) and those under 5 years had a very high mortality rate. The disease was spread by close contact between humans from breath or saliva but could also be acquired by breathing aerosols (for example in the form of fine textile particles impregnated with saliva or matter from pustules). The virus was quickly killed by exposure to sunlight but could remain alive and active for long periods (in ideal conditions, several years) particularly in woollen fabrics. Cotton fabrics did not shed fine fibres so readily.

In an exposed population, unaccustomed to infection, the entire age range was at risk. There was potential for a true pandemic, wiping out large proportions of the total population. Mortality rates were, then, not simply the product of viral infection but of a radically reduced ability to be given or obtain care, if only in the most elementary form of a supply of water and food. This was particularly relevant given that the soles of the feet and the hands could be drastically affected by pustules. Death rates were accordingly enlarged as thirst or hunger came in association with the viral condition. Thus whereas in endemic conditions as few as one-third of infected persons might die, in an exposed population it has been estimated that 60 per cent or more of entire populations might be wiped out. The disease ran a course of perhaps three weeks from first infection to death or recovery and was generally passed from one infected person to some other(s) at about 8–12 days from first infection. In a closely knit group, an epidemic would commonly have run its cycle in perhaps six weeks. These were important reasons why an Atlantic trip could deliver smallpox from Europe to the Americas whereas a trip from Britain to Australia (or even South Africa to Australia) was not likely to yield an infected person capable of infecting others on land. It was possible, however, for infected belongings to be carried ashore and so create a risk for others.

The spread of infection depended on close contact through a chain of human beings. An epidemic naturally followed the path of exposed human beings and movement between them. In sparse populations, the disease would die out — that is, it would not become endemic. A quasi-endemic condition could arise if frequent visits from infected Macassans repeatedly delivered the virus. The trip time from Macassar to the nearest landfall was certainly short enough to allow, in principle, this to happen. On the other hand, Macassans spread along the coast from the Kimberleys to Cape York and, in many cases, the trip time was too long for transmission to be a very easy matter.

Transmission potential from Macassar

It is important that an investigation should be made of any health/disease records or histories in Holland and Portugal. I cannot undertake this task. This might throw light on the prevalence of smallpox in Macassar, in Sulawesi as a whole and in the main Javanese islands. Any such investigation should give close attention to the question of whether there was an increase in smallpox activity throughout the 1780s and 1820s.

The prevalence of smallpox as an endemic problem in the East Indies is, however, taken for granted. In the main islands it appears to have attained endemic status by the sixteenth century, but this might be more carefully assessed from Dutch and Portuguese records. Boomgaard (nd) suggests that Javanese epidemics occurred several centuries before white Australian settlement and the disease may have been endemic throughout the 'Indies' and specifically in the Moluccas in the early sixteenth century. (Boomgaard does not list an epidemic at a time appropriate to the 1829 Australian outbreak.) In these conditions it seems unreasonable to treat the port of Macassar as other than fitting into an endemic system. The circumstances were such that, notwithstanding the small (25 000 or so) population of the port, Macassar must be treated as being at least in a quasi-endemic condition. Integration with the rest of the Celebes was one factor. Dr A. Reid estimates the 1800 population of Sulawesi (Celebes) at 1.8 millions. He proposes that the densely settled area of Sulawesi was, in fact, the south-western peninsula at the head of which Macassar stood. By implication, the immediate region of Macassar contained a very large population. Its size was such as to provide ample conditions for smallpox to become endemic in the immediate region. Medical modelling concludes that a population of the order of 250 000 in a contained area provides the base conditions for endemic smallpox.

In addition there was the status of Macassar as a major and busy port and communications node in both inter-island and long distance shipping movements. Travel by water rather than land was the efficient communications mode and Macassar was closely locked into the epidemic/endemic system of a wider area through its frequent inter-island and long distance links. Moreover, the so-called Macassan fisherman who visited Australia's northern coast did not come only from Macassar itself. The Bugis, who composed a considerable portion of the crews, came in particular from the south-west peninsula of Sulawesi and their movement along the peninsular coast to and from Macassar tied the whole area together. Here again we cannot be categorical until we have concrete medical evidence. Nevertheless, the conditions were such, given endemic conditions elsewhere in the archipelago, as to create endemic smallpox around and in Macassar. If the Macassans brought smallpox to Australia they were much more likely to have implanted and transmitted it in their immediate home environment.

Despite such books as Macknight's *The Voyage to Marege* (1976) we know very little of the circumstances of the carriers of disease, the crew. We do know that they were typically all-male and, in vital contrast with European ships, families and very young children were not included. This has important implications for the spread of infection *en route*. It seems improbable that a high proportion of the crews would have been susceptible to the disease. But were they, in fact, together in other sailing activities throughout the whole year, prior to departure to the trepang areas of Australia? Did they assemble specially for the voyage to Australia from various parts of Sulawesi? How long before departure from Macassar were they in close communication with each other? All these questions have a vital bearing on the period of incubating infection prior to departure for Australia. If they associated with each other for a significant period before departure, we cannot take the mere travel time from Macassar to Australia as anything other than the extreme lower limit of time for transfer. In British conditions, with most of British crews continually associated ashore and on board, the spread of *identified* infections (that is, those diagnosed 10 days or so after initial infection of the primary carrier) occurred very early after exit from the home port. This was in conditions of much larger ships, with more opportunity for separation on board than on Macassan praus.

There cannot be any serious doubt that one very recently infected 'Macassan' could spread the disease among the probably small fraction of crew members exposed and that a potent virus could be delivered to the closest Australian landfall. If the fleets departed during an epidemic in Macassar, it seems likely that the disease could be carried on a substantial number of praus, providing the potential for dotting infection at various points along the northern Australian coast.

If this appraisal is reasonable, a side issue arises that, though very speculative, is too important to pass over. Let us suppose that northern Australian Aborigines were, to a substantial degree, isolated from those in the rest of Australia during the monsoonal period of 3–4 months. If Macassans could relatively easily and frequently deliver smallpox to currently isolated Aboriginal communities in the Top End of the Northern Territory and the Kimberleys, and perhaps towards the Gulf of Carpentaria, a radically different population potential existed there as compared with south-eastern Australia. If these northern communities were *frequently* assailed by smallpox they were unlikely to be able to attain the densities that could have been permitted elsewhere. These northern Aborigines may themselves have acquired, perhaps quite quickly after regular Macassan landings, something of a quasi-endemic condition with populations held quite severely in check. This is obviously highly speculative but the possibility needs to be raised since it would have a bearing on perceptions of relative densities. Anthropologists' perceptions of potential population densities for Aborigines have depended a good deal on observations in the Northern Territory and particularly around the estuaries and southward flowing rivers in that area. These perceptions influence ideas of population/resource ratios and notions of whether Aborigines used Australian resources lightly or not. These conditions, if correct, may not have applied in south-eastern Australia if a regular smallpox epidemic did not occur there.

But how far along the coast was transmission likely to be feasible? We cannot be categorical about any answer to this question. It is impossible to be certain that there was no chance that the disease could be delivered to the head of the Gulf of Carpentaria. Equally, it is impossible to be categorical that such a distant delivery was a frequent risk. Although other considerations arise, three matters are fundamental: the duration of time of the voyage; the potential for on-board spread of the disease; and the period of incubation before departure. In considering these points, it is relevant to reiterate some of the matters raised in *Our Original Aggression*. The trepangers did not carry families with them. This greatly alters the transmission possibilities as compared with British ships. So too do the relatively crowded conditions in the undivided space for the crew. So, moreover, does the *expectation*, in endemic conditions, that only a small proportion of the crews were exposed to risk of infections as the rest would be protected by virtue of prior immunity. Some references are made (cf. Judy Campbell, 1985) to the presence of some young boys amongst the crews. These, in endemic conditions, would be the most likely carriers.

It is useful to take the three points above in reverse order. In the case of most long distance shipping movements by whites around the world, ship visits to any port were typically relatively brief and the crew visited land while living aboard. A stay of two weeks would, however, be ample time to infect a crew member and for that person to spread the disease among the exposed crew members before departure (the period of high communicability might be set at 8–12 days after first infection). This time lapse seems to be a primary condition in the British experience. Typically, identified on-board infections developed as a second round of infection in a few days after departure. The spread would, of course, be accelerated if more than one on-shore infection occurred. The rate of spread on a Macassan prau would almost certainly be much faster.

We know very little about how Macassan crews were made ready for departure for the Australian trepang grounds. A great many detailed questions could be listed as relevant to the matter. For example, were the crews engaged in inter-island shipping throughout the year? Would they then as a group be likely to be frequently exposed to infection throughout the East Indies? Were many new crew members added to the normal complement of each prau for the trepang voyage? To what extent was Macassar their home town? To what extent were the fleets assembled along the whole coast of southern Sulawesi? What contact did crew members have with the southern peninsula of Sulawesi as well as Macassar itself? But one important question seems to be: were crew members in communication with each other for a substantial period prior to their departure from Macassar? If so, this period becomes prominent as time to be added to the duration of the trip to Australia, affecting the transferability of the disease.

Preparation for a voyage of several months clearly took a considerable time. Substantial cargo was loaded and stored. Crew members added their own possessions, including trade goods. It seems that the same or very similar crew voyaged each year, partly because of their interest in sharing in the profits and often because they were in debt to the masters, or might even have been slaves of the masters (Macknight, 1976). The immediate issue is, however, that the departure date could not be set by the clock. It depended on the master deciding that the monsoon had set in. There was some considerable, but not yet statistically determinable, variation in the onset of the monsoon, implying that crews would need to be assembled ready for departure when the master made that decision. It was in the interests of both the crew and the master that they be available and ready. The Darwin Meteorological Bureau (personal communication) suggests that this variation could extend to 3 or 4 weeks on either side of the approximate average date.

Not only did they need to be available for sailing but a system of communication was also necessary to provide, if nothing else, information on the departure date. Macknight (personal communication) believes that those in Macassar itself probably waited around the dock area and that, in some cases at least, may actually have lived in the masters' large residences. Brought into close association with the docks, they were exposed not only to infections developing within Macassar itself but also to those brought ashore from frequently arriving ships and praus whether in Macassar itself or elsewhere. All were linked by the necessity of obtaining sailing information.

I have not been able to find any means of determining the strict statistical variance in the onset of the monsoon in Sulawesi. But the Sulawesi–Darwin weather shift was inter-linked. Again reference to Dutch or Portuguese records might be revealing. Australian meteorological records suggest a considerable variation in the onset of the monsoon. This is, however, to be immediately qualified. It depends, to a considerable degree, on the subjective, albeit expert, evaluation of meteorologists. Thus the Darwin wind-speed data are virtually useless because of the inappropriate placement of wind recorders. It does seem highly unlikely, however, that there was not a considerable period of relatively close contact between the crew prior to sailing. To the 14–15 day trip from Macassar to Port Essington needs, as a typical experience, to be added a considerable potential incubation period before sailing. This might be insufficient to protect Aborigines around Port Essington. But it seems likely to enhance considerably the protection of Aborigines at the head of the Gulf of Carpentaria.

Obviously, accidents could happen and a single crew member be first infected at the moment of departure. To rely on such accidents as a routine, however, is at least as unwise as it is to ignore them. A non-stop sailing trip to the head of the Gulf would take about 4 weeks. But the monsoon very rarely blew continuously for anything like this period and delays from calm and contrary winds occurred. In addition, stopping at intermediate points would extend this time. The more extensive the spread of disease on board, the more likely it would seem, that a master would make an early landfall. In any event, as Macknight (1976) indicates, the fleets broke up into small groups, sharing out the trepang grounds. To achieve a delivery of potent virus to the head of the Gulf would require: a very recent infection of one member before departure; a substantial fraction of exposed crew members; a considerable time lag beyond the likely ten or so 'incubation' days after infection, when further viral communication was to be expected; the survival of the persons affected in the second round of infection to reach the Gulf in an infectious state; and a non-stop trip. The alternative scenario is that an infected prau might make an early landfall and be followed in by a second uninfected one aiming to move on quickly to the Gulf. Transfer of the disease between praus could make delivery to the Gulf possible.

Such events could happen. It is possible that, from time to time, they did. When one adds the in-port delays and risks of prior infections, the probable immunity of high proportions of the crews, the likely speed of the spread of infection in the crews' quarters, the delays and stops on the voyage and the not infrequent foundering of vessels, the risks to Gulf Aborigines, as a general rule, seem to be greatly limited. If the Macassans were able to deliver disease reasonably frequently, why was there not fairly obvious evidence of widespread pock-marking among the whole Aboriginal population along the northern littoral, including the area immediately below the head of the Gulf of Carpentaria? The only piece of evidence we have is a few slightly pock-marked individuals. This does not give strong support to the idea that Judy Campbell (1985) presents of streams of infections percolating through eastern Australia in accordance with the epidemic incidents in Sulawesi.

There is no point in carrying this speculation far. Possibly the greatest effort should be directed to the experience of the praus, not simply in 1828 or 1829 but around about 1825–27. Coupled with this, investigation of Dutch records, in particular, to search for the epidemic experience of Macassar and the other main islands during the 1820s would be important, as would an exploration of climatic conditions in about 1826–7. These matters are not simple. If, for example, there was, as Judy Campbell may be proposing, a peculiar exposure in 1828 — that is an epidemic — it is most unlikely that there was also an epidemic at the more appropriate time, in about 1825 or so. The disease did not operate in this manner.

The potential for an inland spread of smallpox

Let us accept that Macassan fishermen were able to deliver the smallpox virus to the Northern Territory and Gulf coasts with reasonable frequency. If this is a correct assumption, was there any blockage to the southern movement of the virus? Or could we expect the virus to spread widely throughout Australia from the

Macassan visitors? If the latter, we have an Aboriginal population with a high degree of immunity, even though lacking a population size capable of generating endemic smallpox. If, however, there were blocks, it is possible that inland Aborigines to the south were exposed populations even if those at the coast had acquired a substantial immunity.

On the face of it, there seems to be no obvious obstacle to inland transmission. We have the examples of the whole west coast of the United States and the entire American plains areas as indicators of the distances over which an epidemic might travel. The whole of eastern Australia (or most of it) is not substantially different in scale. Fundamentally the spread of any smallpox epidemic was the product of human contact, of the human communications network. In the United States, heavy winter snows severely limited communications in the northern half. The Rocky Mountains provided a strong barrier to the west. No such conditions existed in Australia.

There are, however, three interesting facets of Australian Aboriginal exposure from the north. The first is the timing of the Macassan arrival. The second is the set of climatic conditions that was, virtually by definition, relevant during the period of the Macassan visits. The third is the pattern of normal Aboriginal concentration and dispersion in relation to these climatic conditions, induced by economic considerations.

The Macassans came with the north-west monsoon and left with the return of the south-east trade winds. If the monsoon failed, the Macassans did not materialise. Here we have, apparently, a major contrast with the rest of the world. Insofar as they arrived and brought smallpox, the Macassans transferred it early in the monsoon. Elsewhere in the region the monsoon brought a subsidence in epidemics. The reasons were primarily concerned with altered communications — reduced contact — in monsoonal circumstances. It is also probable that the heat, humidity and rain brought by the monsoon degraded infective material even in urban environments.

Australian Aborigines on the north coast, then, met and maintained contact with the Macassans over periods averaging about three and a half months, with predominant climatic conditions of a great deal of rain, a great deal of sun, a great deal of heat, a great deal of humidity and a great deal of wind. The last characteristic is perhaps least important. The others, however, were significant in relation to the ability of Aborigines to transmit the disease further inland or eastward. Heat and high humidity, particularly in the comparatively non-residential conditions of Australian Aborigines, rapidly degraded the virus in infective material. So, too, did heavy rain and any water through which Aborigines might pass. To this, there might be one qualification. If Aborigines acquired fabrics from the visiting Macassans, if that fabric were infected from close contact with a smallpox sufferer, if that fabric were (like rough woollen fabrics) capable of shedding broken fibres to become aerosols or transmittable to nose or mouth, if the fabric were protected from the weather — then a delayed transmission possibility existed.

These points have no great relevance in terms of some currently infected Aborigine travelling east or inland and carrying the virus. They are, however, of considerable significance if there was any change in the system of communications in monsoonal conditions, as was the case elsewhere in monsoonal areas. If there were a breakdown in communications amongst Aborigines for a couple of months, two consequences followed. First, one would expect, on historical evidence elsewhere, that any local epidemic in a small stationary group would have run its course within the monsoonal period. Hence the likelihood of transfer beyond a given locality would be limited largely to infective materials. Northern Aborigines used little in the way of clothing or other fibrous textile material, though they might possibly hoard or trade textiles (but most probably inefficient cottons). The likelihood that, in normal conditions *after* the Wet, they could communicate the disease by these or other possessions seems to be very considerably constrained, with the risks reduced by the climatic circumstances — the virus was not very likely to survive. Nevertheless, this cannot be a categorical conclusion.

Were there any changes in Aboriginal communications patterns when the Wet began and for how long did these changes persist? There have been some extreme positions adopted on this matter and the evidence may easily be misinterpreted. One such position is given in a 1939 paper by D. F. Thomson (1939). Thomson suggests that some Cape York Aborigines were, for all practical purposes, severely restricted in their movements during December–March (the period of Macassan visits to the Gulf) and probably until as late as mid-year. The reasons given were the combination of the rain and altered access conditions to food followed by growth of high, extremely dense and cutting grass that greatly impeded movement until the flush of growth could be burnt. Aborigines, on this view, concentrated in small, virtually stationary groups during the Wet and only broke out into dispersed patterns of movement perhaps two or so months after the end of the Wet — creating something like six months of isolation.

In a less extreme form, this pattern appears to have applied across the whole of northern Australia, which is heavily influenced by the monsoon. From around late December to March, inland camps were established close to animal and vegetable supplies. On the coast itself Aborigines remained isolated in dune locations or, frequently, on raised sites. It is relevant that animals and birds tended to draw into similar locations. Food conditions would not necessarily impede movement for active adults (though they could for the young and the aged); a human choice on the grounds of resources and convenience would alter Aboriginal mobility. Nevertheless, the 'normal' dispersion pattern was broken.

Such a general pattern seems to have prevailed along the north coast during the Wet. The Aborigines normally ceased to seek resources as a migratory activity but concentrated in small, dense localised groups. Their contact with other groups was correspondingly reduced. It is relevant that congregations for ceremonial purposes occurred at other times of the year, and that these periods of concentration during the Wet were ones largely of isolation.

In effect, the normal picture to be presented at times of contact with the Macassans was an array of localised Aboriginal communities with little contact with each other. This does not exclude contact but implies its radical diminution. When disease was introduced, one might, then, envisage the infection of separate concentrated groups within which the disease would, at least very frequently, be contained. The rest-of-the-world monsoonal conditions, which checked the spread of smallpox, appear not only to have prevailed on the north coast of Australia but probably to have produced a more potent check against the spread of the disease there than in urbanised areas of the world. Again, one cannot be categorical. Even with normal monsoonal conditions, micro-variations could occur in the incidence of the monsoon. It would require very extensive micro-variations to open corridors long enough to permit the escape of the virus during the monsoonal period. This would have strongest relevance in the Northern Territory and the Kimberleys but would be less substantial below the Gulf of Carpentaria. Taking the 25 inch rainfall line as a guide, this line provides a wide belt across Northern Australia, narrowing below the Gulf.

The immediate implication is that Macassan infection of eastern Australia would depend heavily on the ability of Macassans to deliver smallpox into the head of the Gulf of Carpentaria. This point is important when related to the preceding section in considering the ability of the Macassans to deliver the live virus. Let us for the moment continue with the assumption that the Macassans could still be, not infrequently, successful. What did this locational pattern mean for internal Queensland below the Gulf?

In itself, the tendency for Aborigines to concentrate during the Wet limited the direct transfer of smallpox not only east from Arnhem Land but also south from the Gulf and south-east from Arnhem Land to the Darling River. Provided the Aborigines who were normally stationary during the Wet remained stationary when infected, they were very much less likely to deliver the disease inland south of the Gulf. Infection might have broken the normal pattern. Aborigines might have fled. Equally they might have chosen to make pay-back attacks on the Macassans or on nearby, similarly 'stationary', neighbours. If they fled inland they could deliver the disease.

Inland flight is, then, one possibility which needs to be recognised but it would occur in the face of known risks of starvation. Anthropologists would need to answer the question whether such flight was likely, or even to be contemplated by the Aborigines affected. The specific evidence on Aborigines in south-eastern Australia is that if they did 'flee', they moved slowly, with their sick and their families, over limited areas. In the north, Aborigines faced far more severe conditions of climate and potential food shortage in moving. There may, however, be another contact possibility in the north. This possibility is, nevertheless, ambivalent and may rather introduce another block to southern movement. It depends on the locational behaviour of inland Aborigines, particularly in Queensland.

Before considering this, let us look at one special incident. The approach so far taken appears to be at least partly in conflict with the 1868 smallpox outbreak in north-west Australia (chiefly in the Kimberleys and not in Queensland). Reporting it, Foelsche (1882) provides ambivalent evidence: the disease spread throughout 1868 but it died down and disappeared in the ensuing Wet. Apparently one Wet period did not stop the disease but another did. The weather pattern of northern Australia in 1868 and 1869 becomes a prominent matter. In considering this, some subtlety is required. If the monsoon failed in 1867–68, the Macassans did not come and did not deliver the disease. If there was a so-called 'weak' monsoon, the Macassans could come but the rainfall would have been abnormally low, so that the Aboriginal concentration pattern would be weakened and the disease could escape from the coast.

No meteorological records were kept for northern Australia during 1865–68. We have to fall back on Chinese meteorological records. Intriguingly, one of the small number of 'weak monsoons' was in 1867–68 followed by a full monsoonal experience in 1868–69 (Shao-wu Want, 1984). The Darwin Meteorological Bureau affirms that such a Chinese *el nino* year would be closely paralleled in Indonesia and Northern Australia, with wind systems carrying abnormally low rain (letter from Mr R. Falls, Regional Director). It may be possible to confirm this evaluation specifically from Dutch–Indonesian records. In the meantime, it appears by comparing Darwin rainfall over 1869–1962 that the parallelism of Chinese and Darwin weather was close. On only two occasions during 1869–1962 does this parallelism break down in twenty-three possible incidents of major weather aberrations.

How frequent were weak *el nino* years, as isolated events not immediately associated with a complete failure of the monsoon? On the Chinese evidence for 1860–1980 there were possibly only eight isolated weak monsoonal years, a very low frequency. There were, apparently, four years in which a weak *el nino* preceded and was part of a full failure of the monsoon in the following year. In perhaps one year in ten, then, the Aboriginal concentration pattern may have been broken. If the Macassans delivered smallpox in these particular years, the disease was more likely to spread. This appears to have happened in 1868. On the other hand, in nine years out of ten the Aborigines could be expected to have been living in concentrated small bands when the Macassans arrived.

Let us return to the locational pattern of Queensland Aborigines relative to that on the north coast. Unfortunately, I have not found anthropological evidence on concentration patterns in the Channel Country. The nearest is the Darling River, though it seems likely that a similar pattern prevailed in the southward flowing rivers of central Queensland in the Channel Country. On the Darling, Peterson (personal communication) proposes that there was a contrary locational pattern of Aborigines and he suggests that this pattern extended into Queensland. Whereas the Aborigines to the north and close to the coast concentrated during the Wet and dispersed after it, these inland Aborigines dispersed during the Wet and concentrated after it. The pattern was reversed in relation to those in contact with Macassans. It would be important to try to determine how far this contrary pattern extended into the Channel Country.

Clearly, Aborigines who dispersed from the inland might make contact with concentrated, infected coastal Aborigines on the northern Australian coast. It is also possible that Aborigines in the interior attracted, as they concentrated, coastal Aborigines for some ceremonial assembly. It should be possible for anthropologists to assess this likelihood. Insofar as this might happen with some regularity, the transmission system for the disease *from the head of the Gulf* remains a potential. The ability of the Macassans to deliver the disease so far afield then becomes acutely important (see preceding section). However Aborigines from the Darling and southwards (like the north coast Aborigines) appear to have congregated for ceremonial purposes at times different from the more protracted periods of concentration, limiting intercommunication during wet periods.

If inland Aborigines were not likely to contact coastal ones during the Wet, the contrary locational pattern would reinforce blocks to a southward spread of smallpox. As the coastal Aborigines dispersed, the inland blacks concentrated. Contact between the two groups may, then, have remained limited (again anthropologists might assess this). But even if contact from the north were possible, it seems a relatively low probability that, after three to three and a half months, localised coastal Aborigines were a major risk to inland ones. The passage of the disease and climatic degradation of infective sources enhanced the protection of those in the inland.

None of this is intended to suggest an impenetrable barrier to the southward spread of smallpox. No defence system — still less any quarantine defence — is impenetrable. Accidents or breaks in the pattern can happen. It seems that this special concatenation of events occurred in Western Australia in 1868. What is suggested, however, is that climate and behaviour patterns as normal systems operated to constrain, and quite probably to contain severely, the eastern spread of the disease. It is probable, although less firmly, that its southern movement was similarly contained. It bears repetition that this was the characteristic experience of smallpox in the rest of the monsoonal world. Secondly, it follows that the ability of the Macassans to deliver smallpox around, say, the Raffles Bay area, was less significant to affairs in south-east Australia than their ability to infect Aborigines directly at the head of the Gulf of Carpentaria — unless a weak monsoon occurred at the appropriate time.

Evidence of historical frequency of break-out, and direction of movement

The general tendency of the preceding logic suggests a low likelihood of dispersion of smallpox into interior Australia. We do not have to rely wholly on this logic, though it may be important as an explanation of the fact that only three attested outbreaks of smallpox amongst Aborigines south of the main monsoonal belt occurred after 1788. These were in 1789 at Botany Bay, 1829 on the Darling River and 1868 in the Kimberleys. Here we have a periodicity of 40 years. Whatever the source of the disease, this time lapse meant that, on any reasonable assumptions about Aboriginal age structures, about 75 per cent of the population lacked immunity. The only evidence we have in relation to Botany Bay in 1789 is contemporary medical comment that Aborigines showed no signs of facial pitting and, in their judgement the local population included persons aged up to 80 years. Colonists commonly overestimated the ages of Aborigines of advanced years but this strongly suggests, at the very least, a high lack of immunity at Botany Bay in 1788. Since Flinders said that the Macassans had only just begun fishing far into the Gulf of Carpentaria in 1788, it would have been remarkable that their first few visitations there should have been successful in delivering the virus so far south, despite the many obstacles to its progress.

What then becomes of interest is the alternative source of smallpox, the colonists. The outbreak in 1789 occurred 15 months after the arrival of the first settlers, who were known to be carrying viral matter, quite properly, for purposes of inoculation in the event of any outbreak. The 1828 incident was identified approximately six months after the arrival of a smallpox-stricken ship, the *Bussorah Merchant*, at Port Jackson. In the latter case, the ship's contents were removed and supposedly destroyed. We do not know whether destruction meant literally that or merely that material was discarded in the bush, where blankets and other items could have been picked up by Aborigines. We do not know, either, how far the personal belongings of the arriving convicts were retained by them. We do know that a substantial fraction of the human consignment was assigned high up into the Hunter Valley and adjacent to the headwaters of the stream flowing into the Darling, where the outbreak was first identified.

We know little about the spread of the 1789 epidemic (though there are suggestions that the disease reached the southern Victorian coast). We do, however, have much more information about the 1828 incident and, thanks to Judy Campbell's careful research, it is possible to make some interpretation of the direction of movement of the disease on that occasion.

For purposes of establishing whether the 1829 epidemic tended to move south and east or north, we need dated observations of the presence of infection. Four dates, in particular, are reasonably well established in the literature — Sturt's observation in 1829 on the Darling River near Bourke; medical observations of actual smallpox around Bathurst in 1830; similar medical observation around Port Macquarie in 1831; and accounts of events at Port Macquarie indicating that the disease had spread from around Brisbane, most probably during 1831. To these dates, Judy Campbell has added two more. The first is the unexplained heavy death rates on some Macassan praus around Raffles Bay during, perhaps, December 1828 to February 1829; and medical observation early in 1829, of several Aborigines nearby taken by her as displaying evidence of recent but not current infection by smallpox.

In addition, Judy Campbell (1985) has also made a valuable contribution in piecing together a series of locations from south of the Gulf of Carpentaria into northern New South Wales, where some evidence of prior infection, 'around about' 1829, exists. Most of this evidence is from the informants of E. M. Curr, as reproduced in his *The Australian Race*. This evidence was assembled around 1879–80 and depends on recall of the disease either orally or by the evidence of pock-marking on the faces of Aboriginal survivors. Campbell does try to date these locations north of Bourke and Brisbane, though she refers to one date in passing. The pattern is displayed in map 9 (opposite). There are several incidences in the total for which the evidence is strong. She has also made an equally valuable contribution in presenting an array of reputed locations bracketing large areas of north-eastern and western Queensland, where informants were silent on or specifically reported the absence of pock-marked survivors at the end of the 1870s, suggesting some regional differences in incidence. These areas are broadly designated by the word 'NIL' on the map, though it should be stressed that one cannot rule out the presence of pock-marked persons in these areas, or of smallpox having passed through them.

In including these locations, I do not necessarily accept the value or validity of all of them. There is, first of all, no medical evidence in Queensland and no sighting of active smallpox at the time. All are based on recall. Observation by whites of pock-marking does not necessarily mean that infection occurred in the observed areas — Aborigines might have moved. Within these limits, the strongest evidence (not totally conclusive) comes in a relatively small number of cases in which blacks recall a sudden disease incidence with high death rates and in which whites observe pock-marking linked by blacks to that disease episode. Without all these ingredients, reports lose a great deal of their force. On the other hand, the

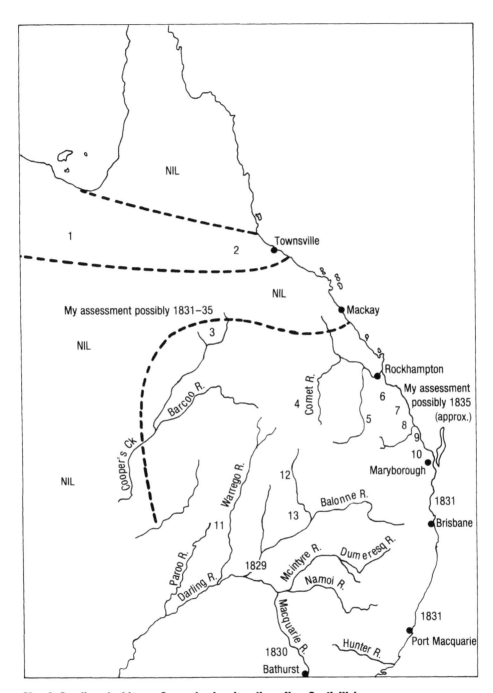

Map 9: Smallpox incidence, Queensland and northern New South Wales

presence of even a small number of 'strong' cases lends support to the relevance of other less certain reports, though not necessarily in the precise locations specified. The disease was such that one might say, reversing the usual adage, that a chain is only as weak as its strongest link.

The array of dated and undated locations is certainly consistent with a spread of the disease from the north. But because there is no attempt to date areas north of Brisbane it is equally consistent with a spread from the south or south-east. The earliest date given in eastern Australia is that of Sturt in early 1829. There is, perhaps, some question to be raised as to why the disease reached Bourke two years or so before it reached Brisbane E-N-E on the coast. The simple answer would be that the disease moved down the Channel Country and then both south and east along the Darling and its tributaries or, ignoring the map and its 'NIL' areas, south-east from Arnhem Land. This seems, for the moment, possible and plausible. But so, also, is an origin of infection in, say, the upper Hunter River in late 1828 (where many convicts from the *Bussorah Merchant* were assigned), moving up the Namoi to reach the Darling in early 1829. So, too, is a possible origin from newly-visiting American whalers near the Murray mouth. Any claim for the Macassan origin rests, so far as this goes, on the persistence of the presence of Macassans as sources of infection on the north coast, not on the recitation of these infected locations. Can we safely make this logical jump?

Let us look first at the implications of the reported events at and around Raffles Bay in late 1828 and early 1829. The report of heavy and unexplained death rates amongst Macassans around Raffles Bay is taken by Judy Campbell as highly probable evidence of a smallpox outbreak. She gives some supporting evidence of medical sighting of several recently pocked Aborigines early in 1829 — if interpreted correctly, the Aborigines had probably been infected during the preceding year.

What can we make of this? It is not clear what is being proposed. Is this outbreak to be linked to the 1829–31 datings in the south-east? Or has the 'information' some other implication? If the former, we must, in all seriousness dismiss it. Smallpox in, say, December of 1828 at Raffles Bay could not be taken seriously as already 'sweeping away' the blacks around Bourke at the beginning of 1829. The reasonable assumption on the basis of rate of spread elsewhere in Australia and in North America is that the disease would take, say, two or three years to reach Bourke (assuming that it was ever likely to do so). One needs, therefore, to be looking probably for a north coast outbreak perhaps around about 1825 or so, not in late 1828 or early 1829. The alternative is a series of panic flights by blacks. A considerable chain of such flights would be necessary to get the disease to the Darling within, say, a few months. As Aborigines would have been travelling with family groups and the sick, rapid movement seems highly improbable. In practice, the disease appears to have drifted quite slowly around northern New South Wales.

The trouble with any notion of an 1828 outbreak among the Aborigines, interestingly enough, is the medical sighting of 'several' allegedly recently pocked blacks. For a medical man to chance on several such persons almost certainly implies that there were most probably others in the region in a similar condition and that they were survivors after a larger number had been infected. They were also adults who were observed, suggesting a relatively exposed population. The substantial smallpox strike that this implies is most unlikely to have happened *both* in late 1828 and also about two or three years earlier. The disease did not operate in this manner. It did not recur with this frequency. It had to wait for a sufficient number of exposed persons (children) to be present. If, on the other hand, there was an outbreak amongst the local Aborigines at the end of 1828 or early 1829, this could not have been the source of the infection on the Darling in early 1829. There is, however, still a problem with this. The medical report did not describe facial *pitting*. The marks observed may not have been smallpox at all. Alternatively, if black skins only slowly took on the pitted form it is conceivable — and may be possible to check medically — that there had indeed been an outbreak as far back as 1825 or so. At this level, the matter must remain obscure, though an 1825 date seems unlikely.

The 1828–29 'evidence' (it is very circumstantial) at Raffles Bay may, on the other hand, be taken to mean that the fleets leaving Macassar for the 1828–29 trepanging season were widely infected. This would be taking two logical jumps. If one group suffered badly, it is perhaps probable that other praus were similarly affected or that some transmission between praus occurred but the other praus reached further to the east along the Australian coast. But if this is the case, we need to consider how far afield such persons could carry the infection towards and into the Gulf of Carpentaria. This particular point has already been discussed. Even if we judged that it was possible for the infection to spread so far, the date is wrong as a source of infection on the Darling at the specified time — almost simultaneous with and possibly even before the Macassan visits to the Gulf in that season.

The Raffles Bay 'information' is, then, most probably a red herring except as a possible indication that the Macassans could deliver smallpox at around that location. It has no implication for the south-eastern epidemic, except on the outside chance that the blacks observed by a doctor had been infected a few years earlier and that Aboriginal skins only took on the pitted form slowly.

Can we, then, date any of the incidents mapped in Queensland? Judy Campbell does not try to do so, though on one occasion when she refers to a date (1835), she does not seem to realise its significance. Any evidence of the disease striking in Queensland after 1829 would raise serious doubts as to the epidemic coming down from the northern Australian coast through the length of Queensland. In considering this matter, we might envisage three broad possibilities of movement of the disease through Queensland. One is south-east from, say, Arnhem Land to the Darling. The second is a passage from the Gulf through the Channel Country (along the Barcoo, Paroo or Warrego drainage systems). The third is along the coast. There would be mixed possibilities of switching to and from the Channel Country and the coast in the process.

The dating prescriptions must, therefore, be made more severe. If the disease moved along the inland river systems to the Darling, travelled east to Brisbane and north up the east coast, a date of infection after 1831 on the coast would not necessarily be convincing, though it would cast doubts on the southward movement. Similarly, a date of infection after 1829 in the upper reaches of the Barcoo, Paroo or Warrego would not be convincing in isolation, since the disease might have travelled down the coast and switched back into the interior, having travelled down into the Maryborough–Brisbane region. In addition, evidence is needed as to whether the disease did or did not travel south-east from Arnhem Land. Evidence on these three points would raise very serious doubts about a southward movement.

It looks as if this evidence can reasonably be proposed, not with certainty but with some substantial support. If correct, there are serious logical doubts about a southern movement (though not quite so strongly about a south-east movement direct from Arnhem Land). The first date is explicit in the source material and relates to infections between Rockhampton and Maryborough:

> Many of the members of the tribe who are over forty years of age bear the marks of small-pox. On this subject the tradition of the Toolooa people is that about the year 1835 they were visited by the Burnett tribes, who brought the disease and gave it to them. (Curr, 1886: 122)

Obviously we cannot take the year 1835 literally. Nevertheless it would require a considerable error by the Aborigines to put the date before 1831 or 1829. Doubts and uncertainties remain; but the date *is* given. The quoted statement also adds another important piece of information: The Burnett tribes were to the south, implying that, at that point, the disease was moving north.

As indicated above, acceptance of this date would leave open the possibility of an inland transmission down to the Darling, with the disease swinging east to and north up the coast. However, the reports on the disease on the Barcoo towards the top of the Channel Country need to be inspected carefully. First, for 500 kilometres or so to the north, all the evidence for a prior infection is negative until one reaches the Cloncurry River, about 150 kilometres south of the Gulf, and the Burdekin on the east coast. Moreover, a similar negative finding is presented west of the Barcoo. This negative evidence is not merely the absence of reports. There are some reports in the sources declaring no pitting on black faces. The broader negative evidence to the north and west casts doubts on a cross-country passage from Arnhem Land. This particular route is, in any event, a weak possibility given the resource conditions of inland Australia and the sparse population there.

The Barcoo evidence is, then, strategic in terms of a passage down the Channel Country. In this case, the report (Curr, 1886: 79–80) is also dated 1879–80. The specific information, from a black policeman, is that amongst his tribe four or five survivors of the disease, then said to be aged about 50 years, were pock-marked. Again, we cannot take this to be exact information. Nevertheless, some qualified inferences can be drawn from it. Typically, whites tended to take blacks to be older than they were. In this case, since the black trooper related the disease and the ages of his tribes-folk to his own birth, the age assessment may have been more accurate (the trooper was fully literate). This strengthens the following appraisal. Let us begin with the assumption that the ages were correctly reported. Persons aged 50 in 1880 had not been born in 1829 when the disease was already rampant on the Darling River. They could not have been infected since they did not exist. The further their true ages fell below the '50 years' reported, the later after 1829 must the disease have occurred. But the rate of spread of the disease implies that we should look to a southward moving epidemic affecting the Barcoo tribes in about 1827 or so. This means that many persons aged 52 (still perhaps 'about' 50 in 1880) were not yet born when the disease would most probably be affecting the Barcoo in its alleged southern movement.

We can go further than this. How far astray would the black trooper need to be in his assessment of ages to open a passage down the Channel Country? Persons aged 53–58 in 1880 would have been aged 0–5 in 1827. Persons aged 58–63 in 1880 would have been aged 5–10 in 1827. (Note that there is no point in pursuing ages below 50.)

Of those aged 0–5, modern supportive experience would imply a smallpox case fatality rate of about two-thirds. In likely stable populations, about 11.5 of every 100 in the population as a whole would be aged 0–5. Of these, fewer than four might be expected to survive on good survival expectancies. Subsequent life expectancy conditions would mean that with no new risks intervening, probably fewer than 1.0 of the original 11.5 would live to be 53–58 years old in 1879–80. This would be a highly favourable outcome. On the other hand, those aged 5–10 would account for about ten in every 100 of a given stable population. Of these ten, 8.5 might survive the disease. Subsequent *normal* life-time risks would allow possibly as many as three to survive to attain age 58–63 in 1879–80. On this basis, the chances are substantially (three to one) in favour of the observed blacks being in the upper age group.

If the disease struck the Barcoo in 1827 or thereabouts, the persons described as aged 'about' 50 would need most probably to have been relatively very old — very considerably above 50 and 'about' 60 rather than 'about' 50. If, on the other hand, they were bracketed reasonably closely towards age 50, the disease most probably affected the Barcoo tribes somewhere between 1831 and 1835 and these survivors were those in fact aged 50 or so in 1879–80. To open the path for the disease to move, at an appropriate time, from the Gulf, requires that Curr's informant must have been radically astray in his conception of the ages of the members of his own tribe.

Obviously, we cannot be confident about the empirical foundations of this reasoning. What it does do is cast further doubt, with some empirical justification. We can, however, go a little further. Curr explicitly proposed that an isolated report from one old Aboriginal woman on the east coast (the Burdekin tribe) should be disregarded — on the grounds that it was her statement only in the midst of a large region in which no pock-marking could be recorded. This illustrates the dangers of imputing the incidence of the disease to the location in which pock-marking is later observed; it has a significant bearing on late nineteenth century claims of pock-marking in Central Australia. Curr also was disposed to ignore reports from the Cloncurry River below the Gulf. Despite Judy Campbell's imputation of this report to Palmer, it was, in fact, from an anonymous source and very obscure (Palmer merely agreed generally with the report). Here, in the frontline of a Macassan entry, so far as Queensland was concerned, the report was of some *slight* marking. It is not evidence on which a strong case can be built. More definitely, it is extraordinary that the strongest pock-marking was not reported close to the Gulf of Carpentaria if the Macassans were the source of the disease.

What is suggested is not a categorical conclusion. It appears quite probable, nevertheless, that the most northerly evidence of the disease (the Burdekin and Cloncurry Rivers apart) would invite a dating of the disease during the first half of the 1830s in Queensland. If we do, indeed, follow Curr and exclude the Burdekin and Cloncurry River cases, the Barcoo and the Comet Rivers are the most northerly known cases (nos 3 and 4 on map 9, p. 115). We must think seriously whether we should not agree with Judith Wright (1981) that these represent the northern limits of the epidemic that began in the south.

Summary and relevance to other diseases

Obviously, we have to be content with a somewhat inconclusive outcome. Despite the fact that there was clearly potential for Macassans to deliver smallpox to the north Australian coast, it seems unlikely that this would have resulted in a frequent infection of the interior. The most plausible interpretation of the 1829 incident is that the disease was moving north not south. This would time it with the arrival of the colonial ship the *Bussorah Merchant*. It seems most probable that the mass of Australian Aborigines represented the typical exposed population, with no immunity. Even with failure of blocks to operate against dispersion of the disease from the north, the frequency of outbreaks suggests that the great mass of the populations south of the main monsoonal belt lacked immunity in any event. The two early outbreaks in 1789 and 1829 are timed with known incidents connecting colonists with the virus. It seems most plausible to model any population on the basis of an exposed population in 1788 and of a dominantly exposed one in 1829, and then to treat smallpox epidemics in these early years, along with outbreaks of other diseases, as predominantly due to the arrival of the colonists.

Smallpox was not the only disease at issue. Given the composition of the crew, Macassans are unlikely to have delivered whooping cough (which the colonists did by 1828), and were probably unlikely to have introduced mumps. They could, however, have brought influenza, pneumonia, tuberculosis and venereal diseases. It is unlikely that there was no sexual intercourse between visitors and residents during a period of some 4–5 months. Tuberculosis and venereal disease would not have been constrained by any monsoonal blocks. They might, however, have been limited by kinship associations. The colonists certainly believed that venereal disease, particularly gonorrhea, was a colonial introduction. Thus, in 1789, Collins (1798: 596) observed: 'The venereal disease has got among them, but I fear our people have to answer for that'. Again, in the late 1830s in Victoria, Fyans (in Bride, 1898: 115) recorded 'Large families of natives — husband, wife, boys and girls — were eaten up with venereal disease. The disease was an introduction from V(an) D(iemen's) Land'.

What is vital is that Australian Aborigines after 1788 were attacked at the two ends of life by smallpox that killed and venereal disease that limited viable reproduction. These are crucial to any demographic modelling. Other diseases — whooping cough, mumps, measles, tuberculosis and pneumonia — seem incidental supplements to the main depopulating agents, agents that had a worldwide significance in the whole of European colonisation. For 'colonisation' one should read, 'the substitution of Europeans for stricken indigenous populations and the consequential transfer of their resources'.

14

RE-ESTIMATING
PRECONTACT
POPULATIONS

Demographic modelling and dynamics of shocks

The steps required for demographic modelling and the re-estimation of precontact Aboriginal populations are:

(a) the determination of the relevant parameters for a stable stationary population;

(b) the definition of the demographic shock effects from population disturbances;

(c) the computation of rates of population decline as the result of combined external shocks;

(d) plausible available estimates of numbers after shocks have been experienced (at the extreme, the level and dating of nadir populations); and

(e) extrapolation backwards from dates of post-contact populations to precontact estimates using the modelled rates of depopulation in (c).

The general perception of immediately precontact Aborigines is that they were in a stable relationship with their natural environment. Though some degree of demographic dynamism might be accommodated within such a concept, it is sufficient for present purposes to translate stability in relation to the natural environment to 'a stable stationary population'. Possible dynamism apart, this does not preclude us from taking into account some precontact disturbances, such as major droughts, that may have created fluctuations in population levels. For the moment, it is assumed that any such fluctuations occurred around a trend condition of a stable and stationary population structure.

A stable stationary population has several essential conditions. A consistent system to generate a stable and stationary population derives from mutually compatible life expectancy by age, gross reproduction rates, fertility conditions and the average age of reproductive women. Obviously, we do not have this information for precontact Aborigines and so have to make assumptions. Thanks to Coale and Demeney (1966), however, we have a vast array of options for populations with different life expectancies and other conditions. In my book *Our Original Aggression* (1983), I experimented with a large number of alternatives and finally narrowed the practical range down to two sets of conditions with a relatively low and a relatively good life expectancy for the late eighteenth century. The basic conditions adopted are shown in table 1 (below), which gives the full age structures for the two assumed systems. In this table, ages are taken in 5-year intervals to age 80, an implausible degree of detail but necessary to ensure the adoption of appropriate parameters to yield populations that are stationary to begin with and that, once shocked, return eventually to a strictly stationary condition. For the same reason, the gross reproduction rates are computed to seven decimals to avoid in-built confusions arising from truncated numbers. Very special procedures have to be adopted to deal with the first year of life. In the tabulations that follow, eo = expectation of life at birth.

The structure shown in table 1, with specified parameters, can now be shocked by isolated incidents (an epidemic) or by some continuing disturbance such as venereal disease, with the demographic effects unfolding over time through the different age groups. In the event of epidemic or endemic problems, we need data

Table 1: Simulated 1788 population structure and parameters

Ages	West level 5 eo = 30		West level 1 eo = 20	
	Females	*Males*	*Females*	*Males*
0–4	11.54	11.89	14.32	14.66
5–9	9.95	10.23	11.29	11.52
10–14	9.50	9.82	10.55	10.85
15–19	9.07	9.43	9.86	10.24
20–24	8.55	8.91	9.05	9.44
25–29	7.97	8.29	8.17	8.51
30–34	7.37	7.64	7.29	7.57
35–39	6.75	6.95	6.41	6.59
40–44	6.13	6.20	5.58	5.59
45–49	5.53	5.42	4.82	4.61
50–54	4.49	4.60	4.06	3.66
55–59	4.17	3.74	3.25	2.75
60–64	3.34	2.86	2.40	1.91
65–69	2.45	1.98	1.57	1.17
70–74	1.58	1.20	0.87	0.61
75–79	0.88	0.59	0.37	0.24
80+	0.38	0.25	0.14	0.08
Total	100.00	100.00	100.00	100.00

WL 5 parameters
eo = 30

WL 1 parameters
eo = 20

Gross reproduction rate males 2.2569725
Gross reproduction rate females 2.0817000
Mean age reproduction female 27

Gross reproduction rate males 3.2343476
Gross reproduction rate females 3.0307105
Mean age reproduction female 27

Other parameters including age specific fertility rates in Coale and Demeny op. cit.

or estimates on the mortality outcome by age. It is also possible to allow for recovery conditions. Aborigines might make special efforts to restore their populations by increased rates of reproduction or reduced birth control, or by constraining any inter-tribal warfare.

Nobody dies twice. Nor can anyone be restored to life. This means that unless disturbing influences are isolated in time, it is not possible to allot a depopulating influence to any particular factor. Moreover, the outcome as a whole can be affected by the order in which different influences are introduced. It is essential, therefore, that known history dictate the order in which shocks are introduced. As the models are constructed, if one introduces each depopulating agent in isolation and allows its effects to run their course, the population would stabilise (except in total resource loss or killing conditions) at a reduced level at approximately 1880.

Fortunately, history goes a long way towards solving or minimising many of these problems. In Van Diemen's Land, there is no evidence of smallpox. The sequence here appears to be the early introduction of venereal disease and the taking of women by sealers, with some killing, from just before the turn of the eighteenth century, followed by a slow resource removal by colonists during 1803–20, and then a rapid and destructive decade of resource removal and organised killing.

In New South Wales and Victoria, the first identified smallpox epidemic in 1789 is timed with the first introduction of venereal infections by colonists. This is followed by a long delay to about 1800, before resource removal or killing becomes significant. Then, after 1815, resource taking and killing gathers pace and in the midst of these two processes a second smallpox epidemic intervenes in 1829. These are the primary shocks. Other diseases are also relevant, including influenza, whooping cough, tuberculosis and pneumonia. Given their sequence in time, however, the net additional depopulating influence of these other diseases is slight, at least up to 1850. The significance of these other factors lies essentially in their preventing Aborigines staging a population recovery after being afflicted by other influences. In the modelling results below, one notional additional disease is introduced to show the likely limited effect.

The crucial depopulating agents on the mainland, but not in Van Diemen's Land, appear to have been smallpox and venereal disease. It is appropriate to take these two, first, in sequence.

Smallpox

For modelling purposes, we need data on age-specific mortality due to smallpox and on overall death rates during an epidemic for the entire population. (It might be noted that the minor form of smallpox had not emerged at the relevant Australian dates and only *variola major* is at issue.) For present purposes, I have chosen the latest available age-specific death rates for an epidemic in India during 1974–75, taken from the World Health Organisation (WHO; table 2, p. 124). There are a good many variants on these death rates, but they have one merit in that they were established at a time when it was medically known that, though no cure existed, patient care could maximise the chances of survival. The WHO data give ten-year intervals after age 20 and I have simply split these evenly to approximate 5-year intervals. It will be seen that there is massive mortality in early infant years, a radical fall in young childhood and a gradual rise again to relatively high death rates in older ages.

Table 2: Age-specific mortality, unvaccinated patients, India 1974–75

Ages	Case fatality rates %
0–4	45.70
5–9	15.50
10–14	5.80
15–19	15.30
20–24	22.60
25–29	22.60
30–34	23.10
35–39	23.10
40–44	30.80
45–49	30.80
50–54	26.90
55–59	26.90
60+	31.60

Source: R. N. Basu *et al.*, *The Eradication of Smallpox from India*, WHO, 1979, p. 65

In a medically unorganised society, with less opportunity for care, it must be assumed that the death rates were higher and typically much higher in an exposed or predominantly exposed population. This is particularly so in Aboriginal society, where economic organisation depended on the daily collection of foodstuffs. An epidemic might be expected to pass through an Aboriginal band within 6–8 weeks of the first infection. It is possible and likely that at about weeks 3–4, the mass of the band would be disabled, unable to walk or use their hands. Even if dependants did not become infected, their likelihood of dying was greatly increased because of lack of food and water. In exploiting the Indian age-specific mortality rates as indicators we do not imply that every person in a given population was infected. Given the shape of the age-specific mortality curve, it is likely that any enlarged death rates would broadly follow the smallpox infection outcome, since death rates generally conformed to level of dependence.

The Indian case fatality rates suggest about a 30 per cent mortality rate for those actually infected. This percentage is far below most records or estimates of death rates during a smallpox epidemic in an entire exposed population. In both North and South America, death rates in large population groups of 50 per cent, 60 per cent and higher have been estimated for the whole population. It bears repetition that this does not necessarily mean that all those dying were infected but that their deaths, which in many cases can perhaps be attributed to lack of normal care, can be fairly ascribed to the epidemic.

In Australia, the Botany Bay estimate was about 50 per cent in 1789. In this case there is some evidence that the disease reached what is now Melbourne; to do so it must have followed the rivers southwards to accord with the human chain required. The disease in Sydney was declared medically, by penal doctors familiar with the disease, as smallpox:

In ... April numbers of the natives were found dead with the smallpox ... It is not possible to determine the number ... carried off ... It must have been very great; one half ... died and ... it must have spread to a considerable distance. (*HRA*, Series I, vol. 1: 159).

Of the 1829 epidemic:

> All the very old men . . . say that . . . it followed down the rivers . . . laying its death
> clutches on every tribe . . . until the whole country became perfectly decimated . . . at last
> the death rate became so heavy . . . burying their bodies was no longer attempted . . . The
> disease, after devastating the tribes gradually died out leaving but a sorry remnant.
> (Beveridge, 1883: 35).

Robinson (in Presland, 1977) reporting on Victoria in the early 1840s, saw
evidence of the total depopulation of a good many tribes, with tiny remnants
joining other bands. One conflicting piece of evidence is that of Dr Mair, who was
sent officially to investigate conditions around Bathurst. Mair arrived to observe
deaths after the epidemic was some time advanced. He reported death rates of the
order of only 30 per cent. This might be questioned. If Mair reported observed
deaths amongst a total population where some bands had passed completely
through the disease experience and others were in the process of infection, his
observed mortality rates would necessarily be an undercount to the extent that he
included amongst the population those who had been infected and recovered. In
these conditions in four hypothetical bands of 100, where one had passed through
the epidemic and had experienced a death rate of 50 per cent and the other three
were in the process of a similar experience, Mair's observations would have
yielded just above 30 per cent mortality rate even though the actual rate for all
bands was 50 per cent!

Epidemics tend to be hit-and-miss affairs. One group will escape lightly while
others will be substantially wiped out. The average may remain very high. We can
model the process by using the WHO age-specific rates from India as a base
mortality level of approximately one-third, enlarge them by 1.6 times to yield an
overall death rate of approximately 45 per cent, and multiply them by 2.2 to give
an aggregate mortality of 60 per cent. In doing so, the extreme mortality for any
age group has been limited to 90 per cent. Historical evidence throughout the
world suggests that the rates may well have been higher and 60 per cent should not
be taken as the upper bound. Equally, the adjustment upwards by 1.6 times to yield
approximately 45 per cent is a conservative interpretation of the explicit Botany
Bay evidence.

In the modelling adopted, the 1789 Aboriginal population of the mainland is
assumed to have been wholly exposed, while in the 1829 epidemic those over age
forty are assumed to be wholly immune by virtue of prior infection (a generous
interpretation since some will have escaped the earlier incident).

For West Level 5 populations, with eo=30, the two epidemics would have
reduced the 1788 Aboriginal population to about 55 per cent by 1850, with nothing
else intervening, if only the base rate mortality is assumed. If the death rate is
taken at 45 per cent, the population modelling suggests a fall to about 40 per cent,
and with a death rate of 60 per cent, the population would have fallen to a little
over one-quarter of its 1788 level by 1850. No marked difference arises using West
Level 1 conditions with eo=20. Females would suffer slightly worse rates than
males because of pregnancy complications.

Venereal diseases

Smallpox killed. Venereal diseases in the main attacked the other end of life by
limiting reproduction or the ability to produce viable children. In this respect,

syphilis was less significant than gonorrhea, which could gradually occlude the fallopian tubes and cause sterility.

In modelling the epidemiology of gonorrhea in Australia, the procedure depends on Caldwell's evidence for Africa. Caldwell's results depend on African sexual and marriage patterns that may not accord with those of Aborigines. Nevertheless, we have widespread evidence of Aboriginal infection and the process may have been hastened rather than slowed by the original spread of sealers around the Australian coast and the extension of colonial settlement inland. Colonial treatment of Aboriginal women may have helped to determine the outcome. For want of any other, Caldwell's evidence has been transferred to Australia suggesting that over a 40-year period fertility is about halved.

When do we date the beginning point? Here Van Diemen's Land and the mainland experience diverge. The former was clearly influenced before 1800. In the latter, despite the observed presence of venereal disease at Botany Bay in 1789, the containment of the settlement until after 1813 at least limited colonial spread of the disease. To be conservative, it is assumed that venereal disease was transmitted from 1815, despite the fact that sealers on the southern (Victorian) coast must have been implicated well before then. See table 3 (below).

Table 3: Venereal diseases (females only)

NSW	VDL	WL 1 eo=20	WL 5 eo=30
1788		100	100
1790		100	100
1795		100	100
1800		100	100
1805		100	100
1810		100	100
1815	1795	100	100
1820	1800	99.28	99.42
1825	1805	97.36	97.83
1830	1810	93.32	94.93
1835	1815	88.86	90.59
1840	1820	82.25	84.85
1845	1825	74.39	77.91
1850	1830	65.75	70.15

It should be stressed that this is intended to suggest the impact of venereal disease in isolation. Just as nobody dies twice, no woman can become sterile having already died of smallpox. This question does not affect Van Diemen's Land, where the modelling suggests that it was possible that population may have been reduced by 20–25 per cent at 1825 when the most vigorous offensive against the Aborigines was undertaken by the colonists. By itself, this was a major demographic loss. It was almost certainly exacerbated by the taking of women by sealers, with consequential disorganisation of the island tribes' society and economy.

On the mainland, in New South Wales and Victoria (and probably already significantly affecting South Australia and Queensland), venereal disease, taken in isolation, may have been instrumental in reducing populations by 30–35 per cent by 1850. The numbers not born because of venereal disease were, of course, fewer to the extent that other killing agents intervened. But venereal disease appears to have been a powerful long-term population deterrent.

Other diseases and population recovery

Populations did not simply decline progressively because of smallpox and venereal disease. Even after a smallpox shock, the high survival rate of girls aged 5–15 presented a deferred opportunity for population recovery. It seems likely that in Van Diemen's Land their exposure to venereal risks was particularly high and efforts to speed up normal reproductive rates were severely constrained there. More opportunity existed on the mainland, and so some opportunity for special reproductive effort may have been possible, at least until the 1820s. By the 1820s, however, the increased speed of ship passage from Britain was supporting the arrival in Australia of other diseases — influenza and whooping cough in particular — to which there was no local immunity. It is difficult to assess how far these particular diseases affected Aborigines. They would have arrived initially in port towns. In both the main Van Diemen's Land ports, there was significant contact between Aborigines and Europeans up to 1820. In Melbourne, late diseases could readily have been communicated to Aborigines in the mid-1830s, while in Port Jackson, by 1820, the opportunities for spread appear significantly reduced unless new arrivals quickly moved inland.

On the other hand, the evidence is widespread, from Western Australia to Queensland, of Aborigines both young and old dying rapidly when in close contact with colonists, and those deaths were commonly attributed to some form of bronchial condition. It is suggested that, given the impact of smallpox and venereal disease, both additional diseases and efforts at population recovery can have had only marginal consequences. Consequently, comparatively simplistic simulations may be adopted to deal with both possibilities. For supplementary diseases, a notional additional disease with a relatively heavy killing rate is inserted at the historical time of 1820 (when the first known incident occurred). The assumed heavy killing rate is stressed because even on this basis the net additional depopulation is comparatively slight. Similarly, in notional provisions for efforts at population recovery, the modelling assumes the prior practice of either abortion or infanticide (both said to have been practised) and the procedure is to lower the mortality rate for infants in the first year. In making this last adjustment, we depart from the strict parameters of a stable stationary population.

Demographic consequences of introduced diseases and population recovery

Table 4 (p.128) shows a range of possible outcomes of the combination of introduced diseases and efforts at population recovery on the mainland for West Level 5 populations with eo=30 (summary 1850 outcomes for 1850 are shown attached to the table for West Level 1 with eo=20). The limited array shown here indicates sufficiently the upper and lower bounds, with a mid-range option, with a series of different major combinations. With smallpox epidemics occurring in 1789 and 1829, resulting in only the base Indian mortality rate; with venereal disease deferred until 1815; and with high efforts at population recovery (col. 1), Aborigines would still have lost about half their 1788 population by 1850. The details are given only for females but the final column shows the male outcome for the year 1850. With similar disease experience but no efforts at population recovery, the 1850 estimate appears as just under 40 per cent of the 1788 level. One additional disease epidemic would have lowered the 1850 population to just on one-third of the precontact numbers.

Table 4: Introduced diseases and population recovery, females WL5 Eo=30

	1 S/pox 1 VD 15 PR 20%	2 As (1) with PR 10%	3 As (1) exc PR	4 S/pox 1 add D20 VD 15 PR 10%	5 S/pox 1.6 add D20 VD 15 PR 10%	6 As (5) PR 20%	7 S/pox 2.2 add D20 VD 15	8 S/pox 2.2 add D20 VD 15 PR 10%	9 S/pox 2.2 as (8) PR 20%
1788	100.00	100.00	100.00	100.00	100.00	100.00	100.00	100.00	100.00
1790	69.24	69.24	69.24	69.24	54.75	54.75	40.33	40.33	40.33
1795	70.77	70.00	69.25	70.00	56.22	56.87	41.96	42.50	43.04
1800	72.95	71.45	69.91	71.45	58.36	59.69	44.22	45.35	46.47
1805	75.45	73.18	70.90	73.18	60.62	62.61	46.41	48.12	49.83
1810	77.59	74.54	71.52	74.54	62.07	64.71	47.45	49.66	51.88
1815	79.53	73.58	71.68	75.58	62.95	66.32	47.66	50.41	53.20
1820	81.24	76.22	71.35	59.86	44.59	47.04	30.43	31.95	33.50
1825	82.42	76.31	70.45	58.66	45.63	46.67	29.55	31.29	33.29
1830	64.00	58.98	54.32	45.03	29.69	31.66	17.82	18.69	19.59
1835	61.62	56.12	50.95	42.33	27.45	29.67	15.82	16.83	17.90
1840	58.48	52.58	47.14	39.10	24.72	27.11	13.52	14.60	15.75
1845	54.26	48.28	42.75	35.37	21.78	24.21	11.21	12.30	13.56
1850	48.93	43.21	37.93	31.28	18.76	21.08	9.06	10.09	11.19
males	51.50	45.37	39.70	34.38	20.39	22.95	9.56	10.72	11.95

Smallpox base rate from India, yielding approx. 30% fatalities
1.6 × base rate approx. 40% fatalities
2.2 × base rate approx. 60% fatalities
Add D = notional disease 1820
VD15 = venereal disease beginning 1815
PR = population recovery
Note that results for WL1 eo=20 yields female survivors in 1850 at:
last row
1 — 46.52
2 — 40.60
3 — 35.17
4 — 29.21
5 — 17.10
6 — 19.50
7 — 7.70
8 — 8.74
9 — 9.87

Were smallpox death rates to have attained 60 per cent with one additional epidemic and venereal disease, the population of 1788 would have been literally decimated by 1850 (col. 7). No efforts at population recovery within the bounds of reproductive possibility would have made any significant difference. In between these two limits, cols 5 and 6 show outcomes in 1850 with populations at about one-fifth the precontact level. None of this has yet taken into account the taking of Aboriginal resources or the killing of Aborigines by violence. These are the model disease outcomes for the mainland. They have little relevance, apart from the table relating to venereal disease, to Van Diemen's Land, where resource taking and killing dominated, especially during the 1820s.

Resource losses and killing

Just as persons only die once so they cannot have resources taken from them after they are dead. Resource taking may be and often was merely another mode of accelerating depopulation — those who lost their resources died of starvation or diet-related diseases. Killing and resource taking were, however, often intimately related, sometimes as two sides of the same penny. Aborigines were often killed to obtain their resources. Sometimes they were killed during efforts to limit their access to their resources. On other occasions they were killed judicially, having committed 'offences' in efforts to protect such access. Resource taking did not necessarily depend on violent killing. Sometimes Aborigines were simply forced off their lands and may have ended in colliding with other tribes. Quite often, remnant Aborigines were employed on colonial properties, but under conditions that limited their access to former resources. In the latter cases, the outcome to colonists appeared inexplicable — Aborigines simply died.

Just as we cannot add separate disease effects together, so it is not possible to identify the independent effects of resource loss and killing when so many other depopulating influences were at issue. Nevertheless, it is useful, initially, to try to gauge some idea of the depopulating impact of resource loss and killing as if no other factors intervened. Subsequently, it is possible to fuse the whole process of disease, resource loss and killing into one.

So far as Van Diemen's Land is concerned, there is little point in making complex modelling efforts. The dominant colonial attempts to withdraw resources and to kill Aborigines were concentrated within one decade after 1820. By the beginning of the 1830s very few Aborigines remained. There can be little doubt that combined and integrated efforts at resource removal and killing dominated the destruction of the Van Diemen's Land Aborigines. The matter is more complex on the mainland.

The processes of resource removal and killing might be seen as broadly a function of the rate at which colonists occupied territory. There are, however, several problems with this approach. First, 'territory' was not uniform in quality and it is as possible as it is necessary to divide areas occupied into coastal, inland river and inland plains areas. We have rough indications of the rate of colonial settlement of these areas from Roberts (1924) and Christie (1979), plausible enough for quinquennial modelling. But to exploit this information we need to convert settlement areas into 'featureless plains', adopting some mode of equating the three types of territory. The general anthropological approach appears to place highest weight on coastal and estuarine areas, significantly less on inland riverine areas and least on plains. Obviously, within each sub-area there are gradations in quality. For a rough approximation, the modelling of resource removal assumes a weight of plains, rivers and coastline in the ratio of $1:20:100$. The quinquennial areas shown as occupied by Roberts and Christie are computed in terms of the lengths of coastline, rivers and land, based on measurements in the *Commonwealth Year Book*. The result gives the relative importance of coastal to inland areas as approximately $3:1$, curiously similar to the estimation of Radcliffe-Brown's concept of relative significance. To this extent, then, the assumptions of the model do not introduce any peculiar bias relative to his population estimates.

The second problem is, who confronted whom? Was it colonists encountering Aborigines as individuals or was it, rather, colonial livestock conflicting with and altering the original ecology? In terms of resource removal, it would appear that the dominant influence was colonial livestock, which destroyed the natural shrubbery; consumed many of the perennial plants, thus supporting the development of annual grasses; ate yam beds wholesale; and indirectly but rapidly changed the habitats of the small animals. Colonists enhanced the process by two main methods. First, they selectively destroyed specially important areas that Aborigines favoured and restricted Aboriginal access to what they regarded as colonial properties. Second, the colonists acted directly in killing Aborigines, mostly in groups, as retribution, to display force in pushing Aborigines off their lands or, at times, merely for sport.

So far as livestock go, an attempt has been made to estimate the quinquennial livestock increase for sheep and cattle, converting each type of animal into a standardised biomass equivalent and weighting the quinquennial areas settled by estimated densities of livestock in each quinquennium.

The third problem arises in terms of the Aboriginal response. In general, Aborigines did not oppose colonists by way of pitched battles. A significant number of colonists were killed by Aborigines and substantial property was destroyed. But the important question is whether Aborigines were relatively mobile or relatively immobile as they encountered colonists and their livestock. This depended, in turn, on tribal and kinship associations. Tindale's efforts at mapping tribes suggest great variety in the sizes of areas occupied and in kin associations. Thus, many tribes on major rivers appear to have occupied relatively small areas where one would expect a relatively low degree of mobility. In the central New South Wales plains, Tindale attached very large areas to a few tribes so that a greater degree of mobility and flexibility of response may have been possible there. Clearly, if Aborigines could slowly yield territory, their populations might survive until, as in Van Diemen's Land, concerted and final action was found to be necessary. If Aborigines were immobile, they were forced to take the brunt of colonial settlement tribe by tribe. In general, the mainland experience appears to favour the assumption of relative immobility.

Colonists did not occupy all territory. Even had they done so there would have been the opportunity for some Aborigines to 'slip through the cracks' of colonial constraints. But the colonists did not have to take everything for Aboriginal society to become non-viable in traditional terms. It is difficult to determine what that point may have been. Clearly some outback New South Wales tribes survived into the second half of the nineteenth century. Equally, the gold discoveries in Victoria in the 1850s were the final demographic blow. For present purposes, it is assumed that the resource take in New South Wales and Victoria by 1860 represented total removal of resources. The process of modelling resource withdrawal then rests on computing the proportion of resources progressively withdrawn up to 1860 during each quinquennium.

Table 5: Percentage of 1860 Aboriginal resources absorbed

	NSW	Vic.
1805–09	0.42	
1810–14	0.33	
1815–19	1.83	
1820–24	4.42	
1825–29	5.42	
1830–34	24.58	14.00
1835–39	27.92	19.00
1840–44	13.14	5.00
1845–49	—	30.00

Table 6: Resource loss and disease

	NSW WL5 Spx 1.6 VD 15 PR 10% Res loss 05	NSW WL5 Spx 1.6 add D 20 VD 15 PR 10% Res loss 05	Vic. WL5 Spx 1.6 VD 15 PR 10% Res loss 30	Vic. WL5 Spx 1.6 add D 20 VD 15 PR 10% Res loss 30
1788	100.00	100.00	100.00	100.00
1790	54.75	54.75	54.75	54.75
1795	56.22	56.22	56.22	56.22
1800	58.56	58.56	58.56	58.56
1805	60.02	60.02	60.02	60.02
1810	60.83	60.83	62.07	62.07
1815	60.74	60.74	62.95	62.95
1820	60.45	42.38	63.58	44.59
1825	58.45	39.95	63.87	43.63
1830	37.65	25.63	41.87	28.50
1835	32.32	21.48	37.64	25.01
1840	24.99	16.10	37.70	19.77
1845	15.70	9.83	20.93	13.07
1850	6.18	3.78	6.18	3.75

Tables 5 and 6 (above) show the percentage of 1860 resources absorbed in each quinquennium, as computed, standardised and illustrative estimates of depopulation, combining resource loss with diseases and efforts at population recovery. One might compare columns 2 and 4 of table 6 with column 5 of table 2. As will be seen, resource loss begins to cut into Aboriginal populations in New South Wales and Victoria from 1830, but even between 1830 and 1850 it does not add radically to the depopulation caused by disease. There can be little doubt, however, that resource loss and the consequent depletion of Aborigines' diets accelerated and exacerbated the effects of disease. Here the confusion about cause of death defeats any attempt to impute contributions to total depopulation. What is certainly clear, however, is that any plausible rate of killing of Aborigines by colonists was largely irrelevant to the process of depopulation.

15

TURNING THE MODELS AROUND

How can we exploit these approximations to estimate possible or plausible precontact Aboriginal populations? If we have reasonable estimates of remnant populations prior to 1850, we can reverse the models and project backwards from these dated estimates to a 1788 base. There are fortunately some numbers, particularly for Victoria and Van Diemen's Land, but much less completely for New South Wales. In Van Diemen's Land we have the official 1818 estimate of 'about 7000' and by the early 1830s a few hundred. For Victoria, there is an array of numbers but essentially they apply to the early 1840s. In New South Wales, estimates for coastal areas are also available for the early 1840s. Though we concentrate on these areas here, it is relevant in extending the picture to the whole of Australia that early estimates are available for parts of Queensland and Western Australia.

Van Diemen's Land

Van Diemen's Land is the least significant and can perhaps be disposed of quickly. Radcliffe-Brown (1930) opted for a precontact population of 2–3000. Rhys Jones (1970) has raised this number to 5000. *The Statistics of Van Diemen's Land* estimated a current population of 7000 in 1818 and G. A. Robinson (in Radcliffe-Brown, 1930) projected a precontact number of about 7–8000. Given the extensive sealing around the island from the later 1790s, its size, and the penetration of settlement by 1818, it is not implausible that the colonists had a reasonably good impression of prevailing numbers by 1818. Not very much activity between Aborigines and colonists occurred between 1818 and 1820, and this official estimate is taken as applicable to 1820.

The venereal disease model would suggest that we might have to add about 1000 to this figure to derive a precontact estimate. But in addition to venereal disease there was undoubtedly considerable violence between the sealers and Aborigines before settlement, and after the penal colony was established significant killing occurred, with Europeans shooting into groups of Aborigines. Some other diseases were also transmitted. It seems possible then that an appropriate precontact number could be of the order of 9000 persons. After 1820 and particularly after 1825, genocide directed and organised by the governor substantially eliminated the indigenous population in an overt struggle over access to resources (Robson, 1983).

Victoria

Radcliffe-Brown opted for an estimate of 11 500 for what is now Victoria. This was the product of choosing between alternative numbers and opting for the lowest, together with some supplementation based on assumed numbers of tribes and tribal size. The available contemporary numbers dated between 1841 and 1845 (one date is uncertain) are:

Portland	(1845)	3500		(mean of 3–4000)
Wimmera	(?)	3000		
Westernport	(1845)	2000	or	3800
Murray	(1841–5)	2000	or	3000
Gippsland	(1845)	1500		
Total Vic.		12 000		14 800

Gippsland is not included in the backward extrapolation of the models. It was isolated, heavily forested and there is no evidence that it was subject to smallpox. From the modelling, we might use the mid-range smallpox kill of 1.6 times the base Indian rate (see Table 2, p. 124) and so choose, within this constraint, upper and lower bound extrapolation factors of eight or five times the 1845 populations. This would yield, adding an unadjusted 1500 for Gippsland, a range of precontact Victorian populations from 54 000 to 85 500.

The conservatism of the assumptions behind these bounds should be stressed. A 45 per cent kill rate was a very moderate outcome and there is a good deal of evidence (c.f. Butlin, 1983) of very heavy mortality rates in Victoria. Were we to use a 60 per cent kill rate for smallpox, the projected precontact population would rise to approximately 120 000. This is far from being beyond the bounds of possibility. Similarly, the treatment of Gippsland derives basically from the fact that smallpox was not recorded there. Yet Aborigines there were subject to violent killing, possibly the most violent in the whole of Australia. Even so, its precontact population was almost certainly very limited — even if we enlarge the 1500 several times.

Adjustments of the order of five times and more particularly eight times seem, in fact, to conform to suggestions made by the authors of several of these regional numbers. Radcliffe-Brown might have taken some of these contemporary suggestions into account. Thus Fyans, who was then Police Magistrate and Land Commissioner for Portland Bay called attention to the heavy mortality that had occurred, particularly before 1835 (that is, before colonial contact). The evidence he presented suggests that he had some reason to believe (though he does not state the figures) that the 1788 population of Portland Bay had once been between

14 600 and 17 600. These figures would broadly conform to a Victorian aggregate of 54 000 if similar adjustments were made elsewhere.

E. M. Curr (1883), a pastoral manager and amateur anthropologist with a deep interest in Aborigines, suggested a different system of modelling. Observing during the 1840s along the Murray and assembling information from elsewhere, Curr drew his own inferences from the frequency and condition of cooking mounds in Victoria. He proposed that the number of cooking mounds operational in about 1840 were made up of one-third consistently used and about two-thirds never used. From this he concluded a recent depopulation after 1835 of between a half and two-thirds. But Curr also observed many other ovens which were no longer operational and through which large trees were growing, indicating, in his view, a prior major population loss about 40 years before 1835.

One may question the grounds for his judgement but it is not possible simply to ignore it. Moreover, Curr's 1835 population estimate of 15 000 for Victoria was based on the assembly of a great deal of information. This would be a low number in comparison with the estimates for the early 1840s given above. But Curr explicitly invites projection back to 1788, with implied numbers between 60 000 and 90 000. These are almost the same as the model extrapolations above, at the medium smallpox kill rate.

Based on recent archaeological studies of the Western District of Victoria, Lourandos proposed a population at 1841 of 7900, much higher than Fyans' estimate for Portland Bay and, more particularly, implying much higher densities per square kilometre. This was an extremely rich area of Victoria. Accepting Lourandos' estimate for 1841 and projecting backwards using the lower multiplier adopted above, we would have a 1788 population for the Western District of Victoria of the order of 30–35 000. Accepting the same density figures that are implied by a 1788 population of only 54 000 for the rest of Victoria would yield a 1788 aggregate for Victoria in the region of 75 000 persons.

G. A. Robinson's detailed field studies in 1841 (in Presland, 1977) produced age data on some 500 remnant Aborigines. There is a marked shortfall in ages 0–14 years and a significantly low representation of persons aged 50–54. Those aged 10–14 and 50–54 in 1841 would have been the groups most exposed to risk from smallpox epidemics at about 1790 and 1830. This is another straw favouring heavy mortality from smallpox on two occasions. Strengthening this, Robinson also identified a substantial number of areas in which no tribal survivors remained.

Population densities in Victoria and some implications

No great reliance should be placed on population densities. Nevertheless, it is of interest that Radcliffe-Brown's estimate for Australia did exploit concepts of 'carrying capacity' and his figure of 12 500 for Victoria implied a density of approximately one person per 18 square kilometres. By contrast, at the extreme, the adjusted Lourandos figures for Western Victoria would imply one person per 1.5 square kilometres. Perhaps the old Aborigine who claimed that his people were once as thick as cockatoos on the plain was not merely indulging in hyberbole. The model range for Victoria implies a lower density for the whole of Victoria ranging from one person to 2.5 for each 4 square kilometres. The Western District was a particularly advantageous area, though the Murray with its southward flowing tributaries and the coastal resources meant that Victoria, apart from the heavily forested Gippsland, was an attractive habitat. Despite this, Radcliffe-Brown accorded a population density to Victoria lower than that in the Gascoigne River of Western Australia, the area with which he was familiar by virtue of field studies. The Gascoigne River area could not, by any stretch of imagination, be equated ecologically with Victoria and it is possible that Radcliffe-Brown adopted an innocent racism — black people thrive only in high temperature areas.

When he turned to New South Wales, Radcliffe-Brown's estimate of 40 000 was not based on available numbers, which he simply discarded. Curiously, his figure yields a population density for New South Wales that is almost the same as (very slightly less than) his estimates for Victoria. He purported to subdivide New South Wales into coastal and inland areas, allotting 25 000 to the coast and 20 000 to the inland, making the aggregate 'to be on the safe side' 40 000 rather than 45 000. In effect, given all his references to irreducible minima, the lowest possible estimates in Victoria were carried over into New South Wales and arithmetically emphasised. This was done despite the richness of the New South Wales coast and the fact that the main river systems of Australia flow through its interior. The result is a warning against area carrying capacity concepts. Even more so is the total estimate for Australia.

The question of New South Wales

Radcliffe-Brown was correct in recognising the much more limited contemporary estimates for New South Wales. Certainly, we have no opportunity to exploit 1840s regional estimates that cover substantially the whole colony. Nevertheless, we do have some and, indeed, some important indicative numbers.

First, let us note that, were we to make a simple extension of the Victorian modelling results to New South Wales (as Radcliffe-Brown *de facto*, did), we would be looking at numbers of the order of 200 000, 265 000 and 320 000 to match the three Victorian model results above. These are five, six and seven times the numbers proposed by Radcliffe-Brown. Are these numbers within the bounds of possibility?

The various regional figures for New South Wales relate to different dates and some are anthropologists' recent reconstructions, based on early estimates. We have numbers from Phillip in 1788 for the Sydney area; for the southern shores of Port Jackson after 1810; from the 1845 Inquiry into Aborigines, which relate particularly to coastal areas (some fragments for inland locations are too scrappy to be used); and estimates for the Darling River based on Sturt's 1829–30 observation of the incidence of the second smallpox epidemic. There are also relevant numbers for the Moreton Bay area in 1845.

The Land Commissioner of the Moreton Bay area estimated an 1845 population of 4000 (New South Wales, 'Report from the Select Committee'). The Commissioner also indicated a drastic demographic imbalance, with a female/male ratio of 2:3, and stated that women rarely had more than two children. The Moreton Bay area had been affected by the second smallpox epidemic and probably by the first. It had been exposed to the effects of a convict settlement with its venereal disease implications. And it had, by 1845, been affected by settlement and killing. There is no possibility that the number 4000, with its attendant densities, could approximate the 1788 population. We probably need on the basis of the modelling results to replace it with a number four to six times this level — 16–25 000 in accordance with relatively conservative model conditions.

This has an important bearing on a large section of the northern New South Wales coast. Belshaw (in McBryde, 1978) used the commissioner's number plus some incomplete estimations for the north coast to re-estimate the area from the Queensland border to the MacLeay River. His resulting number, supposed to be precontact, was 6300. This was in fact, based on the 1845 preconceptions. The area between the border and the MacLeay River is a particularly rich habitat, a fusion of coast and estuarine plains with a veritable network of food-rich rivers. Moreover, the Aborigines had been exposed not merely to the effects of the Moreton Bay convict settlement but also to a similar settlement at Port Macquarie. For the MacLeay River, Massie (1845) clearly displayed a demographic distortion far worse than that at Moreton Bay — a female/male ratio of 1:3, with children accounting for a mere 6 per cent of the population instead of the standard 20–30 per cent. This exceptionally low representation of children is a feature of all the 1845 coastal reports, in fact in some cases there were no surviving children in remnant tribes. Port Macquarie is explicitly listed as a location of the second smallpox epidemic. We cannot leave these distortions unadjusted and relate the aggregate to 1788 as Belshaw proposed.

An adjustment of Belshaw's north coast estimate using only the medium modelling adjustment would be highly conservative. Yet it would invite us to consider a precontact population for this section of the coast at 26–38 000, the higher figure almost equal to Radcliffe-Brown's estimate for the whole of New South Wales.

Apart from a 1788 estimate of about 4000 on the Cumberland Plain, we have no historical information for between Port Jackson and the Macleay River and none for south to the Victorian border. The Sydney area figure suggests a density of the order of one person to 2.5 square kilometres approximately, compared to a north coast density for the higher re-estimated population of about one person per square kilometre and for the lower number at about one person per 1.6 square kilometres. Despite Port Jackson, the Cumberland Plain was not ecologically highly attractive. The Manning and Hunter Valleys in the central coast were certainly much more so. If we apply the lower density of the north coast to this area we would have approximately 20 000 persons in this mid-coast area to be added to the 4000 on the Cumberland Plain — a total from Botany Bay to the Queensland border of 50–62 000.

We have no guidance for the south coast, which narrows greatly as the mountains move close to the sea. The population density was almost certainly much less here but it seems unlikely that numbers could have fallen short of the order of 15 000. A plausible New South Wales coastal population may then lie within the range 65–77 000. Let us opt for the lower number, conforming to that degree with Radcliffe-Brown's caution.

In the interior, we have two guides. First, we can relate the Victorian estimates to the Murray River and probably to the Murray–Murrumbidgee basin. Allen (1972) has appraised sightings by the explorers Sturt, Mitchell and Eyre during the 1820s and 1830s and estimated a Murray–Darling concentration of Aborigines at five persons per 1.6 kilometres of river. He finds this in conformity with coastal densities, without considering the potential of the main inland rivers and their surrounds.

Allen makes no adjustment for possible population loss prior to these sightings. The only adjustment that he makes is for the seasonal conditions operating when the explorers passed by. This is unlikely to be adequate, particularly given that the prime source, Sturt, was consciously describing populations stricken by smallpox and often observed that smallpox had already 'swept away' many of the people. We need both a careful ecological reconstruction of these areas and adjustment for disease and some resource loss. Taking the middle range modelling for New South Wales, including both disease and resource loss and conservatively adopting the 1825 numbers, it seems likely that Allen's densities may need to be about doubled. This would imply a Murray–Murrumbidgee–Darling precontact total of the order of 60 000. Interestingly enough, this conforms to the lowest estimated density for Victoria. At least the two possible procedures lead to essentially the same figure.

For the rest of New South Wales we know virtually nothing. Some of it is desert or near desert, some mountain, some plains country. If we were to take Radcliffe-Brown's Australian mean, given the poor conditions beyond the Darling, we would add only 20 000 to the New South Wales population. This would be merely a stab in the dark. We would then have precontact estimates for New South Wales of 145–157 000. This is well below the 200–265–320 000 derivable by adopting Victorian densities for New South Wales — a transfer that is implicit in Radcliffe-Brown's calculations. Clearly all this needs to be carried a great deal further, but it is suggested that Radcliffe-Brown's number for New South Wales needs to be about quadrupled, on a conservative basis.

Australian aggregates

Within the context of this volume I am concerned predominantly with the present New South Wales, Victoria and Tasmania (Van Diemen's Land) because I wish to confine attention to pre-1850 conditions. Only very limited contact between colonists and Aborigines outside these areas had occurred by that date. Nevertheless, it is essential to appreciate that from Moreton Bay and Port Essington in Queensland and the Northern Territory respectively, venereal and other diseases were being spread by colonists. We have only to read the account of the convict outpost at King George's Sound in Western Australia (Mulvaney and White, 1987) to appreciate how rapidly and completely obscure disease communications could enfold and destroy Aborigines. The second smallpox epidemic appears certainly to have passed through most of Queensland during 1830–35, causing massive mortality. Hot on its heels came settlers pushing up towards central Queensland.

In the 1880s, T. A. Coghlan attempted an estimate of Australian Aboriginal populations. He gave no basis for his estimate which was, nevertheless, 200 000. It is not intended here to try to relate this number to the suggested modelling procedure. Major adaptations are needed, not least because virtually no Aborigines remained in Van Diemen's Land or Victoria and very few in New South Wales. They had passed beyond their nadir into oblivion and one would need a different procedure to estimate their numbers. Here, however, remains a challenge. Essentially, Coghlan proposes by implication that virtually the whole of the remnant lay outside these three colonies: in Queensland, the Northern Territory and South and Western Australia. This 'rest of Australia' needs to be modelled with somewhat different assumptions. It seems better to focus at the moment on areas claimed by colonists. However, it is suggested that the population figures for the 'rest of Australia' in 1880 may need to be increased by a factor of the order of five to yield a precontact total. This would imply an Australian aggregate of the order of 1.25 millions.

The following summary conclusions may be suggested:

(a) Australian Aborigines were in a different position from the indigenous peoples of the Americas in confronting Europeans, particularly because of prior contact with people from the north of Australia.

(b) Northern visitors were certainly capable of delivering diseases, particularly smallpox, and almost certainly did so from time to time.

(c) Despite this contact, the northern visitors were visitors, not settlers. They did not implant endemic conditions.

(d) There appear to have been important blocks to the transmission of disease from the north. These blocks were essentially climatic, social and economic, inducing a breakdown of communication between Aborigines during the monsoon when any disease might arrive. By the end of the monsoon, the epidemics would have passed.

(e) This raises the possibility that Aborigines on the north coast may have been afflicted frequently by disease while the mass of the remaining Aborigines in Australia were literally an exposed population lacking immune defences to introduced diseases.

(f) The first colonists at Botany Bay brought variolous matter with them for proper medical reasons. An epidemic was observed at Botany Bay 15 months after their arrival. In 1828 a smallpox-stricken ship arrived in Sydney and a smallpox outbreak was observed on the Darling in 1829. A potential link arises from the contents of the ship and the assignment of convicts quite close to the point of the observed outbreak.

(g) Colonists brought other diseases — influenza, whooping cough, mumps and measles, together with pneumonia, tuberculosis and venereal diseases. These, with smallpox, appear to have been the prime depopulating agents of Australian Aborigines.

(h) In addition to diseases, colonists claimed Aboriginal resources: evicting them, restraining access and otherwise impeding normal hunter-gatherer behaviour. The result was starvation and the intensification of diet-related diseases.

(i) Killing for retributional, judicial or merely sporting reasons was a factor in depopulation. But it seems unlikely to have been a primary element.

(j) Adjusting for depopulation due to these factors, it seems possible to provide plausible re-estimates for each of Van Diemen's Land and the present New South Wales and Victoria at a level of the order of 260 000 — close to the traditional number proposed for Australia as a whole.

(k) It seems likely that precontact Aboriginal populations throughout Australia lay within the bounds of 1–1.5 millions.

PART IV

THE ESTABLISHMENT OF A BRIDGEHEAD ECONOMY: 1788–1810

16

INTRODUCTION

The story of the early years of the first penal settlement of Botany Bay has often been told. By far the best account is Fletcher's *Colonial Australia before 1850* (1976). I do not intend to examine the details of the first two decades, nor to repeat what was said about Aborigines in Part III.

The First Fleet, landing its complement of some 717 convicts and 273 members of the Marines and their families, together with a handful of civil officials and their families, embarked on a high-risk venture half the world away from Britain. The newcomers were totally different from the Aborigines in lifestyle and approach to life and economy. The foundation process of colonial economy is accordingly introduced here to juxtapose what the newcomers attempted to achieve in the ancient Aboriginal environment. Their arrival punctuated the existence of Aborigines around the arrival point and their impact spread quickly far afield.

The first settlement can be seen from either of two perspectives. One is the beginning of a colonial success story — and a remarkable one it was. This is the tradition. On the other hand, the two decades after 1788 were preliminary, experimental and exceptional, quite apart from the settlement's convict foundations. After 1792, turbulent, uncertain, experimental and exceptional relations and prospects within the colony ended in a constitutional crisis that enforced a new order. Nevertheless, it laid down a pattern of human values, resource use and technology that conflicted sharply with Aboriginal practice and tradition.

Officially, the newcomers were charged to care for the interests of 'the natives'. In fact, there was little option other than that one or other side should be the loser. The colonists, intent on their own objectives, largely discarded the Aborigines and were probably instrumental — most likely indirectly — in destroying large numbers of them through disease. But as a new 'breed', the newcomers and old residents could not survive together. How the first settlement managed to survive and organise its affairs needs to be understood as the counterpoint to Aboriginal society and economy and its ultimate disaster. This part of the story is an integral component — the other side of the coin — in the destruction of the Aborigines. The colonial success during 1788–1809 was truly a bridgehead that flowered into an overwhelmingly destructive force.

With inadequate stores and equipment, the settlers faced severe survival problems. The task of clearing, setting up encampments, initiating some crude preliminary building and putting out exploratory feelers into the immediate hinterland of the Cumberland Plain absorbed effort and the limited support stores. The development of agriculture to provide local food supplies was an urgent objective but little was achieved during the term of the first Governor, Phillip. The colony remained confronting starvation, a risk enhanced by the arrival of the Second Fleet in 1790 with sick and dying human cargoes and inadequate stores and supplies. Public efforts at farming displayed limited productive potential, partly because of lack of farming knowledge, partly due to the need to learn by doing and partly because of the limited potential of the chosen site. There was also the present and continuing awareness and fear of Aborigines.

The adumbration of a policy for land grants (*HRA*, series 1, no. 1: 7) to military officials and a similar eventual prospect for ex-convicts had little significance until 1792. Then, with Phillip's departure, an interregnum followed with colonial control assumed by officers of the New South Wales Corps. From that moment followed a substitution of private farming and private commercial activity by officials, the large-scale assignment of convicts to employment by individual officers and the emergence of a form of competition between two different systems of operation. Shann (1930) saw this as a conflict between communism and free enterprise. Neither label had much application to the local situation and neither would now be accepted. Public productive efforts with organised gangs of controlled convicts was one mode of labour and resource allocation not only in farming but also in the production of a crude infrastructure. In the process, control did not extend to establishing a literal gaol economy — work requirements were far too diverse and required too much mobility on the part of convicts for that to be the case. This mobility exposed the settlers to greater risk of Aboriginal attacks and intensified fears about personal security. Nor could the original efforts by officials to establish their own farming with land grants and assigned convicts, or even their efforts at commercial undertakings, easily be fitted under the rubric of private enterprise in any simple sense. Almost all the 'private' efforts by officials depended on access in some form to public resources and on the authority that derived from their official positions. 'Penal capitalism' does not adequately fit these activities. Rather it was a process of privatising official roles that laid the institutional basis of what eventually emerged as a distinct private sector in the colony.

Combined with this privatised development was the gradual termination of convict sentences, the progressive freeing of convicts, the allocation of small land grants to them and the growth of small farming and trades activities. Fitzpatrick (1933) once saw this as the emergence of a peasant economy, but this does not convey the variety of undertakings by ex-convicts.

With the end of the military interregnum there was a strongly entrenched official interest in their own publicly subsidised undertakings in both farming and commerce. The restoration of conventional government under Governors Hunter,

King and Bligh saw strong contention between private and public interests, leading eventually to the military deposition of Bligh and a second interregnum that continued until Governor Macquarie's arrival in 1810. In the interval, private farming and private commerce, with some private industry, were further expanded not only by the original officials but also by two other groups. One was a handful of free immigrants, most prominent in commercial activities and in the expansion of offshore enterprises. The other was through the efforts of ex-convicts, the mass of whom remained as small farmers and tradespeople, but some of whom formed comparatively large-scale enterprises. Side by side with these private developments went an absolute as well as relative decline in public farming. Both private and public links with the outside world were developed through shipping and agency connections with India and China and the growth of colonial ship movement around the Pacific and Indian Oceans.

If the colony was not absolutely secure by 1810, it displayed a remarkable diversity of activity, an extraordinary structure of wealth and income, a remarkable ability to satisfy a wide variety of tastes and a high degree of civil freedom. Moreover, the original settlement had been amplified by the extension to Van Diemen's Land in 1803. Shortly after, during 1807–8, sufficient effective organisational resources existed to close down the outpost at Norfolk Island and to re-enact something akin to a colonial First Fleet movement in the transfer of the islanders with their belongings in five ships to Van Diemen's Land. The original settlement was not only expanding but also fine-tuning its occupation of Australia, the fine-tuning done not because of failure in Norfolk Island but because of a conscious cost benefit calculation (*HRA*, series I, no. 6: 182–3).

Basically, this chapter is an attempt to explain the conditions of this extraordinary success rather than to deal with the details of the process of change. During 1788–1809 fewer than 11 000 of the eventual 160 000 ever-arriving number of convicts had been landed (*Australians. Historical Statistics*, 1987). Numerically, then, this bridgehead period accounted for a minute fraction of the convict flow. What is important about the flow, and related ones, is the early success of the bridgehead. Given the tiny scale, the interesting questions revolve not around the detail of but the basic reasons for an extraordinary colonial achievement in terms of economic performance, comparative personal freedom and the establishment of individual enterprise with relatively complex institutions and property rights.

The inevitability of the emergence of free elements in this early society, regardless of any British intent, has generally been recognised, given the relatively short sentences of many convicts and the fact that a considerable number had already served significant fractions of their sentences before leaving Britain. The conversion of convicts to ex-convict status certainly meant a growing opportunity for the exercise of choice. It appeared for the first five years that considerable flows of convicts were in prospect, with 4314 arriving in that period. But in 1793–1809 only 6490 were added. This drastic slackening accentuated the emergence of a substantial freed society at a very early date.

Coupled with this evolution in civil conditions, there appear to have been as many as 700 or so free immigrants during the 23-year period. Some were officials' families, some convicts' families, some wholly free immigrants. These alone were a significant supplement to a freer society. But, in addition, it appears possible that as many as 3000 children had been born in the colony by 1809. Even though not all remained or many failed to survive, they made a major alteration to the penal character of the early society. Much has been made of the sex imbalance of early Australia but curiously enough this is least apposite to the first decade of settlement. Apart from free arrivals, many of whom were women, there was no gross sex imbalance in the first five years' shipment of convicts. The 2622 males who arrived during 1788 to 1792 were accompanied by 1792 females. This may not have been equality but the real imbalance followed after 1792 and up to 1809, when 4778 male and only 1712 female convicts arrived (*Australians. Historical Statistics*, 1987). There was sufficient reproductive potential among the convicts, quite apart from official and free immigrant families, to produce substantial numbers of colonial born. Although the mass of these children were labelled with the convicts they nevertheless introduced a large number of persons capable of a good deal of free choice, at least in strictly legal terms.

If freedom in civil status was rapidly emerging in the composition of the population so that, by 1808, the early settlement was predominantly free and freed, the change in institutional structure, property rights and free and flexible allocation of labour was equally if not more striking. The leadership in this second style of change was provided by the early officials, particularly the officers of the New South Wales Corps (cf Hainsworth, 1971). But by 1800 their primacy was challenged by free immigrants and ex-convicts, and the three different groups provided the 'entrepreneurs' of the first decade of the nineteenth century. Beneath them but by no means minor was the mass of free, ex-convict and some colonial born who jointly contributed a large array of private activities in what had, a short time before, been an exposed, threatened and closely controlled penal settlement. The various groups conducted a wide range of activities not merely in farming but also in commerce and trades, building, transport and offshore undertakings (cf Hainsworth, 1971; Felcher, 1976: ch. 3–5; Steven, 1965).

In a mere 23 years there had been a massive transition accompanied by extensive structural change and relatively complex economic development. Yet, by 1809, little in the way of export development had been attained. One possible explanation of this early bridgehead success, through export-led development, is therefore largely closed off. Confined, as most of the settlers were, within the limits of the Cumberland Plain in New South Wales, no very rich natural resources were immediately available to them. Preoccupied with the Napoleonic wars, Britain did not attend closely to the needs of the settlement. We have to look for other reasons. What might they have been?

17

HISTORY AND THEORY

A summary picture in 1805–6

The best, if incomplete, contemporary picture of the first settlement is given in the muster records of 1805–6 (1989). Subsequent musters, particularly that in 1811, give a less informative account. Development certainly continued beyond 1806, so this early muster probably understates the success attained in the first bridgehead efforts. After 1806, with the succession of Governor Bligh and subsequent conflict, information and truth go underground. The 1805–6 muster does not include all the important information and even within its own terms it has several important deficiencies. But it is the one occasion before the 1828 census when it is likely that the mass of individuals were able to report their colonial activity or occupation, whether in current or predominant terms. Let us in any event deal first with this muster, which included a head count of much, though not all, of the Botany Bay settlement and also encompassed land holdings and farming activity.

Table 7 (opposite) is a summary of occupations/industries reputed to be carried on by males according to civil status as estimated from the muster. The muster omitted officials and their activities and some free immigrants were also excluded. In all, just short of half the population is reported in the table, the greater part of the balance being women, children, officials and free immigrants. Although these omissions affect the occupation/industry distributions, they actually serve to underscore the fact that this was not a picture of a gaol, not even a gaol without walls; nor was it very much of a penal colony and there are no indications either of low living standards or still less of imminent starvation. Historically, no doubt, it was a passing condition. The picture may actually have become stronger and sharper up to 1810. Then, with the ensuing high inflow of convicts it changed substantially. But in the meantime the evidence is for a highly — one might say, extraordinarily — successful establishment of a colonial bridgehead economy.

Table 7: 1805–6 Muster: occupation/activity by civil status (males)

	Came free	Ex-conv.	Ticket of leave	Convicts	Not stated	Total record
Farming/pastoral	118	452	56	691	17	1334
Fisheries	1	26	0	0	138	165
Food, drink, tobacco	3	32	0	2	0	37
Dealers	0	0	0	0	0	0
Leatherworking	3	22	6	0	0	31
Clothing textiles	1	20	0	0	0	21
Metalworking	4	0	2	0	0	6
Building	14	96	3	0	6	119
Specialised timber	4	2	0	21	0	27
Other spec. trades	0	15	0	0	0	15
Transport	8	32	0	10	0	50
Apprentices	26	0	0	0	0	26
Public service	2	55	0	41	13	111
Professional	5	13	0	1	0	19
Personal service	0	29	2	0	0	31
Labourers	11	242	0	74	5	332
Self-employed	NA	NA	70	73	0	143
NS (inc. sick, gaol)	11	272	37	461	28	809
Total record	211	1308	176	1374	207	3276
	%	%	%	%	%	%
Farming/pastoral	8.8	33.9	4.2	51.8	1.3	100
Fisheries	0.6	15.8	0.0	0.0	83.6	100
Food drink tobacco	8.1	86.5	0.0	5.4	0.0	100
Dealers	0.0	0.0	0.0	0.0	0.0	0
Leatherworking	9.7	71.0	19.4	0.0	0.0	100
Clothing textiles	4.8	95.2	0.0	0.0	0.0	100
Metalworking	66.7	0.0	33.3	0.0	0.0	100
Building	11.8	80.7	2.5	0.0	5.0	100
Specialised timber	14.8	7.4	0.0	77.8	0.0	100
Other spec. trades	0.0	100.0	0.0	0.0	0.0	100
Transport	16.0	64.0	0.0	20.0	0.0	100
Apprentices	100.0	0.0	0.0	0.0	0.0	100
Public service	1.8	49.5	0.0	36.9	11.7	100
Professional	26.3	68.4	0.0	5.3	0.0	100
Personal service	0.0	93.5	6.5	0.0	0.0	100
Labourers	3.3	72.9	0.0	22.3	1.5	100
Self-employed	NA	NA	49.0	51.0	0.0	100
NS (inc. sick, gaol)	1.4	33.6	4.6	57.0	3.5	100
Total record	6.4	39.9	5.4	41.9	6.3	100
	%	%	%	%	%	%
Farming/pastoral	55.9	34.6	31.8	50.3	8.2	40.7
Fisheries	0.5	2.0	0.0	0.0	66.7	5.0
Food drink tobacco	1.4	2.4	0.0	0.1	0.0	1.1
Dealers	0.0	0.0	0.0	0.0	0.0	0.0
Leatherworking	1.4	1.7	3.4	0.0	0.0	0.9
Clothing textiles	0.5	1.5	0.0	0.0	0.0	0.6
Metalworking	1.9	0.0	1.1	0.0	0.0	0.2
Building	6.6	7.3	1.7	0.0	2.9	3.6
Specialised timber	1.9	0.2	0.0	1.5	0.0	0.8
Other spec. trades	0.0	1.1	0.0	0.0	0.0	0.5
Transport	3.8	2.4	0.0	0.7	0.0	1.5
Apprentices	12.3	0.0	0.0	0.0	0.0	0.8
Public service	0.9	4.2	0.0	3.0	6.3	3.4
Professional	2.4	1.0	0.0	0.1	0.0	0.6
Personal service	0.0	2.2	1.1	0.0	0.0	0.9
Labourers	5.2	18.5	0.0	5.4	2.4	10.1
Self-employed	NA	NA	39.8	5.3	0.0	4.4
NS (inc. sick, gaol)	5.2	20.8	21.0	33.6	13.5	24.7
Total record	100.0	100.0	100.0	100.0	100.0	100.0

Without investigating the minutiae of the table, several important points are worth making:

(a) About half of all the reported males who arrived as convicts had been freed and not much more than one-third of all males reported were actually convicts. This implied a high degree of legal freedom and an ability to exercise choice.

(b) If it is a correct representation, as many as 5.3 per cent (lower third of the table, column 4) of the male convicts covered actually claimed or were represented to be self-employed. It is known that some individuals were able to bring resources with them and buy of form of freedom.

(c) There are no 'dealers' because many of these are hidden behind the labels of 'food, drink and tobacco', 'clothing and textiles' etc., rather than because no local commercial activity occurred. In part, people under these labels either carried out wholly distributing activities or combined trades and dealing roles.

(d) The appearance of 40.7 per cent (lower third of the table, column 6) as engaged in farming/pastoral activity is open to several questions. The 'Not stated' category for convicts contains a large number of persons. Nevertheless, the mass of these were almost certainly engaged in direct public employment in infrastructure rather than, by this stage, in public farming. It seems implausible that farming/pastoral activity captured more than 45 per cent of those represented. When we add all the omitted categories to the workforce, particularly the officials and women, the proportion engaged in farming and pastoral activity almost certainly shrinks below 40 per cent. In any event, this was certainly not an economy committed to immediate self-preservation.

(e) The 5.0 per cent (lower third of the table, column 6) of males engaged in 'Fisheries' is indicative of the prime effort made by the colonists to develop exports, mainly by engagement in sealing in and around Bass Strait. It might be noted that this activity increased to a peak by about 1810 so that this may be some underrepresentation of the significance of these offshore enterprises and hence of commitment to exports. Nevertheless, there is clear evidence of low achievement in exports (a well-known fact!)

(f) The table shows a wide spread of trades activities of various sorts. Here two points should be made. First, it may seem that, however much the occupational skills of arriving persons may have mirrored those of Britain, there is (lower third of the table, column 6) a very muted similarity of reputedly practised occupations in Botany Bay in 1805–6. To that extent, a substantial fractions of skill were deployed outside the skill areas of the settlers and in a technical sense a high degree of concealed unemployment existed. Nevertheless, secondly, there is a marked scatter of trades activities, particularly amongst the ex-convicts, and there is even some unexpected show of some highly skilled occupations amongst the convicts. The central section of the table (column 2) displays a very strong showing of ex-convicts amongst the various skilled trades. It was generally ex-convicts, above all, who provided the majority of males engaged in these trades, in food, drink and tobacco, in leatherworking, clothing and textiles, in building, in transport and in 'other specialised' trades (watchmaking, jewellery, pipe making, bookbinding, etc.).

These were the transportees who could now exercise choice. The fact that they were now a large proportion of the workforce and could choose is a vital pointer to the range of demands that the colonists sought to satisfy. Had it not been for this group, either many tastes would have gone unsatisfied or more persons allocated under direction to farming may have been diverted to some of these trades. A relatively complex deployment of labour implies an active and comparably complex goods market.

(g) Amongst those engaged in farming, we have (top section of table, first two columns) a small number of landholders who came free and some four times that number who were ex-convicts. The farming description generated with the muster shows (see also Fletcher, 1976: ch 3–5) a strongly unequal distribution of landholdings, with officials, ex-officials and a few free immigrants occupying large holdings acquired by grant, purchase or foreclosure for debt. Most of these, by 1806, had moved out of agriculture to concentrate on pastoral activity. Most agriculture was carried on in small-scale undertakings by ex-convicts (though eight convicts claimed to be landholding farmers). This concentrated structure became more marked up to 1810 as the rebellious officers who overthrew Bligh made numerous grants to ex-convicts (Fletcher, 1976: 51). It is a reasonable inference, with dominantly this ex-convict background, that most agricultural as distinct from pastoral production was carried on, on small holdings with little capital or equipment, despite start-up resources being given by government to ex-convict grantees.

A few additional comments derive from evidence outside the musters. Although land-granting by governors had restored much of the bureaucratic selection of farm areas, farms were being restructured by individual decisions in terms of size, specific location, organisation and product (Fletcher, 1976: ch 3–5). Farms were acquired by a combination of grants, purchase, lease and rental, with a broad division between small farmers as grain producers and larger owners as stockholders. This implied quite complex legal structures in the definition of a variety of property rights. So far as labour markets were concerned, efforts to regulate wage rates in the open market were well established, efforts that seem to have been concessions to assigned convicts who were officially acknowledged as now possessing, while still under sentence, a substantial equitable interest in the property rights in their own labour time. In the basic resources of land and labour, rights to private property were firmly ensconced as basic to the operation of the bridgehead economy.

There have been many comments on the 'wealth' achieved by a number of prominent individuals (Macarthur, Marsden, Campbell, Lord, etc.). One needs to be a bit cautious about these judgements. Certainly some prominent persons had access to and control of substantial resources of land and labour and operated considerable enterprises. Whether they could have realised these assets on the open market on the levels sometimes imputed to them is a highly debatable question. Inequality of income distribution by 1806 appears indubitable, though it is inadequately measured by the size of the workforce (even though the size structure of employment implied a considerable inequality). There were substantial differences in labour intensity in different undertakings. In particular, the variety of farming, mercantile and offshore interests implied a considerably greater inequality than labour market measures might reveal.

In more aggregative terms, my estimates of New South Wales, deflated, might be compared with corresponding aggregates in Britain in 1810 (Mitchell, 1988). This can give only a suggestion of the economic condition of New South Wales. It is vitiated by price and quality comparisons, by obscurities about appropriate exchange rates and by the reliance in the colony on many articles imported from India rather than Britain. For what the comparison is worth, it suggests at the level of gross domestic product that, with adjustments for age and sex, output per person in New South Wales may have been about two-thirds that in Britain. But when we convert the comparison to one of gross national expenditure (more appropriate to living standards), colonial real income or expenditure per head appears as actually higher than that attained in Britain in 1810. In the main, similar problems of international comparison apply to both product and expenditure measures. In this respect, the meaningful contrast between relative colonial product and relative expenditure per head is essentially independent of British data apart from sex and age adjustments. But it would require massive errors of comparison to bring colonial real income per head (adjusted) significantly below that of Britain in 1810.

Logically, the difference between colonial product and expenditure per head had to be due to a special capacity to import. This is one of the crucial issues up to 1809. But, in turn, it will be suggested that the explanation of a high import capacity is part and parcel of another core issue, the rapid development of property rights and private access to resources. With those rights and that access came another development — tension, leading to conflict and eventually rebellion.

Two constructs

To attempt to analyse how such a complex well-off society developed so rapidly it is convenient to abstract from the historical detail and to set up two constructs. One is an extreme representation of the colony under Phillip; the other under Bligh. These are drastic simplifications. The object is to attempt to enlighten history by the use of theory while at the same time constraining the theoretical constructs by history. What is at issue is the attempt to separate the different factors that may have contributed to the early New South Wales success.

New South Wales was never a gaol, nor was it a single-commodity farm; there was always a good deal of specialisation of labour. Nevertheless, its public farming preoccupation warrants the first heroic simplification. Let us suppose a modern high-security gaol. Security is tight, there is virtually no contact with the outside world and salaried warders control prisoners under strict direction. Strictly subsistence rations are provided from outside but prisoners are expected to reduce dependence on these supplies by production from a low-quality prison farm within the gaol. There is initially no distinction between prisoners, all of whom have lost the right to dispose of property rights in their own labour time. Provision is made, after some fixed term, that some prisoners may determine the use of that time, but within the gaol walls on the prison farm. No-one, not even the officials, may leave the gaol except after summons from outside.

Rations are issued from the gaol store, which receives external supplies and farm produce. The total supplies are distributed in equal portions to prisoners and warders alike. Incentive is limited to physical punishment. The only inequality is in status and in the earnings of officials that accrue outside the gaol. An external authority makes two special provisions for senior official use: an externally-available fund for the payment of subordinate officials; and the right, in dire emergency, to commit the external authority to some extra expenditure on the gaol. Lack of constraint in the use of emergency funds carries, for top officials, the penalty of the sack. Within these provisions, there is no choice, no specialisation, no interchange, no internal private wealth, no private property. This is an extreme version — for a less rigid construct, see R. A. Radford (1946).

Quite suddenly, this is transformed. Gaol discipline of the original style is gone. For some prisoners, there is a strictly private discipline but the great majority of inmates have acquired the right to determine the use of a substantial part of their labour time. Only the minority work on the prison farm, most of which has been subdivided into private holdings for the beneficial use of officials and some ex-convicts. Cells are used as private workshops, taverns, guest and bawdy houses and in a large variety of other activities. Some very large enterprises are run by some officials and ex-convicts and there is a very large number of small enterprises. Competition for labour is brisk and there is talk of combination among employees. The exercise yard is alive with hucksters. Outside the gaol, there is a turmoil of delivery vehicles carrying many non-ration goods into the gaol and some outside supply agencies have been permanently established within the gaol to coordinate deliveries. Yet, strangely, nothing much seems to be shipped out of the gaol.

This scenario provides a potential for film script that would make 'The Pink Panther', 'Whisky Galore' and 'The Great Train Robbery' seem like tame documentaries. Of course New South Wales was never a gaol. Nevertheless, the two constructs delineate the essential development of the colony during 1788 to 1810. Widespread private property, including rights in convict labour time, economic specialisation, intricate markets and the presence of local wealth and high income inequality were reached within less than two decades. Moreover, this did not depend substantially on the growth of exports. No-one could possibly suggest that New South Wales history was dull, still less that it was uneventful or overwhelmed by vice, rum, convictism or internal conflict.

Let us focus on the first construct. Is it likely that a wealthy and complex settlement could spring, hydra-like, from the internal resources of the settlement?

Privatising the gaol

Historians before Fletcher (1976), Hainsworth (1972) and Steven (1965) have regarded the subversion — deregulation? — of the original gaol as an accident of the interregnum after Phillip's departure and of ideological differences over public and private farming. Traditionally, the officials were seen as rapacious individuals, grinding the faces of the colonial poor. More recently, this has been revised by recognition of the rewards for entrepreneurship and managerial ability gained by a combination of officials, ex-convicts and a few free immigrants.

The claim that increased productivity may flow from private enterprise and deregulation is an important issue to test. Within the original gaol construct, officials faced with some cause for dissatisfaction might contemplate deregulation along several possible lines:

(a) They might free all prisoners, returning to them property rights in their own labour time, seeking thereby to establish an open labour and goods market and, through consequential incentives, to increase output.

(b) They might form a junta to which all property rights in land and convict labour is transferred. In this event, improvements in productivity would depend on the profit incentives of the property-owning junta.

(c) They might combine elements of the two preceding options. They might recognise the property rights in labour time implicit in the termination of sentences and return property rights in labour to ex-convicts, providing them with some share in landed property and in farming activity; but retain rights in convict labour and land themselves. To this might be added the continuation of a small segment of the gaol farm as public production to provide a test of superior privatised performance.

Of itself, the first option would have little appeal to a junta. Such a ruling group would become dependent on the choices of freed convicts and would be exposed to the risk of being reduced to the same level as them. The opportunity for benefit would be drastically limited until rules of sharing and control were established to the benefit of the junta.

To the extent that it is assumed that the junta depended on the internal resources of the prison farm, there would be merit in adopting some parts of the third option. Insofar as their action depended on the superior productivity potential of a deregulated prison farm, the presence of some ex-convicts engaged in small farming would have merit as a control against which their own more concentrated private efforts might be measured. So, too, would the continued presence of a part of the old prison farm. This would not be merely a matter of personal satisfaction; a control would be important to demonstrate to an external authority the public and not merely private benefits of their actions.

Action by a junta cannot be considered merely in terms of behaviour internal to the gaol. The response by the external authority is important. If external control is re-established (a new governor appointed) the matter of the rights of the original junta to retain the benefits secured by their deregulating action becomes prominent. A former junta now possessing substantial property rights and interests in related enterprises would present an interest group in opposition to externally established authority in the form of a new prison governor. Reduced, potentially, to a cabal, the original junta might justify its action and preserve its benefits under three possible conditions. Such a cabal might:

(a) continue successfully to subvert gubernatorial authority;

(b) claim the benefits of increased productivity and the reduced public costs of imported ration goods, hoping for retrospective legislation to continue so as to internalise the maximum share of the benefits of their action;

(c) appeal to some precedent or convention within the structure of the external authority to justify their behaviour.

So far as the first routine goes, efforts at subversion would depend on the scale and significance of the property and enterprise interests of the original junta and the risk of loss from new gubernatorial policies. In turn, action by any new governors would be influenced by the force of external directives, the extent to which the governor relied on the original junta for executing policy, and the degree of dependence of the original junta on access to administrative authority in order to sustain its property and enterprise interests.

The original act of privatisation could not be effective without a limited coalition which would determine authority and provide sharing rules. It might be expected that such a coalition would rest on the original bureaucratic hierarchy. The more rigid that hierarchy, the easier it would be to form a cohesive coalition and to sustain it in the event of the appointment of a new governor. Nevertheless, conflict of interest within the original junta would be expected. Moreover, the original junta could depend on co-opting persons from the ranks of prisoners when special technical or managerial skills were required or where it was necessary to devolve tasks not readily performed by privatised rulers. The more complete the coalition formed by the original junta, the less scope would there be for effective action by new governors to erode the benefits of the original junta or to restore the status quo *ante*. Governors' freedom of action could be enhanced by new arrivals, by a change in the status of property rights as prisoners' sentences ended or by any internal conflict within the ranks of the original junta.

The second routine warrants extended comment later. For the moment, it may be noted as the substantive basis upon which the original junta would depend to protect itself from retribution by external authority. In the meantime, retribution could be delayed, softened or averted if the junta could make effective appeal through the third routine. If, in the practice of the external authority, there was a confusion of public and private interest, there was scope for such an appeal. More strongly, if the convention existed whereby public officials secured private benefit from or through the exercise of public duties, such an appeal could be more confidently made. This does not imply that public responsibility could be disregarded (though perhaps it might in the most cynical conditions) but that private benefits secured through public behaviour should not disadvantage or inconvenience the external authority. Cicero proposed the principle almost 2000 years before the New South Wales settlement: *Quicquid est utile, idem est honestum; quicquid est honestum, idem est utile* (private interest and public propriety are indistinguishable).

Juntas and cabals in New South Wales

Lest it be thought that the notion of a junta (a Spanish word) is alien to Australian history, it may be worth recognising the local provenance. In arresting Governor Bligh, Major Johnston charged that 'These measures, and various other Acts of Violence were projected and supported by the Governor and a junto (*sic*) of unprincipled men' (*HRA*, series 1, no. vi: 209).

Here, indeed, was the pot calling the kettle black! The military group that deposed Bligh was unquestionably a junta, a ruling military clique, that assumed power rebelliously to protect its interests. Less certainly, but still on the basis of their revealed behaviour, even if not of their constitutional status, the military command that (legally) assumed direction after Phillip's departure in 1792 properly attracts the same term. The constitutionality of the original military government weakens the application. So, too, does Phillip's adumbration of some of the privatisation of the gaol pursued by the military command. Moreover, the military did not benefit themselves exclusively — for example, they made land grants to some ex-convicts. One other element, the informality of the land grants ('A. B. has my permission to settle') has been taken by historians as maladministration and carelessness. This might also seem to disqualify the use of the word. This was far from being the case; the military were protecting their flanks, avoiding accusations of a formal takeover.

This informality, as a mode of making land grants, provided strength rather than weakness to the subsequent relations between the military and new governors, provided the relative efficiency of private, compared with public, farming was demonstrable. After 1795, virtually all senior officials were implicated in the original act of privatisation; they were the dominant gainers and they stood to lose from the reversal of privatisation. By their revealed behaviour, the military acted as a ruling clique, concentrating the benefits of actions that encouraged a powerful coalition against future governors. Although the formal positions and their business interests changed in such a way as to make it difficult to capture easily the position at any one time, the roll call at about the turn of the century is impressive. Atkins the Judge Advocate, Palmer the Commissary, Smyth the Provost Marshal, Marsden the chaplain, Balmain the surgeon, Thompson his assistant, Alt the surveyor, Grimes the assistant surveyor, Baker a storekeeper, Amdell a magistrate, Bloodsworth, Fitzgerald and Divine, superintendents of convicts, faced Hunter and King as prime civilian beneficiaries of military land grants (the grants required confirmation). Amongst the military, there were Lt Col. Paterson, Major G. Johnston, Capts Macarthur, Townson, Piper and Mackellar, Surgeon Harris and Quartermaster Laycock. There were few among the ranks of senior civil and military officials who did not look to incoming governors to avoid loss of substantial private property after 1795. (cf Hainsworth, 1972; ch 1; Fletcher, 1976: ch 4).

These people received the lion's share of military largesse in the process of privatisation. It was they who received the substantial land grants and allocations of publicly supported assigned convicts. There were beneficiaries amongst both convicts and ex-convicts. A significant number of the latter received land grants (permissions to settle). But the aggregate of their allocations did not begin to compare with those of the small number of officials. At least as significant, ex-convict farmers had a tiny share in the allocation of assigned convicts, the mass of whom were absorbed by the leading officials (cf *1805–06 Muster*). In contrast with the latter, ex-convict farmers had to depend on their own unaided efforts to achieve results comparable with those of the large-scale operations of the privatised officials. After 1795 this characteristic may have exposed these ex-convicts to the risk of gubernatorial decision to deny their grants and perhaps to join the officials in this respect. More importantly, in practical terms, it introduced the risk or opportunity of having their farms purchased by officials during the second half of the 1790s. Interested as several officials were in this opportunity, they were committed to protect the ex-convict land grants against incoming governors.

Amongst those who profited most from purchase were Palmer, Grimes, Macarthur, Cox and Laycock. These men had a special advantage in controlling access to money, goods or labour, enabling them to accumulate many ex-convict grants.

Incoming governors were forced to rely for administrative support on those most advantaged by privatisation and most exposed to the risk of property rights in land and convict labour time. These officials had become subsidised capitalists and were forced, confronted by Whitehall's instruction to successive governors, to operate as cabals. The more governors sought to execute Whitehall instructions, the more these officials were brought, directly or indirectly, to usurp or subvert gubernatorial authority. Governors were posed with the task of developing such intra-gaol coalitions as they could to resist the demands of the cabals.

So far as the military–civil complex was concerned, there were strong pressures towards consensus of interest. All had a great deal to lose in terms of property rights and assets. The ancient tradition in Australian history was to stress an ill-defined monopoly by these officials. There is an element of both monopoly and monopsony in the position of the officials. But the crucial problem was the protection of property rights. On the military side in particular there was a strong underpinning of the coalition to protect property rights. The hierarchy of command amongst military officials went far to ensure this. From time to time, personal conflict and jealousies might fray but would not destroy this buttress. As between military and civil officials, there was more scope for internal conflict within the cabal given the differences in military and civil functions and the differential opportunities for gain that lay in these functions. Moreover, civil officials were brought regularly into most direct contact with governors and exposed to an immediate personal justification — provided the governor knew of their actions.

Governors were in a position to form coalitions for their own purposes insofar as they could dispense patronage or impose acceptable constraints. Any action significantly eroding the property rights of the military–civil complex confronted disaster. Formally, governors had power over land grants (including retrospective approvals) and assignment of convicts; they could dispense patronage through official appointments; determine licences to trade; and impose conditions of access to goods and labour markets and the administered supply of materials. They could also reward officials for their services (or their promise of support); and they had ultimate power over liberty and life. These powers, so dear to constitutional historians, were nominal rather than real. The authority of governors who lacked adequate administrative support was easily subverted insofar as their support depended on the officials whose behaviour they sought to constrain. Typically, governors' instructions could be contravened without the governor being aware that this was the case.

Draconian measures would have invited reprisal. Governors, less confrontationist, might use powers of appointment, reward or grant to attract the affiliation of some. Such action would attract the opposition of the (relative) losers. Governors might attempt trade-offs, such as offering increased land grants in exchange for reduced trading by officials. At worst, the military–official complex could choose its preferred option but typically ignore the constraint and accept the proffered benefit. Governors might impose limitations on the numbers of assigned convicts and their ration support only to find that the limits ended in unrecognised and unpaid debts to the government.

Short of draconian measures, governors had two other options. They might surrender to the military–civil complex; or they might simply join it. Successively, Hunter, King and Bligh followed a convoluted and frustrated path along the various option lines. Hunter largely surrendered and compounded the privatisation. King made an initial attempt to claw back the public estate and reduce the numbers of publicly supported assigned convicts (e.g. *HRA*, series I, no. 5: 10ff). The result was mounting nominal debt to the Commissariat. Symptomatic of the no-win situation, King, who pressed strongly for the control of the traffic in rum, ended his term as an alcoholic. Only Bligh attempted to take on frontally the military–civil complex. In doing so, he forced them explicitly into the role of a cabal.

Bligh presented three major risks. It was not the rum trade he particularly threatened, despite the stories of Macarthur's stills. Bligh sought to establish a very limited and exclusive coalition and above all limited the access of the military–civil complex to the benefits of the Commissariat. Secondly, he explicitly contemplated expropriation of some private property interests, not only those of Macarthur (*HRA*, series I, no. 5: 403ff). Thirdly, he contemplated the wholesale removal of the New South Wales Corps from the settlement, and with that removal the inevitable distress sale of their assets. Even if civil officials might be in some disagreement, the highly cohesive military cabal was arrayed as his enemy.

Using the rule of three, Bligh also committed three disastrous blunders. He attempted to govern confrontationally with a tiny group of civil and ex-convict advisers who were extremely weak reeds. He exposed his flanks by excessive personal exploitation of the resources of the Commissariat and his powers of granting land and assignment of convicts (*HRA*, series I, no. 5: 359ff). And, finally, he radically misread the implications of a growing body of ex-convicts and of the question of on whose side their bread was buttered.

It will be necessary to return to Bligh's use of the Commissariat as perhaps the key to accessing resources in New South Wales. Underlying this changing settlement was the growing importance of ex-convicts whose numbers, in Bligh's day, substantially exceeded those of convicts. This increase eroded the security of the labour supplies of the military–civil complex. Bligh interpreted the change as offering a potential source of support from ex-convict farmers. Apart from one successful ex-convict, Crossley, these ex-convict farmers were, at best, sources of popularity votes in circumstances in which votes were irrelevant. Far from being a source of gubernatorial strength, ex-convicts were not generally successful farmers. Indeed, the failure of Britain to deliver convicts with farming experience largely ensured the dependent condition of this group. More significantly, the delivery of non-farming skills played, as we shall see, into the hands of those anxious to privatise the settlement (and to its considerable advantage). Most ex-convicts, through their skills, were tied to the expenditure linkages of the military–civil complex and to others with special access to resources. They provided most efficiently and advantageously products that were not, or not as easily, tradeable as those demanded by well-to-do individuals.

The Rum Rebellion as a conflict over mere rum was not even comic opera; it was the worst soap. Not rum but far more fundamental issues were at stake — private property, profit, individual decision-making. Bligh had no chance of success. Johnston's junta proceeded to engage in the final destruction of public farming and in extensive land grants to ex-convicts, together with some supplementation for themselves.

Bligh's failure was the foundation of Macquarie's success. The removal of the New South Wales Corps meant the destruction of the original privatising coalition. It did not mean, however, the destruction of private property and private decision-making. So far as Macquarie was concerned, the removal of the Corps largely created a power vacuum. He could exploit in a way not open to Bligh the fundamental social change in the colony, the rise to prominence of the ex-convicts or emancipists. Whatever Bligh, Macquarie or J. T. Bigge alleged or believed, and whatever the British government contemplated in its post-1815 delivery of masses of convicts, the days of a penal settlement were numbered the day that Johnston arrested Bligh and a junta reigned in Botany Bay.

18

FREE LUNCHES, ANTIPODEAN STYLE

Convention in privatising official roles

The process of privatisation in Botany Bay during and after 1793 depended on, to say the least, an elastic interpretation of instructions received from Whitehall. No doubt the military rules were accorded some protection from retribution by laziness, indifference and ignorance in the Colonial Office. But unless the superior productivity of officer-farming could be demonstrated, the self-interested mode of approach to public service in Botany Bay might still have been exposed to serious risks had the officials been unable to make an effective appeal, explicitly or implicitly, to prevailing mores. This matter was important in relation to the grant by officers to themselves of private property rights in both land and convicts, and in respect of the trading ventures in which they engaged.

So long as prevailing codes in Britain allowed the use of public office for private benefit, an appeal did not need to be explicit. Rather, such codes tended to make ambivalent the evaluations and directives of Whitehall and of subsequent governors' execution of instructions. Colonial Office directives after 1795 often seem muddled and inconsistent, supporting and criticising public farming, complaining of private enterprise yet providing substantial support to it, blaming governors for failure to control yet rewarding those whose activities the governors failed to check. No doubt distance and ignorance contributed to confusion; but many comments by Whitehall are redolent of an admiration for those who were doing well by doing good. This reflected the blurring of private benefit and public propriety in Britain and throughout the Empire.

Privatisation of the British domestic and imperial government was rife. The record of the array of patronage and of sinecures as supplements to official incomes in the eighteenth century is well known. This is symptomatic of but oblique to the issue at hand. Somewhat more directly relevant was the buying and selling of army and navy commissions; the private acquisition of war trophies; the filling of public contracts by officials; and the purchase, sale or bequest of civil positions. Even these practices are essentially only indicative of a more deeply ingrained behaviour pattern. Coming closer to the mark, the practice of fee-taking or of obtaining rewards by deducting sums from revenues raised took the practice of privatisation of government a step further. But even this could be seen as a recognised substitute for official salaries, not necessarily allowing great freedom of individual action.

Within Britain itself, the circumstances that weighted the process of government most strongly towards a privatised business lay most obviously in the many situations in which individuals could acquire unregulated benefits or could gain in a way that was not closely associated with the value of the public service rendered. Many revenue collectors not only received fees but held funds collected for long periods during which additional personal benefits were obtained from the private investment of public moneys. Similarly, spending authorities could and did divert balances to beneficial use, often over long periods. Others responsible for payments to subordinates could not only use moneys due for their own interests but develop businesses to substitute goods for cash in settlement. Those having official positions with respect to estates, whether of deceased persons or of wards, were similarly advantaged.

In many cases, private interest behaviour was recognised and accepted with no overtones of wrongdoing. Indeed, it is important to realise that privatised action frequently provided a free lunch for all concerned. If the official gained, government did not — or certainly very often did not — lose. In deploying funds, officials 'perfected' the capital market to the benefit of the private sector. In the longer run, this evaluation might, of course, be qualified to the extent to which privatised officials stood as barriers to reform and to other more efficient modes of conducting the affairs of State. The opportunities for personal benefit and the condoning of privatised practices were particularly obvious in the army and navy, a matter most directly relevant to the New South Wales Corps and Botany Bay.

At least in large parts of the Empire, much more substantial opportunities for the beneficial use of public office existed. There, access to public office was frequently taken to be the springboard to a private fortune. Though this might apply most handsomely in areas such as India, there were many similar if not fully comparable opportunities elsewhere. In this case, the question of whether there was a free lunch for all was less important, even though free lunches could occur. Thus privatised officials might form partnerships with colonials to mutual benefit and, indeed, to the benefit of the colonial communities. Colonial rule opened, however, the additional possibility of imposing any costs of privatisation on the subject societies. The larger and richer such societies were, the greater the potential for gain by privatised officials. Recognition of the different potential for making a private fortune was indicated in Britain by the differential fees charged to governors on appointment. Indeed, the privatisation of imperial activity can be carried further with the proposition that a substantial part of the second empire was acquired for Britain as an exercise in private initiative.

Nominally at least, the Botany Bay settlement was a planned colony with little to attract officials in search of fortunes through imperial service. There was no conquest, no obviously exploitable subject society, only isolation, convicts and a wilderness. There was an official hierarchy, particularly among the military (some of whom had access to paymasters' funds). There was the central store, the Commissariat. There were convicts available predominantly for public purposes, though with limited sentences and due to recover the property rights in their own labour time on completion of those sentences. And there were crown lands.

The immediate issue for exploitation by officials in this unpromising environment was conflict over the efficiency of public versus private farming. This provided the immediate focus for acts of privatisation. Through this, not merely farming but the whole structure and function of the society and economy came to rest, despite the continued inflow of convicts, not on public decision making but on private property, profit making and individual choice. That the settlement remained a mixed economy does not reduce the force of this evaluation. Given the immediate issue of farming and given also the role ascribed to the use of natural resources and staples in the theory of growth of areas of recent settlement, it is appropriate to address the contribution of privatisation first to farming efficiency in isolation. In doing so, two questions are at issue. First, did privatisation increase efficiency of farming? Second, is it possible to evaluate the contribution of privatised farming to the wealth and complexity of the Botany Bay settlement within a mere two decades after 1788?

The potential for increased farm output per unit of labour

Formally, several possibilities arise that could yield a gross increase in or gross loss of output per head. The net outcome depends on the balance of changes.

The potential for gross increase could be expected to lie in:

(a) a decline in threats from and costly damage by Aborigines;

(b) increased levels of employment or effort;

(c) reduction of concealed unemployment — or the more optimal allocation of skills to tasks;

(d) application of additional capital and embodied technology;

(e) economies of scale;

(f) opportunities for entrepreneurship, including learning by doing; and

(g) inducements to adapt output to conform better to consumer tastes.

There were, however, countervailing possibilities that were partly dependent on the precise nature of the privatisation process. Depending on whether small farming as well as large private farming was developed, and subject to the continuation of some public farming, possibilities for gross losses might arise as follows:

(a) privatised officials might deliberately lower productivity in public farming or neglect public responsibilities in giving preference to their own interests;

(b) resources might be so concentrated as to act to the detriment of small farms;

(c) intra-colonial trade with differences in bargaining power between small farms and those of privatised officials might limit the opportunity of small farmers to plough back capital into their farms; and

(d) the potential for productivity increase might be vitiated if the external authority continued to supply large quantities of those ration goods in which the colony had a comparative advantage (e.g. meat in relation to the pastoral industry).

An attempt at an historical assessment of farming

One can find some manifestation of all these issues in Botany Bay during 1793 to 1810 (cf Fletcher, 1976: ch 3–5). In the first few years, the officer-farmers cleared their lands very rapidly; they offered throughout the 1790s a variety of inducements to convicts to work more efficiently and provided direct managerial oversight of the workers more effectively than was the case in public farming; they deployed capital in their farms and used equipment such as ploughs more readily than did government; they chose farm locations with greater consideration; they allocated to themselves a very large proportion of the convict labour supply, allowing opportunities for economies of scale; they engaged in intra-colonial trade in farm products and adjusted output more in accord with individual preferences; and they purchased many ex-convict grants, adding to the scale of their operation (sometimes acquiring grants in exchange for debts by ex-convicts).

Nevertheless, the officers' farming activities were never dominant. At the peak of their farming activity the officers accounted for less than a third of the grain production (typically much less) and throughout the whole period to 1810 their livestock populations were lower than those of government (cf Fletcher, 1976: p64ff). On the other side of the balance sheet, they degraded the efficiency of public farming by deliberate inattention and a preference for their own concerns, thereby reducing the productivity of public farming below what it would otherwise have been. Almost inevitably, subsequent governors who depended on the officers were presented with the appearance of superior private performance, even more so than would have actually been the case. At the same time, and particularly during 1793–1800, the officer-farmers used their controlling authority to redistribute benefits from ex-convict farmers to themselves, partly through their discriminatory purchasing activities. This did not merely mean redistribution; it meant also that reduced returns to small ex-convict farmers left less to be ploughed back into farm improvements.

With public farming reduced to very small proportions (other than in livestock), the focus on productivity improvements shifts to small farms run by ex-convicts which produced grains and other cultivated crops. Until 1800, these farmers do not present themselves as sources of high productivity (cf Fletcher, 1976). The ex-convict farmers were the immediate beneficiaries of the destruction and dispossession of Aborigines, with the consequential ability to move and settle freely around the Cumberland Plain after 1800. Apart from the influences exerted through farm trade by the officers, very few of the small farmers were equipped by temperament or experience for agriculture, still less for agriculture in novel Australian conditions; they received few assigned convict servants; they could afford little in the way of technical equipment; their farm areas were small; and basically they relied on their individual efforts (sometimes in small partnerships). A substantial proportion were placed in the Hawkesbury area, exposed to successions of droughts and floods. Subsequently, after 1800, the inroads of pests and diseases reduced their farm productivity.

There were three important offsets to these difficulties after 1800. First, King assigned more ex-convict servants to them and provided them with ration support and subsidies of livestock and equipment (see, e.g. *HRA*, series I, no. 5: 171). Secondly, King reduced the supply of publicly rationed convicts to the large farmers, thereby drastically raising their labour costs (*HRA*, series I, no. 5: 10). This change, along with disease, droughts, floods and pests reducing grain productivity, meant that labour-intensive agriculture on large farms became considerably less attractive. With large areas, the officer-farmers were relatively better placed to reallocate their activities to pastoral operations (cf Fletcher, 1976: ch 4). In doing so, the peculiar activities of government farming weighted the balance of decision-making towards this reallocation. Government continued to be prominent in livestock farming throughout 1792–1810. But it chose to preserve its herds rather than slaughter them. The use of livestock as a farming subsidy appears to have been concentrated on small farmers, and it was basically through this subsidy process and not through public slaughtering that the government made its prime contribution to colonial meat consumption. There was, then, particularly after the reduction of public rations to the convict servants of large farmers, a demand incentive for the large farmers to shift to livestock. It appears that domestic meat consumption, not the potential for export, explains the greater part of that reallocation in the first instance.

This reallocation confuses further any attempt to evaluate the relative efficiency of public and private farming. Insofar as the government constrained public slaughtering, it may have contributed to output but not to consumption. It looked to a long time horizon, depending on the willingness of Britain to continue to send large supplies of meat as part of its transfers to the settlement. The private farmers consumed substantial fractions of their herds and hence appear less prominent as holders of surviving livestock populations. Their time horizons were shorter. Given the uncertainties of food supplies, this combination of policies may have been unavoidable.

The evaluation of the consequences of privatisation — or even the mix of private and public action as compared with wholly public farming — is at this level relatively obscure. Within the settlement, governors and not merely privatised officials accepted the superior performance of the officer-farmers. But even this may have been exaggerated to the extent that public farming was to some extent made to seem worse. There remains one factor that weights the issue strongly on the side of privatisation. This is the accession of effective workforce and managerial skills that followed privatisation. Until the end of 1792, the military were essentially an enclave, committed to colonial security and not engaged to a substantial degree in ration goods production. They and civil officials, in conflict over the direction of policy, probably hindered rather than helped local production. Given that significant numbers of convicts had been assigned to them by 1792 (as personal servants), the total enclave made up a very large fraction of the entire colonial workforce. Precise calculation is impossible. But it seems that the effective workforce of the settlement may have been enlarged by as much as 20 per cent or more to the extent that the entire body of officials and their assigned servants were drawn directly or indirectly into ration goods production. This was a handsome addition, even if resources were not used very much more efficiently. But the increment was not merely numerical. The officers brought directive ability and organisation into colonial activity in response to the incentive to acquire private property. One would be inclined to believe that personal incentive combined with managerial ability did lead to useful net productivity gains.

Nevertheless, it is not conceivable that through farming alone one could explain anything other than a tiny fraction of the standard of living and complexity of the settlement by 1806. Neither the human capital nor the natural resource endowments were such as to provide the foundation of that achievement. Few of the convicts had farming skills; all had to learn the local environment by doing; the Cumberland Plain on which the settlement depended lacked rich resources. The 1806 lunch has to be explained from other sources. It was not earned in Botany Bay by local staple production.

Farming and property rights

One cannot, however, dismiss local farming simply with this judgement. It had a fundamental influence in quite a different way. Fitzpatrick's (1933) thesis of a British planned peasantry in New South Wales has long since been discarded. Some form of ex-convict farming would inevitably have developed, subject only to the survival of the settlement. To that extent, the question of the privatisation of farming focuses on large landownership. What the privatisation of 1793–95 did was to establish the institution of private property held by powerful individuals; to introduce to prominence the profit motive pursued by those persons; and to assert the vitality of individual choice in the settlement as a whole, not merely in farming or land ownership alone. Along with this was the introduction of a highly skewed distribution of a privately engaged (whether employed or assigned) workforce — in other words, the acquisition of property rights in labour time by powerful employers. After 1795, the officer-farmers pressed their claims strongly against incumbent governors. From the springboard of farming, the extension of these principles of social organisation to the economy as a whole created a powerful interest group in actual or potential collision with official policy or action that might threaten to undermine the position of that interest group.

The acquisition of relatively concentrated private property in land through grant and purchase led quickly to a variety of modes of land tenure (cf Fletcher, 1976: ch 3–5) so that the institutional forms in which landed property was held soon became complicated and, indeed, sophisticated. The grants were adapted through the operation of the private market into an array of landholdings, including grants, leaseholds, purchased property, tenancies and partnership holdings. Many of the legal forms to which the settlers were accustomed in Britain were established by 1800 (and certainly by 1806). Coupled with these adaptations went comparable complexity in actual land use. Farms were directly operated; handled through managers and supervisors; or established in part or whole as properties operated by tenants-at-will. There were also intermediate arrangements and combinations, including the procedure of allotting small parcels to convicts within larger estates as part of the reward and inducement system. All this was quickly recreating in a wilderness the British system familiar to the settlers. Such property rights may seem to be highly illiquid assets not particularly attractive to transient officials. This was a problem while the settlement failed to develop rapidly or when some officials were transferred after short periods. The rapid development of a local market in land greatly increased the liquidity of these assets. In addition, there was the British government as a possible, eventual (but by no means certain) backstop as a purchaser of improvements from officials facing departure. Moreover, for some at least, acquisition of landed property in New South Wales could be seen as a valuable asset for absentee ownership. This was prominently the case in the exchange of land grants made by Governors King and Bligh to each other as they joined in the privatising process.

Convictism yielded very special forms of property rights. Nominally, convicts had lost the right to dispose of the property rights in their own labour time for the duration of their sentences. As such, they were pieces of human capital to be directed, assigned, hired or bought and sold. The history books seem to pay inadequate attention to these issues of property rights in convict labour. At first sight, it may seem curious that government did not sell these property rights to growing private interests, following American colonial practice with both convicts and indentured servants. The early privatisation of the settlement, combined with subsequent low rates of convict arrivals, largely prevented large-scale government sale. The problem for governors between 1795 and 1809 was to limit existing private title to convict labour, not to enlarge it through sale (this is a continuing theme throughout *HRA*, series I, nos 2–5). So far as privatised officials were concerned, the issue was to retain the public ration support needed to maintain their capital assets intact and to limit the extent to which convicts regained equitable interests in their own labour time.

Labour shortage was on the side of the convicts. As sentences ran out, the officer-farmers faced the possibility that the marginal product in ex-convict activity would exceed that of convicts on farms. Insofar as this was the case, officer-farmers faced problems of re-contracting to retain their workforce. There was an incentive as the termination of sentences approached for increased rewards to be offered to the convict labourers. This might be in the form of supplying over and above standard rations; or it might include allowing 'free' time to convicts who were still under sentence. During 'free' time, convicts could work for their own private reward. To that extent, they regained part of the property rights in their own labour time. Equally, officer-farmers had an incentive to limit the marginal returns to ex-convicts in order to limit the concessions to convicts. It is consistent with this incentive that they exerted their bargaining power and authority to interpose their purchases of grain from small farmers between the ex-convict farms and the eventual outlet in the Commissariat.

Convicts appear to have gained significantly through such redistributive processes. By 1800, standard hours for convicts were 8 hours a day and, in effect, overtime rates were allowed beyond this (e.g. *HRA*, series I, no. 2: 214, 218, 359; series I, no. 3, 37 etc). It is difficult to believe that such an advantageous result could have emerged in circumstances of purely farm privatisation. Here, too, it seems necessary to look to other aspects of the economy for a more satisfactory explanation.

Although the government did not follow the American practice in the disposal of convict labour time, it was deeply affected by the privatisation process in its handling of convicts up to 1809. Any simple dichotomy of government employment and the assignment of convicts makes limited sense of the reality of Botany Bay. It is not possible to recover the precise numbers involved. But it is clear, first of all, that convicts were used as currency to pay a significant number of persons — numbers of convicts were transferred not simply as assigned servants but as rewards for services rendered. Recipients could benefit from such rewards by using convicts as servants, by employing them in farming or by hiring them out. Actual practice is unclear; but it appears that many official functions were such that a significant number of such convicts must have been hired out. Moreover, in some cases at least, convicts could hire themselves out, paying to their assigned master a rent on their property rights in exchange for the right to work either on their own account or for another employer. The record seems to be silent on whether hiring-out on a seasonal or longer-term basis developed between officer-farmers, though the incentive almost certainly existed to do so.

Government went further than this. Newly arriving convicts might repurchase on arrival the full rights in their own labour property — that is, purchase the freedom to work as they chose. Those most benefited were convicts arriving with significant resources, not a wholly rare event. In addition, skilled convicts were also presented with the opportunity, particularly during 1800–09, to repurchase the property rights in their labour time, at least to the extent of buying tickets-of-leave. Relatively standard prices were set for hirings between private employers and between convicts and government. These are indicative of considerable sophistication in the marketing of labour property rights.

Once again, the limits of Botany Bay farming seem too tight to allow such developments. Clues to the direction in which to look for an explanation seem to be offered in the facts that convicts were able to offer their legal employers sufficient reward, and that much of the benefit seems to have accrued to the more skilled. There was little in the way of sufficiently rewarding outlets in farming for such people.

Offshore enterprises

The shift away from convictism in recent writings has included giving some prominence to offshore enterprises, particularly whaling and sealing, as contributors to activity, foreign exchange resources and standards of consumption (Hainsworth, 1972: chs 9–10). It has also brought to the fore the success of some ex-convicts (e.g. Lord, Underwood, Kable) in establishing large enterprises. Certainly, natural resources of the seas appear to offer opportunities for staple industries capable of yielding export earnings. The southern fisheries led to considerable activity from Botany Bay, particularly during the first decade of the nineteenth century. But how far did the colonists share in the total proceeds; and did their intervention produce much change in the local economy?

In the first few years of the century, the total value of the catch from the southern fisheries as a whole reputedly averaged several hundred thousand pounds sterling per year (Banks concluded the level to be about £300 000 sterling during 1802–04). Had the colonists been able to secure natural resources at this rate they would have been wealthy indeed! Unfortunately, the exploitation of these riches required large capital inputs of ocean-going vessels that were far beyond the means of the colonists and were in any event precluded so far as the settlement was concerned by the East India Company.

The statistical evidence of whaling and sealing operations is both limited and suspect. The record of imports into Port Jackson (as given in ship arrival data dispersed throughout *HRA*, series I, vols 2–5 and in Cumpston, 1964) probably overstates the colonial share in the total fisheries. Even so, it seems unlikely that the colonists achieved more than 1 or 2 per cent of the total. The higher limit would accommodate some interest by locals in foreign ships. An implied upper limit of an annual average of £6000 sterling may have been a useful supplement to colonial exchange resources. But the implications of local whaling and sealing are clouded and the benefits more tenuous than even this suggests.

Staple theory is preoccupied with linkages. So, in this context, historians have pointed to the shipbuilding encouraged in the settlement (despite the East India Company); to the provisioning of visiting ships; to employment; and to the high incomes of some free immigrants (Steven, 1965, on Campbell) and ex-convicts (Hainsworth, 1972, on Lord, Kable and Underwood). These maritime activities and their derived demands clearly enhanced the role of the settlement as a port. It appears that, so far as Port Jackson was concerned, the year 1806 precedes the peak in the importance of sealing by a few years. Hence, while the 1806 Muster gives an incomplete view of the effects of the staple, it records an industry not far short of its peak. The industry operated from Port Jackson and declined relatively quickly. This rapid rise and decline is important, not merely because it implies a brief stimulus to the settlement. The more important implication is in its highly speculative nature and in the ignorance of the potential of the offshore industries.

It is important to appreciate that the colonists not only failed to capture more than a tiny share of the output of the southern fisheries but also failed to penetrate the high quality, high productivity end of the industry. Limited in capital relative to the inputs required, the settlers were largely excluded from whaling (they did engage in some bay whaling) and hence from the valuable whale oil products. Colonial maritime activity was focused on sealing. This was a highly labour-intensive activity that depended on considerable numbers of people spread in isolated locations along the south-east coast and Bass Strait. Over lengthy periods of up to two years at a time, the workforce harvested the seals and collected skins and oil. The 1806 Muster suggests that fewer than 200 persons may have been engaged. It seems likely that the Muster omitted others who were actually away at the time. Some of the workforce was probably occupied in shipbuilding and provisioning not exclusive to sealing. Even so, this represented a significant fraction of the total workforce of the settlement.

This indication of numbers understates the total labour inputs into offshore industries and, indeed, estimates of the total workforce available to the colony need to be enlarged. At many sealing locations, other than those isolated by sea, the sealers drew into their activities a considerable number of Aborigines. The purely sexual aspect of attaching Aboriginal women to sealing groups and the killing of others may overshadow other issues. Aboriginal women were efficient sources of labour in catching and processing seals. White competition and the taking of black females led to a trade between Aborigines and sealers, the latter supplying seal products in exchange for kangaroo meat and skins. Here, perhaps, the theory of comparative advantage operated at an early stage, drawing into a market process both Aborigines and sealers.

Exaggerated expectations, the ignorance of the rate at which the seal fisheries were being depleted and the persistent 'lottery' hope that some few individuals might achieve exceptional catches continued to attract both capital and labour into the industry. Most employees were drawn in on the basis of profit-sharing ('lays' or shares in the catch) but the vast majority seem to have received very low rates of reward overall. Rather than supplying a valuable staple industry, sealing was a means whereby excessive resources of both capital and labour were employed and remained in what was, in the aggregate, a very low productivity undertaking. It wasted substantial amounts of the colony's resources, even though it generated some foreign exchange earnings.

External credits and British subsidies: the capacity to import

Access to imports was determined not by offshore staples but by five other means. First, there was the British payment of official salaries through parliamentary appropriations. Secondly, official services not recognised by appropriations were rewarded in a variety of ways that attracted additional British support either in kind or through the issue of bills payable by the British government. Thirdly, Commissariat purchases of colonially produced goods and services were made through the issue of such bills or by barter with direct British goods subsidies. Fourthly, governors and subsequently the Commissariat issued bills payable by the British government in favour of foreign shippers or import merchants. Finally, there was the peculiar question of the control of the 'military chest' of the New South Wales Corps.

These five sources made up an array of quasi-exports and subsidies in cash or kind to support the total expenditures and standards of the colony. It was these that dominated the colonial capacity to import up to 1809 (and, indeed, until 1820). To these four must be added two other supplements: staple export earnings and private capital imports. Though the size of these two supplements is not adequately known, it is inconceivable that they could be very large relative to the other sources.

The estimates of appropriations by the British government made for the Bigge Inquiry do not coincide with actual transfers to the settlement, and the nominal payments include transfers to dependants and creditors (later, pensions of retired officials are included). Nevertheless, the actual payments by the Colonial Agent responsible for the transfers give a reasonable indication of the amounts available to the colony. Directly or indirectly, the mass of these payments made their way to the settlement. We cannot assume that there was an annual correspondence between transfers and imports but in the medium term there was. Since, at the moment, only appropriations for the military are known, it is better to use these for civil officials as well.

Even the more recent approaches to the entrepreneurship of some members of the colony seem to imply that these officials were not members of the workforce. Hence, these appropriations are taken to be subsidies from Britain. Official function was crucial to the operations of the settlement. Since payments were made for services rendered, it was as if these sums were payments for the export of services to Britain. Civil and military services for the gaol may therefore be properly treated as quasi-exports (cf Abbott and Nairn eds, 1969), though they were rendered locally, and the earnings of officials became a vital source of foreign exchange. In technical balance of payments terms, they become current account credits and can equally be treated as capital inflow.

These earnings credits could not be very effectively deployed until ship arrivals made transfer possible, so they had little meaning until 1790 at the earliest. The privatisation of the settlement, by encouraging ship arrivals, speeded the transfer process. Despite the inadequacy of the statistics, it seems clear that these credits were a major contribution to the colonial capacity to import after 1790 and particularly after 1792 (see table 8, opposite).

There were two other types of credits. One was by way of rewards to officials arranged in the colony. The other was the local purchase of goods and services from settlers, requited through the Commissariat. Payments for these were made by a combination of cash and goods. As a result, they are submerged and confused in the Commissariat accounts, which do not disclose the gross barter transactions. They are therefore mixed with bills, some paid locally, some to foreign shippers; and in both cases barter entered the transactions to which these bills related. There may, then, appear to be a confusion of British subsidies in kind with these other credits.

Though we cannot satisfactorily disentangle the various components, the matter is not as hopeless as it may at first sight appear. The accounts of the Commissariat are net transactions. The netting out in the Commissariat accounts therefore, in principle, also netted out all British subsidies in kind where these were used in barter transactions. As an approximation, it is possible therefore to add these direct British subsidies to the recorded operations of the Commissariat and then the two to the credits for official salaries paid by appropriations. Some of the recorded deliveries in kind requited official and other services and goods as other credits. In effect, not all the direct deliveries from Britain were subsidies. But in principle there is no double-counting between the various components.

Table 8 accordingly presents the available information on civil and military appropriations, Commissariat operations and victualling and stores deliveries from Britain. Together these give the closest aggregate that is currently possible of the consequent import capacity of the colony. It bears repetition that imports will not have matched this total on an annual basis. Moreover, there were other British deliveries, particularly ships. This is one reason for believing that the aggregate may be an under- rather than an over-statement of import capacity. There were other sources of exchange earnings — staple exports and private capital inflow. These seem likely to be relatively minor. Whatever the uncertainties, the central point is that the aggregate shown in the table represented a handsome supplement to domestic resources, particularly to a colony not notable for its natural resource endowment.

Table 8: Approximate Import Capacity (£'000)

	British victual supplies	British stores deliveries	Commissariat operations	Salary appropriations	Total
1790	1.8	18.4	1.3	15.1	36.6
1791	25.6	25.6	1.1	17.3	69.6
1792	17.3	31.1	5.1	19.6	73.1
1793	19.8	n.a.	15.8	17.4	?
1794	25.5	12.3	3.6	15.0(a)	56.4(a)
1795	36.7	4.4	32.1	15.5(a)	88.7
1796	31.1	7.9	41.7	18.7(a)	99.4(a)
1797	7.1	4.0	19.5	22.6	53.2
1798	12.0	5.2	27.0	28.9	73.1
1799	6.6	0.1	41.6	22.5(a)	70.8(a)
1800	13.8	11.8	50.9	26.4	102.9
1801	12.1	7.2	10.8	27.7(a)	57.8(a)
1802	93.3	11.2	16.5	25.5(a)	146.5(a)
1803	16.6	16.2	17.0	26.7	76.5
1804	n.a.	0.3	10.2	26.6	?
1805	9.5	10.3	17.4	26.2	63.4
1806	38.8	6.9	9.1	34.0	88.8
1807	21.8	17.1	10.5	44.6	94.0
1808	35.9	1.8	13.8	38.4	89.9
1809	11.9	0.1	25.2	42.7	79.9

(a) Excludes marines.

The total contribution from Britain altered greatly over the period relative to the gross product of the settlement. So, too, did the salary appropriations, particularly for civil officials. So far as the two columns of British supplies in kind go, it appears that the victualling supplies were largely determined by Britain and that a high proportion of the stores were delivered in response to official requests from the colony. This has some significance for decision-making and in the interpretation of behaviour by successive governing groups. It is unfortunate that the stores figure for 1793 are not available.

Nevertheless, the original junta moved, in that year, to make greatly increased use of the governor's right to issue bills. Whether it continued to receive large quantities of stores is not known. Subsequently, it is interesting to compare, through the Commissariat Accounts, experiences under Hunter, King and Bligh successively. Hunter used his authority to issue bills in a massive way, greatly increasing the flexibility of decision-making in the settlement, to the advantage of the military–civil complex. On the other hand, many fewer stores arrived. By contrast, King (who greatly reduced the issue of bills) made much greater use of direct ordering of store subsidies. In this light, Hunter does not seem so spendthrift nor King so economical as attention to the Commissariat's operations would suggest.

Bligh followed King's policy in this respect, keeping a check on the issue of bills. When the junta assumed power, the reversal of the relationship between stores orders and bill issues is striking. During Bligh's governorship, moreover, the salary appropriations for officials rose sharply. The dominant reason for this was an increase in civil, not military, salaries. Here, too, lay the seeds of a decline in the economic significance of the military.

The combination of British direct deliveries, the net Commissariat operations and salary appropriations presented a very substantial opportunity to the settlement, far beyond the earnings potential of its natural resources. Inevitably, support was very high relative to domestic product early in the colony's history. But even at its lowest level, the ratio of the aggregate capacity to import to gross domestic product was very large. Through direct subsidies and the provision for quasi-exports, the British government provided the colony with a very substantial lunch.

This import capability was a necessary condition for rapid development of real income per head, a respectable level of productivity and a complex economy. But it was not a sufficient one. The potential for growth could have been dissipated either through inefficiency or through the choice of imports. There are several reasons, discussed below, for believing that this dissipation would have been serious had the benefits been dispersed widely or according to bureaucratic rule. But it is necessary to look at the other conditions that turned the British lunch to substantial advantage.

The import process

Whether from British subsidies, credits, staple exports or private capital inflow, there was a real transfer process through imports of goods and services into the settlement. This transfer enhanced the capital and current expenditures of the colony. Imports could enter directly and in the form of capital or current or intermediate goods, each with different implications for development. Or imports could arrive after the access to international exchange led to local expenditures on some colonial activities, with import purchases occurring at a second- or third-round stage in expenditure processes. The directness or indirectness of the transfer process also affected the nature of local development.

No adequate statistics of imports exist. There is a reasonable, though incomplete, indication of the initial access to international resources as between government and individuals, excluding public credits and private capital inflow. This is summarised in table 9 (below).

Table 9: International resources (£'000)

	1790–1800	1801–09
Victualling	197	240
Direct stores	121	61
Bills	253	199
Total government	571	430
Civil appropriations	58	91
Military appropriations	143	189
Total individual	201	280
Total	772	710

Despite the fact that the total for the second period was less than the first in table 9, it is a safe assumption that, adding staple exports and private capital, the level increases between the two periods. Nevertheless, government was clearly the major partner in both periods, and particularly so during 1790–1800. Some of the Bills passed directly into private hands in local transactions. Even so, government appears as the likely major importer during both periods. Moreover, more is known of government imports than of imports on private account.

The mass of government imports were of final consumer goods (cf reports of ship arrivals in *HRA*, series I, vols 2–6). Most of the Commissariat Bills were issued to shippers during 1790–1800 and were used for final consumer goods, above all beverages, meat and grains. The victualling deliveries were similarly essentially of foodstuffs. The stores delivered directly from Britain were much more complex but included consumer goods such as clothing, blankets and the like. It is also clear that a substantial amount of private imports were final consumer goods. Was the capacity to import, then, predominantly frittered away in improved current consumption?

Economic development is a complex process. Notions that development is accelerated by large injections of capital goods are not very useful, particularly when applied to low levels of development. Capital goods were certainly included in the import array. Ships were one major item, supplied as subsidies by Britain or purchased through the Commissariat. The capital in ships could also be acquired by hiring, either by partnerships in ventures with foreign shippers or by chartering as was done by individuals. The next most expensive item of capital assets imported was livestock. Livestock were costly not merely because of purchase and transport costs but also and perhaps chiefly because of losses in transit. As to other items of capital goods, the nature of all economies at about 1800 was such that capital goods inputs into production were relatively limited. This was particularly so in Botany Bay. Very limited quantities of tools and equipment were relevant, with given technology, in farming, building and construction or local manufactures.

The Botany Bay settlement needs to be perceived as a 'Crusoe economy', one in which development and increased standards depended on the availability of a surplus in consumer goods. Such a surplus, at the least, allowed the diversion of resources away from the production of the immediate necessities of life. In doing so, it made possible local capital formation and/or diversification of current output. There is another aspect to such a surplus. In principle, it would allow settlers a longer time to wait before they faced the task of feeding themselves or providing other desired goods. 'Waiting' is a fundamental capital concept in economics. It is also one on which historians have placed too much stress in their interpretation of the history of Botany Bay. This stress reflects Phillip's agony in efforts to establish farming. It has little to do with the realities of the settlement, after privatisation was carried through during 1792–95, in the regimes of subsequent governors. Then the record is replete with indications of public effort in the development of infrastructure, building and construction on private account and the increasing diversification of current activity. This shift to local capital formation and diversification is reported frequently in colonial despatches to Britain.

Nevertheless, there are some peculiarly interesting consumer goods in the Botany Bay imports and their presence well illustrates the strangeness of the development processes. Rum was one, the other was meat. Both flowed in in substantial volume (as, indeed, did grains).

Rum was, for long, treated as the source of degradation, debt and violence in a supposedly early convict society and, indeed, as at the root of the Bligh Rebellion. Much of this judgement is suspect (see my 'Yo Ho Ho and How Many Bottles of Rum?' in *AEHR*). There was clearly an active local trade in liquor. For some, no doubt, rum (or liquor more generally) was a source of degradation and debt. Rum has also been recognised as a form of money as it was tendered over and over again in a series of exchanges. To say the least, such rum currency was exposed to the risk of progressive dilution, limiting its universal acceptability. Fundamentally, most colonial transactions other than those with the Commissariat were achieved by barter (and many with the latter were also barter). This was true particularly in wage payments. In such transactions, rum was a superior good to be included in any basket of commodities offered in exchange for services rendered. It provided an incentive to effort. Insofar as it facilitated transactions, its presence in exchange was an added advantage. As an incentive, it served alike for free persons, ex-convicts and convicts. Importation of rum may then be seen, most importantly, as a significant contributor to effort and efficiency. Such an inducement was important in the development of the economy and rum imports are not to be dismissed as the mere dissipation of resources or persons (cf Butlin, 1953: ch 1).

Similar comments might be made, even if with less force, on almost all consumer goods imported into an isolated colony. So far as the importation of meat was concerned, the matter is even more complex. The British government continued to supply the colony with large quantities of meat until 1809. Given the importance of meat consumption as an inducement to local pastoral development, this may seem to be a deterrent to private enterprise. To some extent it was, particularly in the case of large-scale farmers. But imported meat was an inferior good, much less preferred than fresh meat. To that extent the competition of meat imports was muted. More importantly, British meat supplies served three important purposes. First, and most obviously, they allowed the colonial government to pursue the policy of severely limiting the slaughter of the public herds and of building up a nucleus of livestock for further expansion. Secondly, they limited the private incentive to slaughter, particularly by small farmers. Thirdly, they allowed the colonial government to extend the practice, particularly after 1800, of providing livestock subsidies to small ex-convict farmers. In granting such subsidies, the colonial government gave important support to the living standards of ex-convict farmers and thereby helped to underwrite the ex-convict production of grains. The path of development was far from straight.

Finally, the specifically public importation of consumer goods allowed individuals to economise on such international exchange as they were able to acquire. No doubt a variety of counterfactuals might be presented with which to compare reality. Nevertheless, had public imports of consumer goods been dispersed widely to ex-convict farmers from the late 1790s, a great deal of the potential for growth arising from external support and earnings would almost certainly have been dissipated. To the extent that officers, civil officials and a few free migrants and ex-convicts could channel the benefits of import capacity to themselves and concentrate it, the opportunity existed for a more effective stimulus to development. This was particularly the case if these individuals could enhance through their activities the free lunch that Britain offered. If there were such possibilities, there was the prospect of a free lunch for all — not only for the settlers but even for the British taxpayer. This is the issue to be dealt with in the following section.

Improving the British lunch

A central issue in the success of the early settlement was the extent to which government determined the allocation of foreign resources passing to its hands or, by contrast, how far private individuals (or officials in their private capacity) acquired control and ownership not only of the funds and resources directly under their control but also those of the government. To the extent that individuals privatised these external resources, along with landholdings and assigned convict servants, they stood astride the strategic points of control of the local economy. Until the original junta carried through its acts of privatisation, the colonial government clearly dominated decision-making. After 1795, Hunter largely surrendered to the officials, and King, despite efforts to resist them, ended his term of office defeated (he, too, engaged in some significant privatised activities).

The privatisation of all three areas was, indeed, an interrelated process; and similarly the access to publicly supplied resources, both as international exchange and direct British subsidies, interacted with the deployment of private international resources available to officials. The ability of officials and subsequently a few free immigrants and ex-convicts to gain control of goods brought in by government (whether by importation or the issue of Commissariat bills to purchase locally) allowed those persons to economise on their own international exchange, which could then be increasingly diverted into trade. The retention of their own private resources and the diversion of bills to these individuals allowed greater flexibility in expenditure choices. As wealth increased, particularly after 1800, access to bills became more important in the privatising process and served to accentuate the expenditure influences diversifying the range of activities in the settlement. To that extent, Hunter's policy of limiting direct British deliveries and enlarging the issue of bills played directly into the privatising trend. By contrast, King's reversal, limiting the issue of bills and expanding direct British deliveries, constrained choice and increased tensions between the military–official complex. Bligh's continuation of this policy, with a greater show of antagonism towards the privatised sector, appears as a significant element in the collision that occurred (on these changes, cf the patterns of expenditures in table 8, p. 169). What the military–official complex wanted, more than anything else, was a restoration of the international money supply through the Commissariat and/or secure access to Commissariat resources in kind. Bligh not only did not follow this course but, in addition, concentrated the benefits of the Commissariat on himself, his family and a few associates with whom he attempted to form a coalition. This issue was explicit in the junta's justification for its assumption of power in the colony.

The salary appropriations shown in Table 8 imply substantial private access to an international money supply. The marine salary appropriations may have been used extensively outside the colony and hence are best disregarded. For the rest, the civil salary appropriations were considerably smaller than those for the military. This obscures the significance of the civil officials who had other means to exploit. Given the direct civilian control of the Commissariat, it was they who had the most direct access to all goods brought into and passed out of the public store. After 1800, the Commissary directly issued bills. These modes of access offered opportunities for independent privatisation by civil officials or for bargaining to form coalitions with the military. In addition, the local appointment of subordinate officials paid partly by the issue of bills and partly in kind allowed the formation of a truck system within official groups, so that some civil officials could concentrate the benefits of the available bills issued for these purposes. Typically, the issue of a single bill to the senior official from which subordinate salaries were to be met, directly or indirectly, ensured this concentration.

On the evidence of the Commissariat accounts under Hunter's regime, the most important early modes of enhancing privately available international money by civil officials were: through the accumulation of supplementary civil posts with subordinates attached, thereby attracting to a superior the bill due for composite salaries and opening up opportunities for truck payments; and the direct accessing of Commissariat goods by the staff of the store in order to pursue farming ventures and subsequently local trade. Successful farming (or trade in locally produced farm goods) allowed Commissariat officials to ensure their preferential treatment in supplies to the store. The acquisition of interests in ships (particularly by Palmer) allowed officials to deliver goods directly into store on their direct or indirect ordering, even though bills appear as issued to ships' captains. Not all action was legal, even given the mores of the time, and, as Phillip reported, organised theft and trade in stolen public property occurred, quite probably on a substantial scale.

As King abandoned Hunter's practice of issuing bills himself and passed the authority fully to the Commissariat, a much broader exploitation of official position was possible. After 1800, Palmer, the Commissary, appears to have extended his ventures to processing activities, removing resources from the store, processing them and taking as profit the value added by private activity. This may well have been rationally 'perfecting the market' to general colonial benefit. Given Bligh's approach to the Commissariat, to personal land acquisitions, the assignment of convicts to himself, and the grant of rations, livestock and farm equipment to support his farming, he and Palmer were necessarily allied against the junta. Palmer could not have carried out his activities without Bligh's agreement, nor could Bligh his without Palmer's knowledge and acquiescence. Jointly, Bligh and Palmer carried the privatisation of-the Commissariat to a high point that threatened the enterprises of the military or ex-officials.

Military salary appropriations were a much larger privately available source of international money than were civil salaries. For this reason alone, the military were, as a group, more significant in the process of privatisation at the beginning. Their direct rule during 1793–95 made them dominant. The access of a limited number of military officials to the military chest was fundamental to the first stirrings of private development and to the beginnings of commercial enterprise. But the style of the military hierarchy provided the bonds of a solid coalition that largely ensured their success and sustained them as a group after the appointment of new governors. As a ruling junta they could, at least for the period 1793–95, determine their access to the Commissariat and ensure preferential treatment in goods in and out of the store. Subsequently, sales to the Commissariat of their own produce and of colonially produced or privately imported goods acquired through trade were important means of concentrating international money supplies or Commissariat goods in their hands.

The military had special early advantages, at any rate between 1792 and 1800. The mere facts that they were more numerous than civil officials and that their total salary appropriations were larger opened the opportunity, through the formation of syndicates, to a scale of operation that made substantial import trading possible. Some speculative cargoes could pass to lower income groups. But the official positions of the military made it possible to channel these cargoes largely to themselves, and their immediate access to private financial resources gave them a secure priority in any buying queue. Speculative cargoes required the colonials to be satisfied with the attempts by foreign shippers to second guess colonial tastes. Optimal satisfaction depended on direct ordering or, at the extreme, the chartering of ships. Either approach required a scale of financial transaction that only the military, as a group, could achieve.

Even this achievement depended, however, in the early stages, on a process of privatisation within the military itself. The Paymaster was placed in the most advantageous position to exploit, for trading operations, the balances in the military chest. Pending actual payment to other ranks, such funds could be exploited in Botany Bay in just the same manner as was conventional in Britain or elsewhere in the British army. Macarthur was the greatest beneficiary. But, whether for reasons of scale or of long-term political motives, he found it appropriate to join with other officers in trading syndicates, exploiting both individual salaries and the available balances of the military chest (cf Hainsworth, 1972: 26ff).

The use of the military chest might have been relatively severely constrained had the troops been paid regularly and in cash. Neither event was common, and this, too, was the widespread experience of other ranks in the British army. The operation of a truck system in the Corps in Botany Bay ensured the accessibility of balances over sufficiently long periods to engage in quite lengthy trading ventures and also provided supplementary sources of profit to officers through administered prices. It provided an intra-military mode of concentrating wealth while the profits from trade added further to the wealth of officers. A good deal of the profit from trade could be reaped from the sale of imported goods to the Commissariat, thereby ensuring the recovery of proceeds in the form of international exchange (bills) either directly or (more frequently) indirectly.

There were many other opportunities for the concentration of access to resources. Import trade by the military opened opportunities for sales to ex-convicts at administered prices in exchange for ex-convict farm produce. The latter could be disposed of to the Commissariat in exchange for bills, adding to the similar proceeds from the sales of the junta's own farm produce. Either through the acquisition of bills directly or through acquisition of publicly imported goods, the junta could devote more resources to trade either internally or externally. When placed in control of the settlement, they were able to avoid the use of private resources for local enterprises, in farming or otherwise, being subsidised by public goods from the store for their own rations and for those of the labour that they assigned to themselves.

It is important to stress that the store gave the officials an opportunity beyond the mere value of their own output. Their incomes from local activity should be measured as bills received for their entire production plus personal ration support. Given their awareness of this potential during their period of rule and during Hunter's accommodating administration, it may well have been frustrating that King turned to the more controllable mode of direct deliveries of goods from Britain. But it was more than merely frustrating to find Bligh pursuing for his own personal gain precisely the same mode of operation with the Commissariat. Bligh operated in close association with the Commissary and much more severely limited the access of the military to Commissariat goods and international exchange. This they found intolerable. The assault by King and Bligh on the rum trade, profitable as it was, seems to be merely indicative of, rather than central to, the collision that occurred.

The bargaining power of the ex-convicts was severely limited by the elementary fact that the military had control over life and liberty. This was essentially true whether the military governed directly or not. This stark condition, added to the priority of military access to the Commissariat, was enough to ensure the ability of the military to bargain down the price of produce sold by ex-convicts and ensure, where appropriate, the transfer of their grants for debt. The official position of the military ensured that by one means or another this local trade, at least with ex-convict farmers if not with all ex-convicts, would be advantageous to the military, and by direct or indirect means add to the military's opportunities for capturing publicly generated foreign exchange or directly supplied goods from Britain. One can, however, no longer argue that rum dominated in military–settler relations. Rum was significant and as already suggested played a role as an incentive to work for assigned convicts and a further support to the success of official ventures. Indeed, one might well think that the early junta, presented with access to the store and the authority to issue bills on the British government, might have had a grand celebration in which rum might figure prominently. This does, in fact, seem to have occurred. In 1793, the rum stores of the Commissariat were speedily distributed to thirsty officials and more rum was imported on public account. That this was not a wholly exclusive celebration is suggested by an entry in the Commissariat accounts for a stoppage of pay on account of missing liquor stocks. It appears that, briefly, the other ranks along with some convict clerks joined in the celebration. The fine was extraordinarily tolerant (see Commissariat accounts for 1793).

Sequentially, land grants by officials to themselves presented these officials as the successful farmers; the allocation of ration support to themselves and their workforce, together with support in terms of tools and equipment, freed their individual capital; their access to quasi-export earnings opened the avenue for external trade and through that to domestic trade; their official positions ensured a dominance in colonial bargaining with ex-convict farmers on the one hand and subsequent governors on the other; through these official positions they could further exploit the resources of labour and the Commissariat to their own advantage, including the accessing of British goods delivered in kind and publicly-generated international exchange (bills). Ostensible government dominance in resources supplied externally and in international exchange became essentially nominal.

Yet, in achieving this concentration of resources, the officials went a consider-able distance, at least, towards optimising the use of them. Their own official salaries (which would otherwise have meant little to the colony) became important sources of development. By diverting store resources to themselves, they achieved a scale of individual operation that would not otherwise have been possible. By accessing Commissariat bills, particularly through intra-colonial trade, they achieved a scale of activity and a flexibility that seems inconsistent with any reasonable concept of a 'penal settlement'. They prevented resources in cash or kind lying idle, as both were prone to do in the hands of the colonial government. Their actions were undoubtedly self-interested and they may have skirted the edge of legality, even given the mores of their time. But, basically, they comported themselves until 1808 in a manner that was generally consistent with British practice.

Acquiescent as officials in Britain may have been about much of colonial behaviour, time was not on the side of the military. The arrival of free immigrants, such as Campbell, eroded their economic power after 1800. The rise to prominence of a few ex-convicts also presented competition. These other competitors were significant in the development of the economy. But the fundamental problem that the early officials faced in retaining the dominance they had acquired was not, at least until 1806, due simply or primarily to these other potential business leaders. It arose from the fact that sentence terms eventually expired and convicts became ex-convicts, and from the failure of the British to sustain a supply of new convicts on a substantial scale. The progressive emergence of an ex-convict society at the turn of the century posed the officials, in particular, with a new challenge: the fact that the majority of the society could choose, both as sources of labour and as consumers. It was to this social structure that the privatising officials were most effectively adapted and they seem to have responded by increasing their interest in trade rather than farming. In itself, this reflects the importance of the process of privatisation. But the officials still sought to use established modes of access to wealth — the Commissariat with its supply of bills and British direct deliveries of goods. As their convict workforce shrank and as King, in particular, sought to limit ration support, the ability of the military to sustain their wealth was threatened. They might take goods from the Commissariat, as they did, and simply leave debts unpaid after 1800. This behaviour became untenable with a governor who limited access to the store. The officials were forced, then, increasingly back to the limits of their individual resources, particularly after Bligh's arrival.

Something else was in train from the late 1790s. This was the growing requirement for officials to bargain with ex-convicts rather than merely supply their demands through trade. An increasingly private market in both labour and goods, dominated numerically by ex-convicts, introduced the price system as a means of determining shares in available goods. Wealthy and powerful as they might be, officials were faced with bargaining pressures to allow ex-convicts and even convicts to share in the improvement in standards of consumption that had occurred. Botany Bay offers an excellent example of the trickle-down process as the terms of trade shifted progressively from the officials to ex-convicts and convicts, particularly during 1800–6.

Trickling down

Phillip had found it necessary, in the absence of adequate official support, to appoint a considerable number of convicts to positions of trust. In the process, these convicts received a substantial amount of both authority and freedom. So now, in a privatised system, the officials were confronted with the task, first of all, of re-creating an operating market structure. The beneficiaries in this case acquired greater access to wellbeing in addition to greater freedom. This was a situation to rejoice the heart of any libertarian. It could equally enthuse any Marxist.

A few wealthy officials, even when their number was enlarged by a small number of free immigrants and wealthy ex-convicts, could not possibly conduct their multifarious concerns unaided. A producing and distributing hierarchy was essential. Indeed, the demands on the time and attention of the few dominant persons compelled a comparable, if variable, alteration of the modes of operation even in farming. In this issue lay the first trickle-down process, a sharing of the benefits of role and wellbeing, though not necessarily of wealth in the sense of assets. Nevertheless, even though wealth was not directly shared, the opportunity developed, through increased wellbeing, for wealth accumulation at lower income levels.

Military pride apart, an officer could neither direct his farm in detail nor manage the details of purchasing or reselling goods (Hainsworth, 1972: 36ff). The acquisition of part of a ship's cargo might be a reasonable matter for entrepreneurial control, as could the choice of an ex-convict farm for inclusion in a total holding or the determination of an importing order. To purchase and transport grain or meat from ex-convict farmers, and to dispose of liquor stocks or other goods at retail, required a chain of transactions and a chain of subordinate humans. To deal with the Commissariat required association with convict or ex-convict servants of the Commissary. Such transactions required a variety of support. Convicts or ex-convicts were in a sufficient position of scarcity to demand and secure a transfer of part of the benefit that officers transferred to themselves in filling the gaps in the market structure. The terms of bargaining shifted real income above subsistence standard towards, if not necessarily approaching, the level of that of the officials. Within such a transfer, there was scope for variety, so that some gained more than others, depending on their role and scarcity value. It bears repetition that this improvement applied to convicts and ex-convicts alike. Both became agents of the officers; both became transporters of goods; both acquired licences to trade, including licences to operate taverns.

Similarly, in the conduct of farming, officials adapted to organisational necessity. Basically, this adaptation transferred to convicts, in particular, some of the benefits reaped by the officials. This was manifested in a variety of ways in terms of farm organisation: in the introduction of share farming, tenancies or the allocation of small parcels of land to employees. More generally, it accelerated an improvement in convict living standards to above basic subsistence level and restored equity interests in the property rights in convict labour time.

On the production and distribution side, the trickle-down process is clear enough. But benefits reaped by officers were, at least potentially, transferred downwards through demand processes. As unfree labour became scarcer and official wealth increased, the supply price of labour rose and the marginal utility of money to officers fell. In an isolated society, the effect was to concentrate demand on overtly non-tradeables and on goods whose delivery was costly if only in terms of the uncertainty of supply. The demand consequences appear substantial.

Wealthy officials, free migrants and the few wealthy ex-convicts sought personal services in considerable variety, ranging from maidservants to legal counsel, with a wide spectrum in between. But those whom the wealthy had encouraged into well-to-do specialisation similarly sought these goods and services. Housing was an obvious asset. From this demand flowed a derived demand for bricklayers and carpenters, glaziers and painters, limeburners and stonemasons, and similar building trades. Demand for personal services was similarly prominent: house servants, barbers, lodging-house and tavern keepers, coachmen and boatmen, ships' crews, medical and legal services, and schoolteachers were all sought after. All these figured definitely in the 1806 Muster. (See table 7, p. 147.) The demand for luxury goods, including those arising from such esoteric trades as jeweller, gunsmith and jockey, is also apparent in the Muster.

Demand for specific goods and services derived from a few wealthy individuals would not, in itself, be adequate to explain the specialised occupational structure of 1806. Even the higher incomes of those who gained immediately from the few wealthy would not be sufficient. As specialisation was encouraged, further specialisation was induced. The extension of specialised activity was, no doubt, partly an attempt to recreate a structure with which the ex-convicts of 1806 were familiar. But there was an underlying condition: specialisation breeds specialisation. With that development, as Adam Smith insisted, came the opportunity to utilise human capital to maximum advantage.

The problem in explaining early Botany Bay development, accordingly, shifts to the supply side. Were the skills present to satisfy these demands or did the quest for wealth lead merely to unsatisfied demands that were only partially requited by imports of consumer goods? This question requires consideration of the human capital that Britain delivered to the settlement.

The supply side: human capital

Criticism of Britain for its failure to supply convicts with farming skills has run through the history books, as it does through governors' despatches. Indeed, this view of immigration has its echo in Australian policy for most of the first century and a half of white Australian history. This has already been dealt with briefly in the introduction to this Part.

With high quality natural resource endowments, primary activities tend to be emphasised. In conditions of efficient transport and communications, international prices tend to equality, encouraging an array of production in conformity to comparative advantage. Neither high quality natural resources nor efficient international transport and communications were available to the Botany Bay settlement. The Cumberland Plain was a poor resource base. The colony was isolated. Gubernatorial policies attempted to frustrate the exercise of colonial choice after 1795.

Had the British supplied predominantly farming labour, it would have been impossible for the colony to develop as it did. Indeed, given the resources of the Cumberland Plain, so casually supported by Banks, it is possible that a settlement populated by farm labourers would have ended in disaster or at least much larger outlays than the British in fact incurred. Obviously such judgements must be speculative, though they are nonetheless relevant to an understanding of what actually happened.

Farming was undoubtedly vital to the settlement. Nevertheless, preoccupations with farming can blind one to the extraordinary success of the early settlement. Farm inefficiencies due to poor natural and human resources kept farm productivity low; Britain's willingness to continue to supply foodstuffs limited further the rewards to agriculture in the settlement; and the behaviour of the military–official complex kept returns, particularly to ex-convict farming, in check. There was not a great deal that King could do to alter that position.

Privatisation, private access to resources and the sharing of those resources would also probably have come to nought but for the fact that Britain supplied not farming but urban skills. In itself, this did not generate a complex specialised economy. There is a suggestion that some officials sought a significant degree of self-sufficiency, directly engaging a variety of skilled labour. The demand for varied skills for assignment was persistently strong, a fact that led to the government both charging for the assignment of skilled servants and offering skilled convicts the opportunity to buy out the property rights in their labour time. As, however, the majority of convicts became ex-convicts, they, too, had the opportunity to choose. In these circumstances, the final condition for a flexibly operating economy fell into place.

The convicts and free persons arriving in Australia were far from presenting a replica of the structure of British skills. Nevertheless, there were many skills embodied in the convicts. The 1806 Muster reveals reasonably well the extraordinarily wide variety in early skills, through teachers, doctors, lawyers, carpenters, bricklayers and brickmakers, painters, glaziers, limeburners and stonemasons, tinsmiths and gunsmiths, shipwrights and sailmakers, and the like (table 7, p. 147). The ability to deploy a substantial fraction of these skilled persons flexibly and so early had a peculiar significance. This was the stage at which a successful bridgehead was established by whites on the Australian continent. Subsequent development depended heavily on this early success. The ability to indulge in high expenditure by some colonists, and indeed even if only to a somewhat less extent by a significant fraction of the settlement, was matched by the circumstances, particularly after 1800, in which these skills could satisfy local demands by a relatively free supply response.

It was not rich natural resources or staple industries but the wealth of human capital that formed an essential ingredient of the remarkable early success of the colony. It was because of skills and re-acquired freedom that one finds prominent in the 1806 Muster a peculiarly large proportion of the total workforce of the settlement engaged as self-employed in skilled occupations. Since they chose to deliver these goods and services, it seems a reasonable assumption that they shared sufficiently in the wellbeing of the settlement.

Comparative natural advantage may be seen as, at least briefly, to a large degree turned on its head. Of course, much of the activity was in non-tradeables. Moreover, the specialised trades of Port Jackson in 1806 were protected by isolation and the uncertainty of deliveries. But even in competition with imports, a high proportion possessed skills that allowed effective competition in many areas. Given that economies of scale were not particularly prominent in craft activities in

1806, the ex-convict colonists were well-equipped to compete with imports. To a substantial degree, they were aided by the accessibility of certain major types of materials locally — timber, stone, lime and so on. For the rest, comparatively slight importations of materials supplied the necessary imported base.

The general conditions of success

Summarising, it may be suggested that the early achievements of the settlement may be seen as the product of seven major conditions:

(a) the early elimination of threats from Aborigines and their almost immediate depopulation;

(b) the early privatisation of the settlement and the firm estabishment of private property, privately employed labour and market choice in the settlement;

(c) the accession of substantial British support in kind, through the authority to issue bills payable by the British government, and through the presence of substantial quasi-exports (these were, however, more effective to the extent that a substantial control over the deployment of these resources fell into the private hands of relatively few);

(d) the desire for non-tradeables and for goods that could not be readily tradeable;

(e) the supply of human capital with skills appropriate to a relatively advanced society;

(f) the lack of economies of scale in large areas of non-food production; and

(g) the recovery of property rights in labour time by the majority of convicts.

PART V

THE TAKEOVER
PROCESS:
1788–1850

19

INTRODUCTION

Conventionally, the initial British settlement of Australia in 1788 is seen as a public project to establish a distant convict colony in the Antipodes, though there is increasing debate as to whether the intention was merely to establish a convict settlement or was influenced by considerations of imperial strategy and trade interests. This Eurocentric approach is heavily influenced by the long accepted belief that British settlers, whether convict or free, entered an Australia that was occupied by only a handful of Aborigines. There is less clarity on the legal evaluation of the day: in particular whether Aborigines who lived in Australia did or did not, in fact, occupy it because they were not 'farmers' in the accepted European sense.

These highly parochial attitudes to Australian history have had many far-reaching consequences. They have embedded almost all historical writing about Australia in a very narrow perspective. They have led either to a concentration on the alleged sordidness of the convict settlements or to the extraordinarily rapid and successful development of a pastoral Australia during the first sixty or so years, along with extremely rapid rates of expansion of population and economic activity. For economic historians, then, in particular, Australian economic history is seen as the development of 'an area of recent settlement' in which a great deal of wealth came relatively easily.

There is another perspective, radically different from the convention. First, there is the fact that British entry was into a continent that had been occupied by Aborigines for several tens of thousands of years. Far from being an area of recent settlement, Australia was an area of very ancient settlement. As I suggest in Part II, the Aboriginal economy was a stably ordered system of decision-making that amply satisfied the wants of the people. British occupation resulted (note that there is no indication of intent) in the destruction of Aboriginal economy and society and the decimation of its population. We have, then, two counter-balancing experiences — a rapidly expanding British society and a rapidly declining Aboriginal society between 1788 and 1850. Over this period, Australian history seen from the point of view of human beings as a whole is a dual process, not simply one of European expansion. The substitution of British for Aboriginal society and economy meant a transfer of resources from losers to gainers. This transfer is properly to be seen as a takeover.

Takeovers can be friendly or hard-fought battles, frequently presented in terms of the substitution of a more efficient management, a new product or productive process, or the transfer of available assets to some other activity. Seen in this light, British settlers establishing enterprises in Australia may have had a much more challenging task than is usually conveyed. They may have faced much higher costs through Aboriginal resistance or even fears of Aborigines. There may then be a much more exacting account of European 'success' than is usually represented. Similarly, an attempt to understand the outcome for Aborigines requires an exploration of the events unfolding for the losers. The reasons for and conditions of that loss are matters of prime interest in any account of Australia as a whole. Why conditions of Aboriginal society made British success possible and the nature and scale of the loss to Aborigines need to be investigated if we wish to move from an essentially Eurocentric view of the world.

There is, however, yet another dimension to the takeover process. We could still, in considering a takeover, confine our attention to the late eighteenth century and the first half of the nineteenth. This would continue to limit discussion to immediate problems of Pacific and Indian Ocean conflicts between imperial powers and traders, to the nature of British society and law in the later eighteenth century, and so on. It is important to perceive the stage and speed of development of the two societies, British and Aboriginal. Once we do this in long-term perspective, we do indeed have a radically different mode of approach. From the point of view of human history, the Australian takeover was carried out by one of the most recently established societies (possibly the most recently established) in the world and the transfer of resources came from one of the most ancient. A very different picture and a different set of issues arise when we treat Britain, settled perhaps 20–30 000 or more years after Australia, as 'an area of recent settlement' and Australia as 'an area of ancient settlement'. Such a perspective brings into sharper focus the extraordinary speed of British and the extreme slowness of Aboriginal development. It is an intriguing question as to whether, in the very long run, the former was innovative and successful and the latter backward and archaic.

It bears stressing that in discussing the economic history of Australia from 1788, it is not assumed that Britain intended, through the settlement at Botany Bay and elsewhere, to destroy Aboriginal society and economy. Indeed, as we shall see, official intent and the attitudes of many individual settlers may have been designed, insofar as Aborigines were considered at all, to achieve some form of merger rather than a takeover. The gulf between the two societies, the one new and the other ancient, was, however, too large to be bridged and the outcome as a consequence of British settlement was the destruction of Aboriginal society and a demographic disaster for Aborigines.

20

BRITISH DEVELOPMENT
IN THE LONG RUN

T he southern coast of England lies approximately 5 degrees farther from the
equator than does the south of Tasmania and the northern limit of Scotland is
about 18 degrees farther. The Australian prehistorians are impressed by the ability of
Aborigines to occupy Tasmania perhaps as far back as 30 000 years ago. During
the ice age a vast ice sheet extended from Scandinavia across the North Sea to
cover most of Britain. Human occupation was severely limited, though some
settlement in the extreme south may have been possible. There is still a good deal
of debate on this issue. Perhaps by 12 000 BP, definitely by 10 000 BP, England was
colonised more generally by *Homo sapiens*, as one of the last areas of Europe to be
settled. Initially, early hunter gatherers trickled across the land bridge from Europe
until the melting of the glaciers led to the final rising of the seas, re-forming the
English Channel about 8000 BP. Thereafter the slow flow of human beings that
persisted came by sea, as they had come from island South-east Asia to Australia
several millennia earlier (Starr, 1974). Less than 8000 years after the English
Channel re-formed, this primitive 'British' society had become the richest, most
powerful and most technologically advanced nation on earth, incidentally rolling
the ancient Aboriginal society into substantial oblivion. While the Aborigines at
one end of the earth acquired an exceptional accommodation to nature in local
terms, their distant relatives at the other extreme were able to develop an
exploitative technology and mode of handling their environment to gain a form of
mastery over much of the globe. Yet curiously, the per capita standards of living
200 years ago in terms of food consumption probably then favoured Aborigines
(Collins, 1798; Curr, 1883; Eyre, 1845; Grey, 1841; Manning, 1882; Mitchell,
1839; Petrie, 1904). It seems possible that conditions of physique, health and life
expectancies may also have favoured Aborigines (Collins, 1798; Mitchell, 1839;
Plomley, 1966). Economists who tend to think that progressive improvement in
wealth depends on the generation of a food surplus need to rethink the theory of
economic growth, at any rate in the very long run.

Separation by sea from Eurasia appears to have favoured Britain, while the comparable separation of Aborigines left their society to become a technological backwater open to takeover. Isolation does not seem to be the answer to comparative development. Similarly, proximity to change does not appear as a sufficient determinant. Rapid change in human social organisation and technology appears to have occurred during about 8–5000 BP in three prime locations — in the 'fertile crescent' of the Eastern Mediterranean, in the Indus Valley and around the Yellow River in China. Here, agricultural development, the domestication of animals, population concentrations, urban societies, hierarchical social structures, smelting of metals and the development of metal objects, military organisation, rent-taking through tribute, slavery and various forms of unfreedom developed (Starr, 1974). The Eastern Mediterranean and the Yellow River cores lie very roughly equidistant, respectively, from Britain and Northern Australia. The tide of change poured — with important stops, starts and reversals — over Britain, projecting it beyond its near neighbours. It appears to have passed Australian Aborigines by or been rejected by them. At a far greater distance from development centres than either Britain or Australia, complex urbanised–agrarian and strongly hierarchical societies were established in Central America despite distance and isolation.

Before the Roman invasion (Donnell, 1983; Salway, 1981), Britain had received flows of people transferring technology and forms of social and economic organisation from the Middle East up the Danube Valley and along the Mediterranean and French Atlantic coast. Organised into petty warring kingdoms, these immigrants had nevertheless developed substantial agriculture, pastoral activity and craft industries as well as the exploitation of soft minerals. Trade was well established with Europe and there is some evidence of early 'British' trading links beyond the Middle East. Barbaric as the Romans may have regarded the 'British', it appears to have been partly the known natural wealth of Britain that prompted the Roman invasion.

Roman occupation, the *Pax* and *Lex Romana* were the first, if forcible, efforts to weld at least England into some degree of national entity. As inheritors of the technical, economic, social and political conditions derived from the Eastern Mediterranean, Rome had the essential springboard from Italy to develop a vast network of imperial control extending over much of Europe and the Mediterranean. For 500 years, these traditions were injected into England. On the one hand, Rome delivered a military market, a money economy, organised administration, a villa system of agriculture married to the Celtic farming of Britain, improved agricultural productivity, urban centres, transport systems and extended trade contacts with Europe. On the other hand, it imposed military control and confirmed more rigidly the hierarchical organisation and exploitation of unfree labour on which the ancient world depended (Salway, 1981), including the continuation of slavery. Despite the transmission of comparable socio-economic organisation to Java from the Asian mainland and despite very early Javanese development of very advanced ship-building technology (Macknight, 1976; Manguin, 1987; White, 1982; Wiseman, 1977), it is scarcely conceivable that a transfer of influences corresponding to those of Rome on Britain could have been spread by Asians to Australia.

The withdrawal of Rome from Britain meant reversion in many areas, both internally and in the exposure of Britain to renewed European migrations and invasions, just as the eventual sacking of Rome capped a vast trans-European movement of people and substantial economic retrogression. Christianity was one of the most important legacies of the Roman Empire in Europe and Britain, serving as a new unifying source, a new means of concentrating power and wealth, a new support to agriculture through localised security, a new means of concentrating power and wealth, a new support to agriculture through localised security, a new stimulus to trade and a new influence in the preservation of forms of unfreedom. Particularly on the European mainland, the Church in combination with temporal organisation gradually restored authority and stability over large areas, particularly in Western Europe. One of the most important outcomes of the decline of Roman military power, even though delayed in the Eastern Mediterranean, was the eventual exposure from the eighth century AD of the Middle East and the entire Mediterranean to Muhammadan intervention. This change disrupted though did not stop long-distance trade with the East, and increased the costs of trade around the Mediterranean itself. Indeed the Byzantine Empire contributed to the trade links of the new city states of Venice and Genoa with the East. But once the Turks captured Constantinople and occupied Egypt in the early seventeenth century, there were intense pressures on European long-distance trade with the East and a consequent impellent demand for alternative ocean routes (Clough and Cole, 1952).

The crucial thrust of these changes was to move the centre of economic and social development within Europe towards central-western Europe, particularly France, and the Atlantic seaboard. Initially, for Britain, the outcome might be encapsulated in terms of the re-formation of petty kingdoms with remnants of villa agriculture exposed to Viking trader–warriors and eventual invasion. In the process, a significant innovation was imparted in the form of ship design and construction, a matter of primary significance given Britain's geographical position and equally significant for the continuation and development of British trade (Wilson, 1978). As feudal order developed in Europe, particularly in France, the next major intervention in the form of the Norman invasion reintegrated England with the centre of Western Europe. It restored a form of centralised authority and hierarchy and established in England Norman forms of feudality, unfreedom, focal points of control and security, French manorial agriculture and systems of taxation and tribute. It also enhanced, through feudal security and the establishment of population centres, the opportunity for an extension of long-distance trade. Nevertheless, it was not until the end of the fifteenth century that England began to establish a unified national state (Clough and Cole, 1952).

Nation-states had preceded that of Britain and, in 1500, even England was still a relatively underdeveloped and regionalised economy, particularly by comparison with France and Spain, where centralised regal and church authority had been established earlier. Nevertheless, England had developed further in several key respects, particularly in the breaking down of localised feudal strongholds, the commutation of feudal dues and the extension of personal freedom. In these respects, England was better equipped in the long run for international trading competition. In the course of the sixteenth century AD, in particular, English shipbuilding technology moved ahead of its European competitors.

One specially important commodity, wool, had already laid the foundation for long-distance trade in Europe through the Merchant Staplers. Increasingly, Britain became not merely a recipient of external influences but a source of intellectual and institutional change to other countries. Early development of science and technology (cf Charles II and the Royal Society), the evolution of sophisticated market institutions and the orientation of free individual activity towards increasingly specialised market behaviour allowed Britain to develop rapidly in terms of both domestic and external activity. Compared to most other European nations, Britain freed itself relatively early from a highly centralised form of mercantilist state. As a precondition for these and other vital changes from 1500, Britain had been able to escape from much of the continental conflict that had helped to preserve there church and temporal authority combined with feudal order, with their accompanying unfreedom.

One major problem England, in common with other urbanised societies, had not been able to escape was disease (Creighton, 1965). Communicable diseases extended back into the ancient world of city states as major causes of mortality and morbidity (Starr, 1974). Plague has been, historically, the most notorious, the source of the so-called 'black death' that carried massive mortality in the fourteenth century. But plague was not the only major communicable disease and, indeed, it disappeared early from Europe. Wherever sufficient population nuclei developed, Europeans were exposed to epidemics of varying degrees of intensity with different implications according to the age and sex of victims. Once their significance was revealed after the disappearance of the black rat and plague, prominent sources of mortality and morbidity included smallpox, tuberculosis, influenza, whooping cough, measles, dysentery and, later, venereal diseases. These were all 'crowd' diseases transferable through relatively close contact, their effects enhanced by poor nutrition, lack of medical care and poor hygiene. They were the price of population aggregation, and in the main rare in relatively sparsely populated areas. Europeans gradually developed forms and degrees of immunity to many of these diseases, so they tended to concentrate their influence on children. For some diseases, such as dysentery, pulmonary diseases or venereal diseases, no such explicit immunity developed, though it is possible that resistance to some of these diseases developed (or that the diseases changed their form and severity).

In greater or lesser degree, British (and other European) populations accommodated to these diseases. Survivors of some infections acquired lifetime immunity; some 'crowd immunity' developed; and diseases in some cases were attenuated. Many tended to become diseases of childhood, with heavy early age mortality tending to sustain high death rates at early age and produce only slow population increase despite high birth rates. Once Europeans, including the British, broke their dependence on land and acquired global mobility, they carried these infections throughout the world, including to Australia.

The sack of Constantinople and occupation of Egypt by the Turks, and the extension of Muhammadans into the Mediterranean had several important implications for this particular history. The Turks were able to increase the costs of long-distance trade with the East — trade particularly in spices and precious stones — and directly to tax goods transfers, making radical inroads into Venetian and Genoese trade. Muhammadan presence in the Mediterranean similarly increased the costs of trading within the Mediterranean itself, particularly for traders on the Mediterranean littoral. Competitive advantage in trade shifted to the west, including Britain, in intra-European trade. But, in addition, the net benefit of investment in sea-going transport to achieve contact with the east rose sharply. Britain, participating in the Crusades and thereby maintaining contact with the East, was one of the eventual gainers from this alteration of relative trading costs by land vis-à-vis sea passage.

21

THE HUNTER GATHERERS OF EMPIRE

From the fifteenth century, European maritime technology responded to these pressures and opportunities. Improved ship-building construction and the development of the astrolabe, the compass and mapping methods were all vital to this belated European response to leave the land and attempt ocean travel, a feat that Aborigines had, with inferior technology, achieved tens of thousands of years earlier, as had the Chinese with superior technology. First the Spanish and Portuguese, then the Dutch and finally the British and French developed into major imperial powers, hunting and gathering under their control vast areas of the rest of the world. If the original object was to respond to the increased costs of trade in and via the Mediterranean in order to seek the highly prized and largely luxury goods of the East, found benefits on the way progressively altered imperial and trading ambitions. Trading objectives on this scale and with this order of risk were not easily achievable by individuals. State-directed and supported corporations were crucial instruments and trade and imperial interests became closely inter-twined. National and corporate action, individual trading, naval operations and piracy became components of a complex imperial and trading play with fine gradations separating them. In the course of 300 years after 1500, the five nation states of Europe competed for and, in varying ways, dominated most of the nations outside Europe. State intervention in and, at the extreme, state direction of commercial activity provided the foundation for so-called mercantilist policies.

The initial interest in Eastern spices, silks and precious metals was qualified early by access by the Portuguese to slave dealing down the African coast and by Spanish access to gold and slaves in the Caribbean and central and southern America. In turn, wealth from growing colonial empires affected the reality and perceptions of relative national power in Europe itself, so that imperial competition became, in part, an extension of intra-European competition. Once the Cape of Good Hope was rounded and India attained, the desired resources of the East lay open to sea transport. To secure the high profits on these and American traffic depended on a variety of responses by competing trading and imperial interests. Conquest, killing and enslavement of many indigenous populations; the intercontinental transfer of slaves as a labour force to imperial areas; European settlement of 'newly discovered' areas, including the transfer of convicts and indentured servants; the formation of trading posts and naval establishments; State-organised enterprises with governing powers; naval confrontation on the high seas and the capture of booty; the sacking of competitors' trading posts; imperial transfers consequential on the outcome of European wars and royal marriages — all these indicate the variety of devices employed to attain imperial interest.

Spain and Portugal were the first of the imperial hunter gatherers — Portugal tracking along the west coast of Africa, Spain crossing the Atlantic to the Americas. In fact, both soon joined in a movement in both directions, with uneasy alliances and a fragile duopolistic division of areas of interest. For Portugal, the first reward was African slaves followed, once the Cape was rounded, by Eastern spices acquired through trading posts rather than Portuguese settlements. Portuguese exploitation of South America was slow in contrast with actions by Spanish military and merchants, freebooters and the Spanish Crown, for whom Central America spelt gold.

Innovators are always exposed to risk by copiers. In the case of imperial expansion, maritime lines of communication were progressively lengthened and exposed to attack. British and French privateers, in particular, preyed on these lines of communication as well as following the paths first shown by Spain and Portugal. Wealth could be obtained by attacks on competitors' shipping, without the expenses of conquest, exploration and settlement. The transfer of wealth through these modes could then be seen as enhancing the wealth of the individual European nations represented by the naval victors. This was basic to the first forays by both Britain and France.

Britain was slow in the imperial race. From the early seventeenth century, the British Crown and British business interests turned their attention primarily to the Americas. They were followed quickly by the French. In the Americas, a protracted conflict for empire followed, continuing to the end of the eighteenth century. In the process, Britain showed a peculiar predilection for imperial organisation, not wholly unique in European adventures but nevertheless particularly prominent in British behaviour, in the transfer of nationals to occupy and settle non-European colonial areas. Britain showed another relatively special characteristic in a larger tendency to devolve not merely trading interests but actual ownership and governing authority to private individuals and corporations. By comparison, other European competitors tended to exercise more direct control by the Crown and to fail to encourage, if not positively to discourage, emigration of their nationals to settle in numbers in colonial areas. Some of the reasons for this difference are taken up below.

Portuguese entry into the East was followed most importantly by the Netherlands, both nations in pursuit of a highly profitable trade in spices. While Portugal lacked both the population base and the wealth to invest heavily in empire, Holland rapidly attained prominence in the seventeenth century, first at Antwerp and subsequently in Amsterdam, as the financial centre of Europe. From this vantage point and supported by large-scale investment in advanced shipbuilding, Holland succeeded, over Portugal, in dominating the spice trade and the spice islands in Ceylon and our old friend, island south-east Asia, from which Australian Aborigines had come (Spate, 1979, 1983).

Coming late into the Indian–Pacific Oceans, Britain was left to conflict primarily with France and Portugal for the control of India. Here, the East India Company (established in 1601) progressively expanded its interest and control until it fell heir to substantially the whole of the Indian sub-continent by the end of the seventeenth century. By comparison with the spice trade that Holland controlled, India might have appeared for some time to be second prize. In fact, however, its resource advantages fitted domestic British industrial development, particularly in providing a supply of textile raw materials and a mass export outlet for finished textile goods. Moreover, by comparison with other resource advantages accruing from European 'expansion' into the rest of the world, spices became of dwindling significance. With the British East India Company accorded not merely governing rights in India but a monopoly of trade in the Indian and Pacific Oceans as against other British interests, the significance of India and the Company loomed increasingly prominent throughout the eighteenth century (Spate, 1988).

It is worth pausing to recognise the array of goods (Clough and Cole, 1952) accruing by sea transport to European nations as a result of imperial acquisitions from the fifteenth to the eighteenth century. In doing so, it is important to appreciate, notwithstanding the presence of mercantilist states, the scale and range of opportunities offered in business terms to traders. Any nation might gain, through imperial control, the opportunity to turn the terms of trade in its favour. Similarly, by gaining advantage in these traded goods to the detriment of competitors, a successful imperial competitor could hope to reduce the national wealth and hence the military power of others within Europe itself. Most importantly, within such national designs, individual traders of successful nations could expect to maximise a personal advantage in the expansion of business and the accumulation of wealth. In turn, the growth of their trading activities supplied materials for industrial restructuring, a process that expanded as goods acquired from overseas changed progressively from luxuries to items of common consumption. It was in this last process that Britain gained most after 1700 and increasingly throughout the eighteenth century. Many interests were at stake in imperial development and it is unfortunate that historians have tended to focus so closely on cabals of policy makers in order to find reasons for action.

The list of goods flowing by sea into Europe or transferred by Europeans to the colonial empires is a long one. It should be stressed that what follows is indicative and far from exhaustive. So much attention has been given to gold and spices that it is appropriate to stress that both declined in significance after the mid-seventeenth century, even though they continued to offer incentive. The growth of colonial slavery partly by enslavement of indigenous populations but more importantly by the intercontinental transfer of slaves in large numbers to colonial settlements became a massive operation. Britain participated in this trade along with other nations, and as the American settlements of British nationals enlarged so too did their dependence on slavery, particularly to produce cotton and tobacco. To these slaves, Britain added other forms of unfree labour for colonial development in the form of indentured servants and convicts. All re-created, in different institutional circumstances, the fundamental institution of unfreedom necessary to support economic and social hierarchies, an institution from which Britain had largely freed itself by the seventeenth century. In the light of Australian settlement, it is worth noting that convict transfers were a minute component in what was a long-sustained and large-scale transfer of unfree people for the purposes of colonial development, made by all the imperial nations.

Beyond gold, spices and slaves lay a wide and growing spectrum of commodities. Some were not new, having been carried in small quantities overland from the East. Sea transport opened up the opportunity not merely for an alternative route but also and more importantly for mass transport. Though high-value and low-volume goods were originally preferred, sea transport allowed and encouraged the large-scale shipment of bulky commodities. The significance of trade and empire shifted progressively from satisfying the tastes of upper income groups to providing the means to transform the consumption patterns of mass consumers. In turn, this implied growth in the scale of business enterprises interested in trade in these commodities. This was most particularly the case with Britain.

Tobacco, coffee, chocolate, cane sugar (and an important derivative, rum) and some additional spices such as vanilla came particularly from South and Central America, along with such novelties as potatoes and tomatoes. From North America, including the Caribbean, came sugar, cotton, tobacco, maize, a large variety of animal furs, timbers particularly important to naval and general maritime development, turpentine, pitch and tar. Offshore, the seas provided a rich harvest, particularly of cod and whales, the latter's oil important for lighting and the lubrication of industrial machinery, a matter increasingly and acutely significant to Britain. As whales became depleted in the north Atlantic, the supply from 'the southern fisheries' became increasingly important. The East supplied a rising volume and growing variety of spices. It delivered, also, some significant plants and drugs, including rice, tea and opium poppy. India, particularly, was a source of fine cotton. Different dyes, influencing the development of textiles, replaced the old European dyes. New perfumes, china and porcelain (as trading extended to China), and new timbers for fine furniture were added to the list of European industrial products and consumption patterns.

It is interesting to speculate as to what might have been the course of European — and world — economic history if either:

(a) such a goods flow had not occurred;

(b) the supply price had been much higher; or

(c) volumes had been significantly less.

What in fact happened depended on the very special steps taken in enforcing imperial power throughout the world and, to a very large extent, on displacing masses of indigenous populations, particularly in the New World.

This illustrative list indicates that the hunters and gatherers of empire were, therefore, in competition for rich game and harvests, and not merely concerned with abstractions of empire and power or with the welfare of indigenous people. Increasingly during the eighteenth century the competition focused on the French and the British in both the Americas and the East. The Seven Years War greatly weakened France, particularly in terms of fiscal commitments and debt, laying the foundations for the French Revolution. Britain, on the other hand, confronted growing American opposition to Navigation Acts and the imposition of local taxation for imperial purposes. In both countries, these developments carried the death knell of mercantilism by weakening the authority of the centralised State.

For Britain, however, other basic internal changes were occurring, carrying development in a similar direction. The British, particularly the English, economy was in the process of more rapid and widespread structural adjustment than was the case in other European countries. The progressive enclosures extending from the sixteenth century accelerated a decline in the labour intensity of agriculture. The growth of industry, conventionally regarded as centred on iron and textile industries but almost certainly incorporating other manufacturing activities derived from the widening array of goods carried by ocean transport, speeded a shift of labour and activity to urban centres. Reduced labour intensity in agriculture and rising industrial demand for labour did not necessarily mean offsetting changes so far as the labour market was concerned. Indeed, the early removal of constraints on the freedom of workers in Britain — a form of deregulation of the labour market — made more prominent in Britain than in the still feudalised countries of Europe a problem that was already clear to the Tudors and became increasingly of social concern in Britain throughout the eighteenth century: a labour market that did not clear readily, leaving substantial problems of unemployment and pauperism. To this, mortality added social difficulties arising from dependants. And the concentration of population in the towns, particularly in the eighteenth century, increased special problems of slums, sweated labour, unemployment, disease and crime.

Britain was restructured away from agriculture far more than any western European country by the middle of the eighteenth century, and this contrast increased over the following 100 years. It is not surprising, therefore, that Britain was, of all imperial nations, more interested in allowing, encouraging and forcing some of its nationals to occupy colonial areas. Workhouses could not cope with increasing pauperism and the largely privatised gaols could not deal with the increasing convictions for crime. Britain found one outlet of prime importance in North America, for paupers, for convicts and for migrants of greater substance who created colonial jobs for British nationals. The loss of the American colonies after 1776 largely eliminated the opportunity to export not only convicts but also paupers — hence the traditional explanation of the origin of Botany Bay in terms of convict settlement.

Counterfactually, other European nations might have settled Australia. Britain appears as having the distinctly stronger incentive even as compared with the French. Its internal restructuring was one major difference, and French fiscal problems after the Seven Years War also operated to British advantage. So, too, in certain respects in a positive way, did the loss of the American colonies. In particular, the American Revolution went far towards transferring the long-distance whaling industry to Britain and hence a much stronger whaling interest in the 'southern fisheries'. It is indicative that the First Fleet was essentially composed of whalers. But, fundamentally, the British economy by the late eighteenth century was structured strongly towards trade in and processing of goods received and sold by sea. In such a structure and with such a dependence on sea transport, the security of distant operations and lines of communication was fundamental.

Extensive bases were required to protect and facilitate ship movements around the Indian Ocean and the East.

In dealing with the settlement of Australia, one should cease to be preoccupied with Botany Bay, interesting as First Decisions may be. The speed with which efforts were made to extend settlements and their location is indicative in part of a pre-emptive objective — not merely to spread population for activity reasons but also to pre-empt directly the entry of other nationalities into Australia and to contain their activities in the Indian and Pacific Oceans. Moreover, and more importantly, it was not merely action by Britain and its imperial competitors that determined the takeover process and settled the fate of the Aborigines. Other groups and nationalities, engaged more literally in hunting and gathering, impinged on other parts of Australia at times very similar to the British arrival and occupation.

22

BRITISH, AMERICAN AND MACASSAN PRESENCE IN THE TAKEOVER

Aboriginal control of the Australian continent was, in fact, affected from three different directions. British entry at Botany Bay on the east coast in 1788 was followed within a decade by American whalers and sealers initiating their activities on and off the south-east coast and in Tasmania (Steven, 1983). In this, they were soon joined by the British (including persons from the Botany Bay settlement). Both groups followed, in time, Macassan fishing visits that spread their presence along substantially the whole of the northern coastline from the Kimberleys to Cape York (Macknight, 1976). These Macassan visits, in search of trepang, may have been regular annual ones for perhaps as long as a century before 1788 and may have been sporadic well before then. By 1788, it appears that the Macassans had only very recently completed their westward extension of fishing as far as Cape York into the eastern side of the Gulf of Carpentaria. As the British settlement spread from Botany Bay north and south along the coast, to Van Diemen's Land (Tasmania) in 1803, into the plains of eastern Australia after 1813, to Moreton Bay (Queensland) in 1824, to Fort Dundas, Raffles Bay and Port Essington (Northern Territory) in 1824, 1826 and 1838, to Swan River (Western Australia) in 1829, Port Phillip (Victoria) in 1835 and to Adelaide (South Australia) in 1836, this movement of settlers was simplified by the effects that whalers, sealers and the Macassans had on the Aborigines, even though the dominant intervention was British. The three sources need to be seen together as leading in different ways to the eventual success of the British takeover.

Within a little over ten years after the Botany Bay settlement the Aborigines were almost surrounded, even though neither they nor the other actors were aware of it. Once sealers reached Rottnest Island off Perth, not later than 1825, the pincers were closed. Within twenty-five years after 1788, the British were poised to occupy the plains and riverlands of the southeastern mainland and Van Diemen's Land. Within fifty years, Aboriginal society was devastated in the southern half of Australia. Within 100 years, only scattered remnants remained throughout the whole continent, chiefly in areas not then prized by Europeans.

Some of this destruction was intentional; incidentally, perhaps, by the Macassans, not infrequently by Americans and much more frequently by British settlers (including the colonial born) and by colonial authority. Most of the outcome was inadvertent in terms of the causation that actually unfolded. Had unintentional consequences not intervened in a massive way, it remains an important question as to how Aborigines would have been dealt with. Given apparent British persistence (determination?) with the settlement of Australia after the end of the Napoleonic Wars, this question turns on the possibilities of mutual accommodation by or conflict between Aborigines and Europeans. The implied 'game' issues are central to the discussion to be developed below.

In the meantime, it is important to understand the possible sources of significance of the Americans and Macassans in the eventual outcome. The Americans not only directed whaling and sealing expeditions into Bass Strait and across to Kangaroo Island; they also traded with the Botany Bay settlement. In establishing links between Botany Bay and Bass Strait, they provided opportunity for convicts and ex-convicts to provide part of their whaling and sealing workforce and also demonstrated to Botany Bay settlers the sealing potential that could be pursued independently. After 1798, groups of sealers were dotted on the Bass Strait islands and on the Van Diemen's Land, Victorian and South Australian coast, located in isolated groups and dependent to a large extent on their own resources for survival for long periods.

The consequential inroads into seal populations (McBryde, 1978; Plomley, 1966) were the first significant reduction of specific major supplies to Aborigines in the area (corresponding to the problems created by the use of seine nets in Port Jackson a little earlier). Sealers, both American and British, also acquired Aboriginal women not merely for sexual but also for sealing and other hunting and gathering purposes (a process repeated later in Western Australia). Whether the transfer of women was always by force is obscure but the loss of women was important to Aborigines not only because of the role of women in gathering but also because of their expertise in handling seal carcases. One mode of accommodation to this indicates a considerable adaptability by Aborigines and perhaps a conscious trading accommodation at least for a few years after 1800. A trade developed, with Aborigines providing variety to sealers' diets in the delivery of kangaroo meat in exchange for seal meat. Even at this primitive level, comparative advantage operated with some effect.

Sealers were not, however, merely peaceful traders and hunters. There was soon violent confrontation on both sides and more persistent violence by sealers towards Aboriginal women. Sealers, however — less perhaps directly from Americans and more from persons brought by them from Botany Bay as well as the British shippers who followed the Americans — carried with them communicable diseases. In the absence of explicit evidence, one cannot be categorical about the Americans. It is highly improbable, however, that they failed to pass directly or indirectly to Aborigines the pulmonary and venereal diseases that were common in Europe, certainly existed in Botany Bay and were characteristic of European ships' companies. Both these groups of diseases were almost certainly transmitted at a very early stage to Aborigines in Van Diemen's Land and along the Victorian and

South Australian coasts. How Aboriginal women who cohabited or were forced to cohabit with sealers were dealt with after any group of sealers left is unknown, despite allegations of mayhem. It is extremely unlikely that all failed to be reabsorbed into Aboriginal groups, those who were would have extended these diseases more generally into Aboriginal society. Later, we can return to the wider demographic implications of these diseases and their ability to spread widely over long distances amongst Aborigines.

As has already been discussed, the Macassans appear so far as any information goes, to have been much more welcome but much more numerous and regular visitors on the northern Australian coast. The trepang that they sought for trade with China do not appear to have been highly prized parts of the Aboriginal diet and to this extent they did not disrupt Aboriginal production and consumption behaviour. There are suggestions of episodes of violence between visitors and residents, but the indications from language and goods transfers and Aboriginal travel to Sulawesi are that the seasonal Macassan visits were comparatively amicable. Unlike sealers and settlers, the Macassans did not outstay their welcome, remaining in north Australia only for a few months of each year.

Like the sealers to the south, however, the Macassans also carried communicable diseases. As wholly male crews, the Macassans most probably cohabited with Aboriginal women and may have transferred venereal and even some exotic tropical diseases. We do not know. But one disease can be regarded as having certainly been delivered to parts of northern Australia and possibly more widely from Macassan praus. This was smallpox (Butlin, 1983, 1985; Campbell, 1985; Cumpston, 1914). Again, the wider demographic implications of this disease are left for later. Nevertheless, it should be noted here that, if, as has been proposed in the past, smallpox was introduced by Macassans and spread throughout the whole of Australia, the role of the Macassans in simplifying the British takeover was of prime significance. It might be noted in this context that American whalers, having first fished the tropics north of Australia before passing into Bass Strait, cannot be ruled out, without any question whatever, as possible sources of the same disease.

23

THE MAJOR PLAYERS

A series of quite different acts were played out in Australia in the substitution of a British for an Aboriginal economy and society, and significantly different explanations are required for important parts of the process. Nevertheless, there were some common ingredients throughout and it is convenient to bring these to the fore at the outset. In particular, we need to appreciate the scale and nature of the differences between the two cultures insofar as these differences affected the takeover process.

The following tabulation endeavours to lay out a limited array of preconditions and modes of operation relevant to the British and Aboriginal economies and their interaction. In each item, opposing conditions of each side in the confrontation are entered in very summary form to try to capture the general array of opportunities for accommodation and conflict. Obviously it is impossible to incorporate variety and detail. What are perhaps more important to appreciate are firstly the range of contrasts and secondly the fact that neither side understood the variety and depth of the differences. In other words, the cost of information required to span the gulf between the two sides made errors of understanding virtually certain and, in the last resort, was a price that neither side was willing to pay.

British in Australia	*Aborigines*
1. Market activity, trade and exchange	1. Limited trade and exchange
2. Profit-oriented business	2. Satisfaction of ends in common
3. Specialisation of activity	3. Joint quasi-household functions with gender division of labour
4. Fixed residential and work locations	4. Migratory activity and associations
5. Directed tasks by employers	5. Variable and adaptive group tasks
6. Monoculture	6. Multi-resource use and management

7. Domesticated pastoral animals	7. Hunting including use of fire
8. Extensive unfree labour (in most locations)	8. Free workforce subject to non-deviance
9. Written language and rules	9. Unwritten tribal laws and ritual
10. Hierarchies in work and society	10. Limited hierarchies
11. Both central and privatised order	11. Group order and enforcement
12. Private transferable property	12. (Essentially) communal property
13. Enforceable private contracts	13. Inter-group obligations
14. Communicable crowd diseases	14. Few communicable crowd diseases

Had the Aborigines possessed some tradeable objects, the outcome might have been different, though even in the case of the Amerindians, for whom such items as furs were available for trade, the social and demographic change was catastrophic. Indeed, it is possible that the immediate obstacle to a peaceful outcome was rather that the British had little of esteem to offer the Aborigines. Unaccustomed to major differences in natural endowment between areas within Australia and hence to extensive specialised interchange, Aborigines could not easily be drawn into a transaction network by the British. At the initial points of contact, there appear to have been a few trade items — for example, British axes in exchange for kangaroo meat or Aboriginal women. It is indeed possible that these few items helped to stave off confrontation for a brief period and contributed to the apparent 'peaceful' perception of Aborigines in the first instance. In the (not so very) long run, however, it appears that it was only after Aboriginal society had been radically disrupted that some British goods came to be widely valued by remnant Aborigines: first liquor and subsequently blankets, flour, sugar and tobacco, drawing Aborigines into a (dependent) market or welfare relationship.

Equally, in the absence of strong hierarchies and centralised government, Aborigines could not readily organise concerted resistance in such a way as to present effective battle lines to the British. This is not to imply non-resistance. Resistance tended typically to be piecemeal. This seems to be true even of the strong resistance offered after the first few years of the original Botany Bay settlement and in Van Diemen's Land. It is doubtful whether the British had much superiority in military technology and it seems likely that concerted attacks by spears could have imposed heavy costs on troops and settlers armed only with muzzle-loading rifles. But Aboriginal dependence on hunting and gathering, with limited storage potential, as well as commitments to sacred sites and ceremonial gatherings largely enforced the diversion of groups to peaceful production, consumption and other tasks, in other words away from sustained warfare. This frequently exposed them to risk of British attacks on dispersed hunting and gathering bands and ceremonial gatherings, and even to British misinterpretation of hunting bands as war bands. One possibility of sustaining warfare was open — transferring British foodstocks to Aborigines, thus allowing fighters to combine warfare and food acquisition in one. It was not until late in the confrontation in eastern Australia that some efforts at concerted resistance appear to have been made by Queensland and New South Wales Aborigines; the same condition applied in Van Diemen's Land. By then, however, only a rearguard action was feasible and in conditions in which the Aborigines had, in any event, no place to which to retreat.

Historical options for Australian Aborigines appear then to have been narrowed largely to either substantial integration within a dominantly British economy and society by adaptation to British modes of behaviour or both social and demographic destruction through starvation or violence. Small numbers might seek traditional behaviour in isolation. Given that it had taken the British several thousand years to attain their social and economic structure and institutions, it may seem inconceivable that the first option was a realistic one for Australian Aborigines *en masse*. Transfer by Aborigines into low-paid activities did not, however, demand such a massive technical transformation. Indeed, given the pressures on British migrants to learn by doing in terms of the Australian ecology, Aborigines possessed information of high value to the British. Aborigines were, in fact, frequently employed for this purpose by government, explorers and settlers. What a sustained transfer required was, however, a fundamental cultural debasement on the side of the Aborigines and willingness on the part of the British to accept them even at the level of low-paid labour.

Whether interaction was by way of trade, violence or Aboriginal submergence in or by the British economy and society, the terms of that choice and the conditions of its outcome depended on the prevailing law and its enforcement. Effectively, two and perhaps three legal systems operated, neither known to or understood by either side. Two were formal British and Aboriginal law, with the British possessing a defined mode of enforcement in relation to personal and property infringements and the Aborigines adopting a less explicit and unqualified stance dependent on verbal communication. The third was a privatised law, the law of the frontier, the application by individual British immigrants of the law of force rather than the force of law. At times, British privatised law was supported or condoned by formal authority, confusing the Aboriginal interpretation of their opponents. These issues applied to land rights, access to resources (including women), and concepts of trespass, damage to property and personal injury and killing. Whereas, in theory, formal British law demanded punishment of the specific wrong-doer, Aboriginal law was less discriminating or specific; it applied to members of groups rather than to individuals. In fact, in the application of frontier privatised law, the distinction largely disappeared and, indeed, privatised British action tended often to become pre-emptive or preventative rather than a requital for wrongdoing.

Law, economics or warfare apart, contact between the British and the Aborigines exposed both sides to a different array of social problems in the form of any diseases carried by the other and to which either side was not immune or resistant. These issues had earlier unfolded for indigenous populations in the Americas, with disastrous results for American populations. Aboriginal populations were not quite as isolated from the rest of the world as the people of the Americas. Nevertheless, the cost of isolation through their exposure to European–Asian diseases was extremely high. In contrast with Africans, Aborigines appear to have carried few diseases to transmit to Europeans. At this level, the exchange in Australia appears as wholly one-sided, favouring the eventual victor in the takeover process.

It is convenient to leave disease aside to begin with and concentrate on economics, law and violence. The two latter issues are the most prominent in the historical literature and, indeed, in modern Australian perceptions of race relations and of the prospects of the Aborigines. Nevertheless, as we will see, disease, law, economics and violence are all interrelated. Because it is essentially a precondition of British–Aboriginal interaction, it is useful to begin with law.

24

ABORIGINES AND BRITISH LAW

For both the British and the Aborigines, conventional law dealt with property rights and relations between individuals and groups (Castles, 1982; Hanks and Keon-Cohen, 1984; Williams, 1987). In the British case, it was supposed to be declared, knowable and capable of enforcement (granted any physical difficulties of policing). So far as Aborigines were concerned, law was customary, not written, and handed down gradually between generations. For both groups, international law and law relating to conquest were obscure issues.

Whatever other matters may have been involved, law relating to land rights was fundamental as the basis for Aboriginal hunting and gathering, the location of sacred sites and hence the foundation of much of their ritual. British entry into Australia inevitably impinged, to say the least, on those land rights. In fact, British acknowledgement of indigenous land rights was an obscure legal matter. Moreover, there was a basic problem of interpretation of the appropriate action to be taken as between centralised British (Whitehall) authority and colonial British authority. British (Whitehall) professions that they sought to protect the welfare of 'the natives' conflicted with their action to enter and occupy Aboriginal areas. British colonial authority dealt with both Whitehall and the immediate processes of resource transfer from Aborigines to local settlers, to whom British (Whitehall and colonial) authority to occupy land was given.

For their part, Aboriginal land areas belonged to traditional occupiers, a word that British entry made ambiguous. So far as Aborigines were concerned, entry into areas owned by any group might be made by permission, and the exchange of gifts and resources might similarly be exploited if appropriate compensation were made. Even so, the presence of foreigners, whether other Aborigines or British, was tolerable only within severe time constraints.

The recognition of land rights was basic to the Aboriginal response to British arrival. That recognition was accorded in the case of the Maoris in New Zealand.

A private attempt by Wentworth to buy massive parts of the south island of New Zealand was ridiculed as 'a job to end all jobs' and thrown out by the New South Wales governor, Gipps. Basically it conflicted with imperial objects and the rights of the Crown. Formal recognition of indigenous rights was accorded by the British government in the Treaty of Waitangi in 1840. The contrast between rejecting private action and approving public action is notable. It reflects the conflict between British government (Crown) views of its relations with indigenous people on the one hand and with its own nationals and their relations with indigenes on the other. The Treaty of Waitangi did not prevent British takeover or avoid extensive racial violence and warfare. It excluded any private initiative to pre-empt Crown rights. It did little to secure indigenous rights.

When possession of (a geographically undefined) New South Wales was taken, four distinct sets of legal relations were involved. One was the Crown in relation to indigenes; a second was the Crown in relation to its own nationals; a third was the Crown's nationals vis-à-vis indigenes; a fourth was the Crown versus other nationals. Here was fertile ground for confusion and legal sophistry. Until the middle of the eighteenth century, British law in respect of colonial areas was essentially medieval. It recognised a distinction between colonies acquired by conquest and empty areas that were merely 'entered'. As variety in imperial interests developed, a new concept emerged, an appeal back to *lex Romana*, proposed by Vattel in 1758. This was a special interpretation of the Roman concept of *res* or *terra nullius* — a thing or land of nobody. Vattel introduced the distinction between indigenous populations who tilled or did not till the soil, a distinction determining on this form of legalism whether an area was occupied or not.

As hunter gatherers, the Australian Aborigines did not 'occupy' Australia though they were accorded the rights — and obligations — of British citizens, nominally protected by but also subject to all British law. Influential as Vattel's views may have been, they were not codified in statutes or appealed to as justification in case law until well into the nineteenth century. The early case decisions appear to have been discarded by colonial governors (particularly Gipps), whether they rested on concepts of *terra nullius* or not. Gubernatorial evaluations appear to have been swayed by governors' own perceptions of relations with British authority; by their own perceptions of colonial invasion of their authority; by perceived immediate risks, physical or political, within the colony(ies); or by inability to contain settlement and achieve administrative control of private actions. In this confused climate, the British authorities could instruct governors to 'care' for 'the natives' and, at the same time authorise land grants to their own nationals, free or ex-convict. Moreover, a governor (Hunter, Arthur) might and did authorise settlers to take all appropriate action to protect themselves against Aboriginal attacks and, in Arthur's case, declare martial law, freeing British settlers from normal penalties for killing or maiming persons (Aborigines).

Recognition was indeed threatened in Australia when John Batman attempted to purchase land from Victorian Aborigines in 1835. Though Batman's purchase offer was trifling, the principle of recognition of land rights was anathema to the colonial governor. Rights reserved to the Crown and the authority of the governor were threatened. In fact, Batman's project collided not merely with gubernatorial or regal interests but with many other private interests then intent on occupying the interior grasslands, woodlands and riverlands of southeastern Australia. So far as

Aborigines were concerned, British law — with its rights and it obligations — was circumscribed within the limits of conditions of peace or by the delimitation of authorised areas of settlement. British settlers might occupy Aboriginal lands within those limits, could by implication deprive Aborigines of resources and could buy, sell or receive as grants areas of land within those limits, subject to the (very) distant Whitehall admonitions to care for Aboriginal welfare. The inconsistencies between these ends were never squarely confronted.

The execution of several whites for the Myall Creek massacre in New South Wales seems an aberration due to one man's conscience (Atkinson and Aveling, 1987). Where private British settlers, in effect, defied or ignored British colonial authority and moved beyond prescribed settlement areas — squatted — an essentially privatised 'law' prevailed. A similar privatised 'law' was relevant to the Bass Strait sealers and to all Van Demonians when martial law was declared. Without martial law as protection for Europeans, private solutions persisted without government intervention. Even when Port Phillip was accepted as an area for settlement in 1835, the physical problems of administration meant that private 'law' largely prevailed over the pious advice of Whitehall or colonial legal or administrative attitudes. But this was a general outcome. At the frontier, where the contest was most heightened, it was typically private 'law', the law of force not the force of law, that prevailed. Not uncommonly, in Tasmania and Western Australia and, later on, in Queensland, private 'law' formally loosed by authority was applied to Aborigines who resisted or got in the way (Kennedy, 1902; Loos, 1982; Plomley, 1966; Stannage, 1981).

Victors do more than write history. They also write the law. Privatised or official law was weighted overwhelmingly on the side of British settlers. The Myall Creek massacre apart, British settlers could encroach on Aboriginal resources with impunity from British (though not from Aboriginal) law and could commit acts of violence, including killing, substantially with impunity. They could charge Aborigines with offences against British property, including the killing or maiming of livestock. If Aborigines reacted to a loss of resources by attacking British persons or their property it was a one-sided legal matter for the settlers. Under British law, Aborigines as non-Christians could not give evidence against British individuals or in their own defence. One might be tempted to conclude that the ambivalence and sophistry of formal British law and the application of privatised 'law' was a sufficient condition for the destruction of Aboriginal society and economy, given Aboriginal dependence on resources available from the land. In fact, the options of compensation or of Aboriginal incorporation in the British colonial economy could have altered substantially the legal conflict between the two sides.

25

THE ECONOMICS OF TAKEOVER

Australian history writing on Aborigines has moved from one extreme convention to a second. The first, a long-established one, is that Aborigines were of no significance in British settlement but largely faded away without resistance and with little in the way of incorporation in British economic activity. The second is a very recent revisionist story of extreme violence on both sides, with strong Aboriginal opposition and official and private violence by British settlers (Blainey, 1982; Elder, 1988; Loos, 1982; Reynolds, 1981; Robson, 1983; Turnbull, 1974). The first reflects the fact of Aboriginal depopulation, without inquiring into the reasons. The second derives from an exclusive focus on acts of violence and tends to create an impression of a noble Aboriginal defence of homelands and vicious behaviour by intruders, whether individuals or officials. It is suggested here that both interpretations are open to serious doubt. Let us look first at the mutual economic opportunities that could have led and did lead along two different paths, one to Aboriginal integration and at least partial compensation, the other to violence. There can be little doubt that British entrants did seek to acquire access to resources formerly used by Aborigines. Since they sought to produce their own food supplies and later to produce pastoral products for export, they necessarily sought to occupy Aboriginal lands. Economic interest in a takeover process must be recognised as a major determinant of the outcome. It should be stressed at this point, however, that this economic approach takes no explicit account of either racism or what appears to have been a fundamental problem, communicable diseases.

Given Aboriginal multi-resource use and seasonality of movements, British entry into Aboriginal areas could create major resource problems in a variety of ways (Altman, 1987; Berndt and Tonkinson, 1988; Blainey, 1985; Christie, 1979; Dawson, 1880; Jones, 1980). Habitats could be disturbed and strategic resources destroyed either by British persons or by livestock. Only a few such resources needed to be disturbed for a traditional 'equilibrium' to be upset or even for crisis to develop. There might then be a greatly limited seasonal fallback for Aborigines. Secondly, the mobility of Aborigines could be constrained through denial of access to specific areas, thereby exposing them to seasonal shortages. Thirdly, Aboriginal production methods (particularly the use of fire but also their dependence on mobility) might be constrained by private rule and enforcement, thereby reducing the volume or seasonality of their harvests.

By contrast, Aboriginal presence on, near or in passage through lands that the British occupied or sought to occupy exposed settlers both to personal risks and to the likelihood of destruction of property, particularly livestock (Bride, 1898; Flanagan, 1862; Reece, 1974; Rowley, 1972; Ryan, 1981). This destruction might be general, as when Aborigines killed or maimed animals *en masse*, either as retribution for entry or in recognition of the ecological changes wrought by animals. Or it might be limited where Aborigines sought to exploit such colonial animal foods as were available. Fire threatened British possessions and persons and potentially exposed them to high settlement costs. It was not recognised as an instrument of resource management. Given Aboriginal communal attitudes to property, there was the frequent and indiscriminate potential for action that British settlers classed legally as theft and a punishable offence. Finally, Aboriginal assemblies for ceremonial purposes could create uncertainty and fear.

In what follows, one word that runs through the old and the new convention is crucial. This is the word 'settler', applied indiscriminately in the literature to the British who exploited Australian land resources or engaged in conflict with Aborigines. 'Settlers' need to be disaggregated into convict, ex-convict and free; into agricultural, pastoral and urban immigrants; and into large and small land-owners. All had quite different interests and motives (racism apart) and these need to be uncovered.

In the first major settlement locations, predominantly convict groups were established in New South Wales and Van Diemen's Land and there was a substantial convict presence initially in Victoria (and later in Queensland). These settlements were at first relatively compact. After the end of the Napoleonic Wars, the first two began to expand rapidly into their respective hinterlands and to go through a major socio-economic transformation. Despite convict influx, free and freed individuals came rapidly into prominence. Initially, in both cases, access to landownership was by Crown grant, supplemented by Crown sales, with some aggregation made possible by the emergence of a private land market. By 1820, in New South Wales, immigrant occupation of land came increasingly to rest on illegal squatting, which tended to emphasise large holdings engaged in relatively non-labour intensive pastoralism. Though settlement focused on riverlands, it fanned out widely in dispersed areas in the inland. The New South Wales workforce to 1840, particularly at the moving frontier, was then a mix of convict and ex-convict employees, with some free wage earners, comparatively few in number, on each holding, all engaged by relatively large landowners. Multiple ownership of properties necessarily meant a high degree of absentee ownership, with direct and immediate responsibility resting on employees. Agriculture, as distinct from farming, tended to be concentrated in coastal locations. These features were broadly replicated in Victoria.

In Van Diemen's Land, by contrast, access to land was dominantly by Crown grants made in relatively restricted acreages (the Van Diemen's Land Company was special) with a high proportion of the recipients ex-convict. Pastoralism was a significant activity. But, relative to New South Wales, rich inland river flats and rainfall and climatic conditions favoured agriculture. Hence a comparatively large number of small ex-convict settlers were spread north–south through the centre of the island, many of them engaged in relatively labour-intensive agriculture. Given the size of holdings, even allowing for some private market aggregations, small numbers of employed wage earners, convict and ex-convict, were engaged on individual small farms. In contrast with the dispersed settlement in New South Wales and later Victoria, Van Diemen's Land farming became much more geographically concentrated throughout the 1820s, closing on a central rectangle of the island. As a food resource, this farming also became vital to the pastoral structure of the New South Wales economy.

Up to the 1840s, the severest violence appears to have occurred in Van Diemen's Land (Plomley, 1966; Roberts, 1935; Turnbull, 1974) and south-east Victoria (Bride, 1898; Presland, 1980), though there had been early conflict at Botany Bay (Barton, 1889; Collins, 1798) and along the New South Wales coast, and there was scattered and substantial physical confrontation in interior New South Wales, particularly during the late 1820s and into the 1830s (Atkinson and Aveling, 1987; Blainey, 1982). On the other hand, the coastal violence was quite long delayed and a similar experience of comparative quiescence occurred in Van Diemen's Land until the 1820s. Within that timespan, a good deal of peaceful interaction between the two sides occurred, with intermittent violence. After 1820, violence in Van Diemen's Land rose rapidly to a peak. By 1830 only a tiny fraction of the original Aboriginal population remained. Whether the depopulation was due primarily to violence or other factors is a central question. What is immediately important is to observe the switch in race relations and the change in attitude to the presence of Aborigines on lands claimed by the British.

In all areas, there is another characteristic. This is that large frontier landholders often appeared to accommodate Aborigines, to allow their presence on properties and to employ them in a variety of ways. We cannot achieve a census of this behaviour and clearly less is known about smallholders. In New South Wales and Victoria, at the inland frontiers beyond the coastal fringe, smallholders were almost necessarily few, pastoralism demanding relatively large properties. Despite the absence of completely satisfactory information, it is nevertheless clear that one can recite a substantial list of largeholders (or free managers of large holdings) who appear to have attempted a substantial degree of integration of Aborigines — Ogilvie, Dangar, White, Petrie, Curr, Durack, Dryden, Robertson, Bell, Taylor and so on. *The New South Wales Inquiry into Aborigines, Bride's Letters from Victorian Pioneers* and Robinson's *Journals* (Presland, 1977) give ample testimony on both the New South Wales and Victorian frontiers during the 1830s and 1840s. The terms of integration may have been stern but some largeholders did attempt to employ Aborigines as well as allow dependants to remain on their properties. By contrast, absentee ownership exposed British employees to decisions about accommodation, integration, restriction and violence. In Victoria, Robinson's *Journal* again indicates violence and aggression from employees. In New South Wales, the famous or infamous Myall Creek massacre was wholly the work of an uncontrolled band of employed convicts and ex-convicts (Atkinson and Aveling, 1987; Elder, 1988).

We cannot penetrate adequately the incomplete record and the information and misinformation now available to us. So-called 'battles' were fought, but the reported dead on either side seem remarkably few. Many accounts of settlers' killing of Aborigines strongly suggest the same incident being reported and reapplied to several locations, exaggerating the actual violence. It is not suggested that aggression was solely initiated by the British — far from it. In Botany Bay, in the central grasslands of New South Wales, on the river flats of Van Diemen's Land, there is ample evidence of Aboriginal initiative with a considerable killing and destructive efficiency. To this extent, at least, the attempt to generate a picture of Aborigines coming eventually to fight for their possessions is unquestioned. But if we cannot penetrate into the record and cannot rely on the limited evidence of differences in behaviour patterns, it is worth exploring whether, in different sets of circumstances, there were *a priori* reasons for expecting the little that we know of history to have developed and to be more general. Let us concentrate on frontier conditions and on mainland southeastern Australia. To begin with, we exclude considerations of overt racism, inbuilt prejudice or idiosyncratic behaviour — all of which may have been important.

As the frontier developed it spread out, leaving behind it an enlarging area relatively securely occupied by British immigrants, whether as urban and village locations or integrated farms. Within these settled areas, there remained few Aborigines and here the greater proportion of employers and employees were to be found. Within this settled area, colonial order was reasonably effective, including colonial rules with respect to work conditions and wage rates for convicts, ex-convicts, colonial born and free British immigrant wage earners. British settlers and employees clearly recognised the considerable risks of confrontation with Aborigines in extending the frontier. For mainland settlers, moving beyond declared counties of settlement, this risk was offset by zero land price (a condition that applied also at an early stage in the Botany Bay settlement) and by the fact that, as settlement extended inland, they could often avoid personal exposure by being absentee owners. On the other hand, absenteeism meant reliance on managers and/or overseers. In Tasmania, the issues were different. Grants were the predominant mode of access to land and entry to the frontier was typically made by new grantees — to a large extent, ex-convicts whose terms had recently expired. Whether as relatively small-scale pastoralists or farmers, these frontier grantees sought only a limited employed workforce.

The first issue is, then, to contrast the supply conditions of the employed workforce in 'settled' versus 'frontier' conditions. The incentive for wage earners to move to frontier locations required a substantial margin over employment in settled areas. So far as the free or freed workforce was concerned, substantially higher wage rates were demanded. Even for convicts, who could be directed, greater freedom, provision of dwellings and arms for protection meant higher rewards for them and thus higher costs for employers. But as convicts neared the date of expiry of their sentences, attractions were necessary to retain them — in other words, their rewards were shifted progressively towards those of free and freed labour. Within a timespan of a few years, one might, then, submerge the different employee groups into one. A general condition then applied: the elasticity of supply of wage earners to frontier employment was significantly less than in settled areas.

The relatively low elasticity of supply of labour tended to leave frontier employers on the mainland with a labour shortage. Rewards demanded by employees tended to leave them with an inadequate workforce, even for high labour costs. The availability of convicts helped them to suppress wage demands somewhat and it is possible that they colluded to ensure some wage restraint. This collusion would have been supported by the harsh Master and Servants Act, even if these Acts were not very efficiently enforced. Frontier employers almost invariably had an unsatisfied demand for labour. Complaints about convict rural assignment in the 1820s and 1830s were widespread.

Some employers, like the Australian Agricultural Company, directly imported free labour. There was also a general pressure for the introduction of indentured labour (not only in New South Wales but also in the supposedly free colony of South Australia). Both were expensive sources of labour. The alternative was Aboriginal labour.

So long as Aborigines had preserved at least a substantial part of their resource supply intact and behaved largely in a precontact manner, their behaviour pattern (in actual hunting and gathering as distinct from the allocation of time to other activities of ritual, education and so on) generated a supply-side response in hunting and gathering that matched broadly that of the British employees in relation to frontier employment. Aborigines, substantially undisturbed, could garner food within limited work hours and preferred to allocate time in other ways beyond that limit. They, too, had a highly inelastic supply curve for labour in hunting and gathering. All available evidence suggests strongly that their dietary supplies, in undisturbed conditions, exceeded those of the British. If they were to become employees on pastoral properties, it was essential that their ecological conditions be significantly disrupted.

This disturbance was achieved most directly by the introduction of sheep and cattle, destroying yam supplies, breaking down shrubbery, consuming grasses, disturbing river systems and so on. As British animal populations increased, this disturbance grew, reducing supplies from both hunting and gathering. Under these conditions, Aborigines within traditional locations were forced to allocate more time to hunting and gathering as a first option. In other words, the supply curve of Aboriginal labour time in hunting and gathering flattened or became more elastic. More time was required in these activities and less time was available for other desired ends; their society was under pressure.

If the Aboriginal response was not violence in an attempt to preserve their resource supplies, the opportunity then developed for frontier pastoralists to offer employment to at least part of the Aboriginal workforce. Depending on how far animal destruction of resources occurred, British pastoralists could cover their labour demands at *or below* the British wage rate even though Aborigines began with a superior consumption level. In other words, there was a potential for Aborigines to be used to undercut British wage earner standards. This would be the case even if the Aborigines selected as pastoral workers did not themselves benefit wholly from high wage rates. Their communal sharing rules would tend to redistribute benefits accruing to those not employed and, in fact, help to preserve a surplus labour force on the properties. But this introduced an added issue. Aboriginal employees, in forgoing directly the personal benefit of earnings as a result of communal sharing, reduced themselves to the dependent remnant — in other words, continued to attract the evaluation of 'inferior'.

Pastoralists frequently complained about the apparent inability of Aborigines to provide a sustained labour effort. This raises an interesting issue of major significance to twentieth century perceptions as well as early race relations. Aborigines were accustomed to migratory activity and this may be at the foundation of pastoralists' claims in the nineteenth century (as it is frequently 100 years later). But there is another possibility which should be explored in both historical and modern contexts: were and are Aborigines so subject to malnutrition from ecological disturbance (and perhaps from nutrition-related diseases) that they sought or were compelled to seek at least part of their traditional food resources to try to cope with malnutrition? It seems, intuitively, likely that both conditions operated then and now.

Pastoral employers could act to ensure severe constraints on resource supplies. Aborigines' use of fire could be prevented or limited. Access to water resources could be controlled. Gathering of foods over pastoral properties could be constrained. Actions of this type would be most effective if the pastoralists' control prevailed over large areas — that is, if large pastoral properties existed or pastoralists acted in collusion. Small farmers had less individual control and the larger the number of small owners required to command substantial areas the less efficient would such economic coercion be.

We have, then, different sets of relations between different groups of Aborigines on the one hand and different British groups on the other. Large-scale pastoralists had an incentive to go a considerable distance in destroying the ecology of the Aborigines but to preserve at least substantial numbers alive, dependent and living on their properties. This incentive would alter if Aborigines responded with violence, destroying either British property (including livestock) or British individuals, but subject to this, large pastoralists could be expected to focus on forcing an increased elasticity of supply of Aboriginal labour in Aboriginal hunting and gathering. This would enhance the pastoralists' latitude in bargaining on work conditions for Aborigines on pastoral properties. Large pastoralists had, subject to Aboriginal violence, a limited desire to destroy Aborigines. This proposition conforms to the known statements of attitudes and experience of many large British pastoralists.

Frontier wage earners could, in some degree, act independently to disrupt Aboriginal ecology. But that would weaken their own bargaining power. Their interest would tend to be concentrated on destroying Aborigines, particularly male Aborigines. This could be qualified by absentee ownership. Where British pastoral-owners were rarely on a given property, employees could take on Aboriginal labour to do the work for which they were employed and, by paying them in kind (with sheep meat), do so without loss of reward to themselves and without costs being known to owners. This latter outcome collided, however, with the interests of strictly convict employees who were allowed and even encouraged to deliver their services, for pay, to surrounding employers, subject to the conditions of their servitude. In this event, convict employees had an incentive to destroy Aborigines on neighbouring properties. This latter tendency may have been one of the issues underlying the Myall Creek massacre, where convict and ex-convict employees killed Aborigines on a neighbouring property.

There were other factors in wage earner/Aboriginal relations that arose from work conditions on either side. Pastoral wage earners were exposed to isolation in tending sheep and hence to the direct effects of Aboriginal violence, sheep theft or killing. They could be held responsible for depredations by Aborigines. Equally, they could transfer blame to Aborigines if their own inefficiency resulted in stock losses. These conditions added to their tendency to violence towards Aborigines.

Small farmers had an interest comparable to that of employees, though the mechanisms differed. Not demanding much in the way of employed labour, they had little regard for Aborigines as a potential workforce. Moreover, since they occupied comparatively small areas, they could not individually or in small groups control Aboriginal behaviour patterns. Small settlements tended to lie, for a considerable time (until 1820 approximately in both New South Wales and Van Diemen's Land), close to sources of military or police protection, often an ineffective support to individuals but, when applied, a vigorous physical reprimand for Aborigines. The settlers were exposed to Aboriginal presence, a sense at least of threat and a reality, sporadically, of Aboriginal attempts to acquire settlers' belongings, including livestock, and of violent Aboriginal attacks. For small settlers, even limited property damage by Aborigines could be disastrous. Small settlers' responses were almost invariably antagonistic.

Small settlements spread around the coastal areas of New South Wales and up and down the central spine of Van Diemen's Land after the end of the Napoleonic Wars as the flow of convicts increased. As settlement became more concentrated, their joint rather than individual extension placed rapidly rising ecological pressures on Aborigines. On the New South Wales coast, Aborigines were able to retreat into the mountains for food and a haven after violent encounters. In Van Diemen's Land, however, there was no such potential for relief from pressure for either side. By the mid-twenties, small British settlements collectively prevented the seasonal movements of Aborigines from the coast to the inland river resources. Aborigines had no option but to attack in an effort to reopen access to the rivers. Their choices had a curious cultural constraint in that, for reasons that are obscure, Tasmanian Aborigines refused to eat scale fish, relying on shellfish. This was an inadequate annual resource. In Van Diemen's Land, then, the Aborigines and settlers were placed in direct and increasing confrontation throughout the 1820s. There was considerable loss of life on both sides, though the numbers are impossible to estimate. Thus in one month in 1828, at Oatlands in Van Diemen's Land, twenty inquests were held on British killed by Aborigines (Robson, 1983). So far as the latter were concerned, we have the official population estimates of 7000 Aborigines in 1818 and only a few hundred remaining in 1833. What we do not know is how far this depopulation was the product of settlers' violence. Clearly, in Van Diemen's Land such violence was prominent.

Aborigines everywhere, but particularly in Van Diemen's Land, had another socio-economic problem in their relations with the British, though not primarily with the settlers. This was the taking of Aboriginal women, particularly on the north coast, by sealers. As indicated in Part II, Aboriginal women were crucial in securing food supplies for Aborigines. Though an early trade in women for goods appears to have occurred, the rise in the numbers of sealers to 1820 led to increasingly violent abductions of women not merely for sexual purposes but to supply a workforce for the sealers (the abduction and rape of Truganini and the killing of her husband and two relatives is a well known example). Robinson's surveys of Aboriginal populations cannot be accepted as accurate. Nevertheless, his report of one Aboriginal group in Van Diemen's Land in 1831 as composed of approximately 700 males and only two women (Plomley, 1966), even if the sex ratio is radically wrong, implies the potential for drastic reduction through non-reproduction. Imbalance between the sexes is represented almost everywhere in the southern half of the mainland by 1840, indicative in part of the transfer of Aboriginal women from their tribal groups to serve British purposes.

South Australian and Western Australian occupation by free settlers was supposed to be different from the eastern convict colonies. In fact, essentially the same sequence unfolded and similar economic tendencies appear to have applied. In Western Australia (Stannage, 1981), the fragility of the early settlement of free persons led rapidly to antagonism, progressive conflict and the forcing of Aborigines away from settled areas into country with poorer resource supplies. After 1835, the provision of military support to individual settlers enhanced this process of compelling Aborigines to withdraw to seek sustenance outside traditional areas. By the beginning of the 1840s, the remnants of south-west Australian Aborigines were substantially subject to British law and enforcement.

In South Australia, the early establishment of wheat farming in the south east at once eliminated a vital resource for Aborigines and made it necessary for the (small) settlers to prevent wholly the use of fire by Aborigines and remove them from settlement areas. This was merely a peculiar twist to a general tendency towards a violent outcome where small settlement existed.

By the beginning of the 1830s in Van Diemen's Land and by 1840 on the mainland, moves were well underway to remove remnant Aborigines from exposure to British violence. Protectorates, missions and the allocation of reserves were the common remedy (Rowley, 1973). In Van Diemen's Land and the south of Western Australia, Aborigines were essentially locked up — on Bass Strait islands and, in the West, on Rottnest island. Here small remnant bands played out the last of their lives. On the south-east mainland, protectorates failed to contain the Aborigines, whose numbers dwindled after contact with a variety of diseases. As settlement moved northwards, remnants continued to survive as partially employed, partially dependent groups on pastoral properties, and disrupted bands attempted to maintain their traditional ways of life in the bush but subject to British locational and mobility constraints and, generally, drastically undernourished and demoralised.

It awaited the second half of the nineteenth century for a substantial repetition of conflicting interests, attempts at accommodation and violence to accompany the drastic reduction of the northern Australian Aboriginal populations, particularly in Queensland. In South Australia (Rowley, 1973) Aborigines had a brief moment of integration when the discovery of gold denuded pastoral properties of British labour. For a few years in the early 1850s, Aborigines became the essential workforce for pastoralists until the decline of alluvial gold and the return of labour eliminated their opportunities. In general terms, in any area occupied by British immigrants, Aboriginal populations were decimated and the remnants generally degraded within two or three decades of frontier settlement. But we still have to face the question whether this was due primarily to violence and resource transfer or to some other factors.

For those interested in a possible technical if very simple representation of the essential issues, Figure 4 (opposite) may help to encapsulate the economic issues of possible accommodation and probable conflict. In this figure, there are three

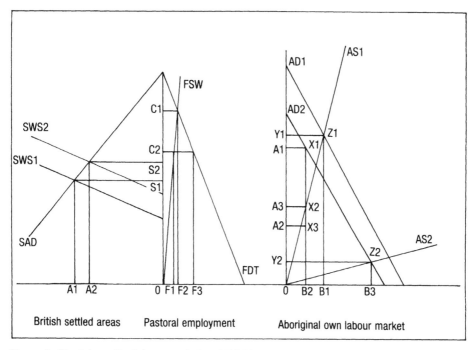

Figure 4: Aborigines, the labour market and British settlement

interrelated panels. The first panel relates to employment in areas fully under control of British settlers and from which Aborigines have been eliminated, the second to frontier pastoral employment and the third to Aborigines' own economy and a concept of Aborigines' own labour market. In the first panel, the 'settled area labour market'. SAD, indicates the demand for labour and SWS1 the supply of (British) labour prior to opening the frontier. Wage rates settle at OS1. With the opening of the pastoral frontier in panel 2, the line FSW indicates an extremely inelastic labour supply. With demand conditions indicated by the line FDT (total frontier demand for labour), workers will seek to demand OC1 rewards. Pastoralists are assumed to appeal to legal constraints or collude in limiting wage offers to OC2 at which level they will attract only OF2 British labour. But at that wage level, they would wish to employ a total workforce of OF3. Potentially, the difference might be supplied by Aborigines. This labour shortfall might be greater or less depending on whether Aborigines were, or were regarded as, inferior or superior to British employees. Let us assume for simplicity that there was no quality differential.

In panel 3, the Aborigines are assumed to place a high value on the absorption of their time in ritual, leisure, education and the like. AS1 then indicates a highly inelastic supply of their own labour in communal hunting and gathering to satisfy their communal food, clothing and housing needs [= potential wage goods]. In precontact conditions, their demand for this labour time is represented by the line

AD1 [it reflects the need, in certain seasonal or ecological conditions, for Aborigines to divert increasing amounts of their time to hunting and gathering but cannot for viability reasons go to the base line]. The unit 'reward' of OY1, at a high level, represents the conventional understanding of high living standards for Aborigines.

However, pastoral [strictly animal] intervention in the ecology so degrades Aboriginal resource conditions that they are forced to adapt to a more elastic labour supply condition in their own hunting and gathering activities. But this implies a greater Aboriginal willingness to be integrated and accept some employment on pastoral properties. Let us assume that some Aborigines are willing to accept employment contracts. If pastoralists offer Aborigines a reward of OA1 initially, equal to the wage rate offered to British employees, OB2 Aborigines are willing to be integrated. With communal sharing rules, the 'tribal' demand for own labour falls, say, to AD2. Pastoralists, at this wage level want OF3–OF2 of Aboriginal labour, which might be greater or less than the supply offered.

Tribal Aborigines can now reap only OY2 rewards per head on their own part. This implies some damage to and possible destruction of their traditional values, and their leisure time shrinks. There is then a large differential between OA1 and OY2 per head, within which pastoralists might bargain for an Aboriginal labour supply. Indicative possibilities are shown at OA2 and OA3 as two levels at which pastoralists might expect to acquire the same delivery of Aboriginal labour. The threat to British wage earner standards is clear.

Two points are important. First, small settlers were not individually in a position to drive down the supply curve in the Aborigines' own labour market to AS2; only largeholders could do this. Small settlers could do it as concentrated groups but had no employment offers to make to Aborigines. Pastoralists, on the other hand, could manipulate the gradient of AS2 beyond the level achieved by their own livestock. They had an incentive to retain a (short-term viable) Aboriginal group on their property. Secondly, it was extremely difficult, assuming high precontact rewards for Aborigines, for pastoralists to alter the Aboriginal supply curve in such a way and to a degree that would allow a pastoral wage rate offer in combination with sufficient remnant hunting and gathering to leave the Aborigines satisfied. If the demand for ritual and so on (time allocated to non-wage goods) were highly inelastic, Aborigines would prefer some of their number to die. They could also have a strong incentive to violence, at least towards British livestock, as a compensation for food losses or in order to contain the losses of their traditional food supplies.

26

THE COMPOSITION AND DEMOGRAPHIC IMPACT OF DISEASE

In 1971, D. Barwick produced an excellent study of the mortality records of Victorian Aborigines who died between 1876 and 1912. She also made a study of the age structure and sex composition of tribal remnants in 1863, allowing a projection back of dates of birth. This study showed high mortality at early ages, high infant mortality and generally poor health conditions for 'protected' Aborigines throughout the period. Low birth rates (imputed back to the early nineteenth century) were ascribed to the prominence of venereal disease, which was prevalent until the 1850s, and the overwhelming cause of death for adults was respiratory disease. Liver, gastric and heart disease, along with a general category of 'infectious' diseases, were also signficant.

Barwick's study related to experience after the British takeover was completed. But it quantified and generally conformed to the comments by British settlers and protectors before 1850 — widespread venereal disease, early age mortality related to venereal, respiratory and other infectious diseases, low birth rates together with a sex imbalance in favour of males. The settlers and protectors before 1850 were impressed by the ease with which Aborigines died, as if they had lost the will to live or even 'willed themselves to die'. This was, apart from Van Diemen's Land, an Australia-wide assessment and applied in south-east Australia, in South and Western Australia, and later in Queensland.

This list of medically described diseases omitted one important infection, smallpox, as did most of the earlier commentary, and it did not give explicit consideration to the possible importance of tuberculosis. Equally, the generalised category of 'infectious diseases' did not clarify the relative importance of those regarded as childhood diseases in 'developed' societies (whooping cough, measles, mumps and the like) or the more general relevance of influenza. But it also focused on specific disease, going so far as to relate disease in many instances to malnutrition. It omitted, then, another basic issue, the psychological and emotional disturbances that accompanied the destruction of Aboriginal society.

The questions firstly of malnutrition and secondly of psychological disorders need to be recognised. Webb (personal communication) has shown that evidence of nutritional stress for Aborigines in the Murray Valley extended back over centuries but is non-existent elsewhere. He has also shown that this stress, while implying relatively dense precontact populations, was intermittent and not perennial. Elsewhere, early evidence of explorers testified to high nutritional standards (subject to some seasonal shortages) through the length and breadth of Australia *prior to British settlement*. After that settlement, the references at the frontier to 'blacks in a starving condition' abound. In general, malnutrition was a consequence of the British takeover.

So, too, is it likely that psychological disorders escalated after 1788. The violence and more importantly the loss of their lands and resources as a result of the British settlement of Australia represented a devastating blow for Aborigines. The other enforced adjustments of their migratory way of life, constraints on movement, the denial of the use of fire, the constraint on opportunity for ceremonial gatherings, the destruction of sacred sites and the taking of Aboriginal women were all elements in the takeover. For Aborigines, these changes eventually left no purpose in life, except for the relatively few willing and able to be integrated in the British–Australian economy. Here we are obviously on speculative ground. But between resistance and submission there may not have been much difference — both meant an early death — with the qualification that resistance could impose costs on opponents. Integration also meant close exposure to British-borne diseases. The takeover game was a no-win situation.

If problems of malnutrition and psychological disturbance were visible to frontier settlers, they were also dominant at the end of the takeover process. What was not necessarily visible — or at most partially so — were other infectious or contagious diseases that appear to have determined the numbers and composition of Aborigines who might resist, submit or integrate when they came in contact with the British.

Progressively over the years 1788 to 1850, Aborigines were exposed to introduced diseases. They were not unique in this. Worldwide experience suggests that the arrival of Europeans into the Americas, South Africa and the Pacific Islands brought depopulating diseases to which the indigenous populations were not immune (Burrows, 1958; Butlin, 1983; Cook, 1982; Cook and Borah, 1948; Kroeber *et al.*, 1925; Laidler and Gelfaud, 1971; Mooney, 1928; Stearn and Stearn, 1945). The Aborigines had little to return in kind. Insofar as Europeans did introduce diseases, the disease consequences should be treated as a significant functional — if unintended — part of the takeover process (the matter of smallpox is open to debate). The only question that one might ask about Australian Aborigines is why their fate might have been different from elsewhere.

Some of these issues have been discussed in my book *Our Original Aggression* (1983) and in Part III of this volume. Since I wish to focus on a particular experience as illustration, it may be helpful if some further repetition occurs here to help reference and recall. Sequentially, in eastern Australia, there were medically identified smallpox epidemics amongst the Aborigines at Botany Bay (but with some later evidence much farther afield) in 1789 (Collins, 1798; Hunter,

1798; Tench, 1961), and much more generally throughout eastern Australia during approximately 1829–31; venereal disease, both gonorrhea and syphilis, amongst the convicts and Botany Bay Aborigines at the beginning and subsequently among Aborigines in Van Diemen's Land before 1820 and throughout New South Wales and Victoria in the late 1820s and into the 1830s to 1850s; tuberculosis amongst convicts in the first settlement and, subsequently, colonial epidemics of influenza in 1820, 1826 and 1838; and whooping cough in 1828.

Australia was protected for a time by distance and ship size. It appears that increases in the speed and/or size of ships exposed the eastern continent by the beginning of the 1820s to the array of what were usually regarded as childhood diseases but which, in the case of the Aborigines, were potentially disastrous at all ages (Belcher, 1982; Butlin, 1983; Stannage, 1981). Except for smallpox, these diseases were easily transferable to Van Diemen's Land after 1820, and deliverable to Western Australia after 1829 and South Australia after 1836. In the case of venereal diseases, they were transferable to Van Diemen's Land, Victoria and probably South Australia by as early as 1800. The taking of Aboriginal women by sealers and the intrusion of escaped convicts into the bush accelerated transmission in Van Diemen's Land, Victoria and South Australia at an early stage.

In addition to these, British immigrants might be expected to be unwitting and unaffected carriers of diseases secreted and inactive in mucous but transferable as active diseases to exposed Aborigines. To add to the list of health problems assailing Aborigines, their tendency to die quickly of respiratory problems may have been due also to contact with atypical pneumonia or, as their resources were reduced by settlers and they came to rely more on birds for food, to psittacosis and meningitis.

In *Our Original Aggression* I attempted a simple modelling of some of these disease incidents using population dynamic models. These models are relatively crude *and apply to large areas, not localised ones*. Most epidemics are hit-and-miss processes, with some groups drastically affected and some lightly or not at all. The models do not assume that all persons were infected. The assumed mortality rates are averages for all areas, conforming to widespread experience but also setting low and high bounds for the outcome. Clearly, it would be sensible to pay more attention to mid-range outcomes. The mortality rates assumed are derived from a combination of recent Indian experience (for age- and sex-specific effects) and from world reports of mortality in areas in which the diseases were not endemic. These latter reports incorporate lack of care and support for both the infected and their dependants. Death rates from all diseases were typically strongly influenced by the availability of care and support systems. In Aboriginal societies, these systems were not available. Moreover, illness or death of members of the workforce carried the exposure of dependants to the risk of starvation. All these issues have to be taken into account in considering the impact of an epidemic in these conditions.

In the case of venereal diseases, the resulting reduced reproductive capability derives from Caldwell's studies in Africa (personal communication). The modelling is not intended to yield literal historical experience but to indicate what plausibly might have happened. Injection of these diseases might be proxied by the rise of sealing activity in and around Bass Strait, particularly over the years 1798–1820.

Table 10: Projected effects of introduced smallpox and venereal disease

	Lower Limit Exposure VD & Smallpox	Medium Limit Exposure VD & Smallpox	High Limit Exposure VD & Smallpox
1788	100.00	100.00	100.00
1790	69.55	55.05	40.82
1795	69.47	56.20	45.01
1800	70.36	57.95	45.55
1805	71.51	59.63	47.80
1810	72.08	60.26	48.51
1815	72.11	60.17	48.51
1820	71.60	59.75	48.00
1825	70.45	58.96	47.56
1830	52.67	58.55	26.36
1835	49.15	35.80	24.37
1840	45.00	32.55	21.39
1845	40.27	28.85	19.15
1850	35.17	24.95	16.31

For a long time, until 1820, the most important disease problems were smallpox, tuberculosis and venereal diseases. Taking the first and third only, some indication of the modelling outcome is illustrated in table 10 (above). (For more detail see *Our Original Aggression*.) This relates to a stable stationary population with a life expectancy at birth of 20 years (my book also deals with a life expectancy of 30 years). The projections are estimated as relating to a base population of 100 (or 1000 or 100 000) females with a life expectancy at birth of 20 years. Males are not quite so severely affected as females (for contrasts and for detailed assumptions see *Our Original Aggression*). The simplified assumptions allow the intrusion of venereal disease only from 1815 as an extremely conservative condition. Hence only the effects of smallpox are shown to 1810, indicating the potential for recovery in the absence of venereal disease. Venereal disease either physically limits reproductive capacity (in the case of gonorrhea) or, for syphilis during its primary and secondary stages, tends to yield very short-lived offspring.

This modelling has no relevance to Van Diemen's Land or Western Australia. It is designed to relate primarily to south-east Australia as a whole. Nevertheless, it is instructive in indicating the possible range of depopulating influences of introduced diseases, without any intervention due to the effects of reduced malnutrition from resource losses by Aborigines or of killing. It does not include the effects of tuberculosis, likely to be accumulative in its incidence as malnutrition worsened for Aborigines.

One cannot conclude from this table that it shows the numbers of a specified population dying. First, it is a depopulation model, taking into account those not born because of disease in adults as well as those dying from disease and related care and support problems. Secondly, people only die once. If, for example, killing is introduced some may not have the chance to be infected by smallpox or to fail, from disease, to reproduce. Similarly, the introduction of other diseases such as influenza, measles or whooping cough may override the sequence. The addition of more and more diseases may, then, have only a comparatively slight effect on the projections because the diseases are not additive in a simple way.

The diseases modelled and many others can spread along a human chain over long distances, certainly far beyond any frontier. Many of their effects would be imperceptible to settlers except in immediate close-quarter terms. Yet these effects would have been fundamental to conditions confronting Aborigines when they had to choose between resistance, integration or submission.

There has been some debate about the origins of smallpox and even the possibility of smallpox epidemics among Aborigines prior to European settlement. For present purposes, this question is not particularly important. Even if the Macassans delivered smallpox a long time before British colonists arrived and even if these infections travelled throughout the Australian continent, there is no possibility that smallpox could have become endemic amongst Aborigines. Populations were too small and dispersed to permit this. *Nor could any such hypothetical early infections have been spread frequently and widely over large areas.* Smallpox requires a non-immune human chain; infection provides, for survivors, life-time immunity. We have the evidence of three epidemics — 1789, 1830 and the late 1860s (the latter only in north-west Australia) — with a time interval of about 40 years between them. With this disease alone, it would have been possible for Aborigines over about two generations — about the 40-year gap between the three known epidemics — to rebuild their populations and in the process build up a sufficient chain of non-immune persons. It seems a reasonable assumption that in 1788 they confronted the first British landing with their precontact population substantially intact.

In the takeover process, the infections occurred at extremely opportune times for the British. Added to venereal disease alone, they simplified the first bridgehead task at Botany Bay and the later acquisition of the riverlands, woodlands and grasslands of the interior at just the right times. There is not necessarily anything sinister in this proposal. In demographic terms, the Aborigines suffered massive losses in 1789; and in or about 1830 the losses were catastrophic. No violent killing that actually occurred in the south-east could possibly begin to approximate these disease losses. Indeed, it would appear that the Aborigines were so severely weakened at relevant contact points as to ensure that resistance could only be short-term.

The appropriate model for Van Diemen's Land is essentially a non-reproduction one (Plomley, 1966; Robson, 1983). Venereal disease and the taking of women began before actual colonisation and rose to a peak while the colony was tiny and relatively static. The results here were, then, quite different in that the predominant outcome was to leave (essentially) the initial male population intact but subject to ageing as women were removed or were unable to reproduce because of venereal disease. By the time settlers sought to make pre-emptive claims on the central river systems, the impacts of venereal disease and the abstraction of women had most probably reached their peak. Even this may be an optimistic picture from the point of view of the Aborigines in that there is some reference to respiratory diseases before 1820.

In Western Australia (Stannage, 1981), it seems unlikely that smallpox played any role before the 1860s. Even if the 1789 epidemic had reached so far afield, populations would have substantially recovered by 1829. No-one has suggested that the 1830 epidemic reached the west. In the West Australian case, respiratory diseases appear prominent at a very early stage, with rapid depopulation due to high mortality over a short period. In this case, the most preferred area for both

Aborigines and British settlers was the south-east triangle. Within this confined space, confrontation, integration or submission made little difference in terms of communicated disease.

In fact, Aboriginal problems developed before formal settlement in 1829. Certainly not later than 1825, sealers (of whatever nationality) were established at Rottnest Island and had acquired Aboriginal women. Preceding the formal settlement, the New South Wales colonial authorities had despatched an outpost, including convicts, to the King George's Sound area. We know that at a very early stage Aborigines were infected with venereal disease, perhaps from these convicts, perhaps also from the subsequent settlers. But the most damaging disease effects were a series of influenza epidemics in 1830, 1836–37 and 1843, together with whooping cough in 1832. This last introduction was substantially combined with the more exotic disease of cholera, due to the proximity of Western Australia to India. No measures of death rates are available, though reports assert many Aboriginal deaths. Even in the accommodating conditions at King George's Sound, depopulation appears to have followed British entry with extraordinary speed.

These aggregative pictures of the likely demographic consequences of introduced diseases do not nearly convey the problems that Aborigines faced in the takeover process. We need some sense at least of disaggregation into age and sex and the implications of different disease consequences in order to relate disease to the Aboriginal options of resistance, integration or submission.

27

THE INTERACTION OF DISEASE WITH RESISTANCE, INTEGRATION AND SUBMISSION

I t is convenient not only to begin with but also to concentrate on the early experience at Botany Bay. When the smallpox epidemic occurred there in 1789, Phillip for reasons that are obscure delayed until the following year any report to Whitehall. He wrote two despatches, in each case with a brief reference to the epidemic submerged in a lengthy outline of the state and problems of the settlement. Phillip reached three conclusions: (1) about half the local Aboriginal population died; (2) the disease must have spread far inland and along the coast; (3) less military force would be necessary for protecting the settlement than he had anticipated. In the event, he was wrong on the last point. In the meantime, Aborigines had been infected with venereal disease. As Collins (1798) observed, 'I fear our people have to answer for that'.

Given the relatively tight geographical constraint on the first settlement within the Cumberland Plain for the first 20 odd years, we have the chance to consider, in microcosm, many of the interrelations between diseases and the takeover process in general. Some important lessons are to be learned. Before the smallpox epidemic, there was spasmodic and isolated violence by Aborigines, particularly towards convicts and their guards sent to isolated job locations. From late 1788, Aborigines appear to have broken contact with the British settlers, except for two captured for purposes of communication. After 1789, when the settlement was threatened with starvation, some commodity exchange appears to have developed between the two sides, with the settlement receiving kangaroo meat in exchange for such items as alcohol.

As the settlement became increasingly privatised after 1792, its agricultural activity spread, initially on relatively poor land and then increasingly during the late 1790s into the prime river flats (Fletcher, 1976). From 1795, the settlement appears to have encountered three characteristic patterns of responses from different groups. One was submergence and submission; a second was isolation and non-resistance; and a third was violent opposition rising to a climax during a few years centred on 1800. In the third response, all the subsequent patterns of Aboriginal resistance emerged from isolated spearings of British persons, destruction of livestock and other foodstocks, burning and even attacks on hamlets. After 1805, Aboriginal resistance was largely ended. Some remnants became degraded urban fringe dwellers; other small remnants withdrew into isolation; and a few were integrated. Of the latter, officialdom employed Aborigines as boat crews, to help recapture escaped convicts, not only around the Cumberland Plain but also at Newcastle and even as far afield as Van Diemen's Land (Collins, 1798; Robson, 1983).

To reiterate: smallpox kills, rapidly and in large numbers. The 50 per cent loss estimated by Phillip (and others) is typical of experience elsewhere in the world where non-immune populations were infected. This was not merely the result of direct infection but, as already indicated, the direct effects of smallpox need to be joined with inadequate care and the accompanying starvation of dependants. Gonorrhea tends progressively to reduce reproductive capacity as persistent and increasing inflammation affects the uterus and occludes the fallopian tubes. Syphilis limits the ability to produce viable children.

There are, however, some linked age-and-sex-specific effects of smallpox. For pregnant women, smallpox was substantially a death sentence. With relatively high birth rates and hence a significant fraction of women pregnant at any time, more women than men can be expected to die in a smallpox outbreak. Because women were the gatherers of secure food supplies, their illness and death would have immediate effects on dependants and on the ability of males to hunt or fight. Subjected as a result of venereal disease to declining reproductive capacity, the ability of survivors to reproduce children who died during a smallpox outbreak was then greatly reduced. One might expect this to be the case, within such a limited area as the Cumberland Plain, well within the timespan of 1789–1805.

Limitation on reproductive potential would remain likely to be true despite the age-specific influences of smallpox. In conditions of care, one might expect about 20–25 per cent of infected persons aged 20–40 to die. With inadequate support systems, the mortality rate would very probably be higher. On the one hand, those aged 5–14 would have a high survival expectation, at about 90 per cent. In the course of 1790–1800, however, young girls with a high recovery rate became the ones most exposed to venereal risks and so the reproductive capacity of those least devastated by smallpox was likely to be the most seriously limited and the most important. In a resistance situation, in other words, they could not grow up to produce the future girls and women to deliver collected foods to ensure adequate nutrition, nor the future Aboriginal warriors to replace those lost in fights with the British.

Most immediately, their inability to replace the mass of the very young dying directly or indirectly from smallpox meant that a major age gap developed, arising from the deaths of those aged approximately 0–4 years in 1789. In 1800–05, this early age loss in 1789 meant a serious reduction in the number of spear-carrying males aged 15–19. But in 1800–05, the Aborigines were also minus other younger potential fighters not born after 1790 because the number of women had been reduced by smallpox deaths. British settlers and the military did not need to achieve a high kill rate of Aborigines by 1800–05. The colonists then faced a ghostly echo. Once we add the attrition due to British killing, the ability of the Aborigines to resist for long or even to consider extensively the question of integration was drastically undermined after 1800.

Aborigines had a temporary relief. Given the expected high survival rate from smallpox of *males* aged 5–14 in 1789, the Aborigines actually had a special if limited stock of young males from their 1788 (full precontact) population moving through and into the warrior ranks. So far as potential male warriors were concerned, leaving aside losses in fights, the Aborigines were almost as able to resist in 1800–05 (when they understood their exposure to resource losses) as they could have been in 1788 (when risks to resources were unclear). After 1805, the echo effect of the smallpox epidemic suddenly punctured the supply of males and their ability to resist, a reversal confirmed by the continuing declining reproductive ability of females.

This may be a major part of the explanation of the ending of conflict by 1802, a sudden flowering of the British settlement and its ability to extend agricultural areas and move more freely. On the other hand, the brief substantial recovery of numbers of warriors in the last year or two of the eighteenth century may also be a significant part of the explanation of the increased intensity of effort by the military and settlers to kill Aborigines, including Hunter's advice (despite Whitehall admonitions) to settlers that they were free to take all measures necessary to protect themselves and their property. In other words, these latter actions did not arise merely because of the spread of the settlement and the increasingly private interest in settlement success. They reflected the fact that there were briefly more warriors to confront as compared with Phillip's assessment after the smallpox epidemic.

Aborigines do not seem to have pressed their attacks strongly, even with partially recovered numbers. This has been seen as their style of fighting. It may also have been a product of their dependence on diurnal hunting and gathering and the absence of storage systems. Both factors seem to have been relevant. On the other hand, by the end of the eighteenth century, Aborigines appear to have pressed attacks even on hamlets. Were these characteristics partly disease-related?

Disease introduced one additional element arising from the effects of both smallpox and venereal disease on the supply of female labour to provide the (basic) gathered foods. As in the case of infant males, smallpox destroyed the mass of infant girls as well as pregnant women, leaving a major shortage of gathering females in the second half of the 1790s. It is possible, then, that there were inadequate non-meat supplies even apart from British claims against Aboriginal resources. Aboriginal groups may have been more dependent than normally on male activity, even male gathering, making even more compelling the need for hit-run tactics. This matter is speculative, however, in that reduced total populations could, even in relatively poor Botany Bay conditions, have increased the resource/population ratio and may have made it easier for hunters and gatherers to acquire essential food supplies.

In the last years of the eighteenth century, as young female gatherers were partially restored (along with the numbers of young male hunter/warriors), Aboriginal traditional food supplies were more secure and so more concerted fighting was possible. This appears to conform to the more organised Aboriginal attacks at the turn of the century. Their misfortune was that it prompted the official loosing of military and settler forces, the advice to shoot on sight and the ability of the colonists to kill Aborigines — males, females and children — with impunity, regardless of Whitehall's nominal beneficence towards 'the natives'. In the Botany Bay encounter, the colonists were under special pressures to be successful in the takeover. Private fortunes and life were at stake as they were, subsequently, in the interior. But colonial officials faced, then, a heightened risk from Whitehall of more than severe reprimand if the settlement could not sustain its existence.

In a stable stationary population of the estimated 4000 Aborigines occupying the Cumberland Plain around Port Jackson–Botany Bay, Aborigines might have been able, in 1788, to assemble a total warrior force aged 15–49 at about 20 per cent of the total population — in other words about 800. Smallpox would have reduced that number to about 550. Had no killing intervened, the warrior force might have recovered to a little over 700 by 1800. No such collected force was ever assembled and some killing did intervene after 1789. Even so, of this hypothetical 700, about 45 per cent were the survivors of the age groups 5–14 in 1789, only lightly affected by smallpox mortality. After that group, there was a massive gap. Even though such a warrior force was never assembled, it was a potential threat to a military group numbering only about half the potential Aboriginal warrior force and guarding a convict workforce that could not safely be armed. With considerable trepidation, the ex-convict farmers were armed.

This hypothetical picture makes more understandable the need for Aborigines to conserve their forces and their ability to achieve a rising intensity of violence as 1800 approached. It seems only reasonable to believe that they were aware of their demographic weaknesses. As Hunter directed open season on Aborigines, and the settlers and military attacked Aboriginal camps, killing both males and females as well as the young, warrior recruitment was more efficiently interdicted than by open war with Aboriginal males. Indiscriminate British attacks then may be seen — from their side — as efficient. Given that not all Aboriginal groups resisted, no massive killing was required to demoralise the opponents of the British. Certainly, there was no killing that came anywhere near the numbers of Aborigines destroyed by smallpox.

This episode makes it easier to understand the much more limited violence in the interior of south-east Australia between 1825 and 1840. There is some evidence that the first smallpox epidemic penetrated into this mainland area. Depending on mortality rate limits postulated in *Our Original Aggression*, this first smallpox epidemic would still have left a somewhat reduced Aboriginal population, relative to 1788, as late as 1829. Given only this intervention, interior Aboriginal populations then may have ranged up to as high as 80 per cent of their precontact numbers. But the spread of venereal diseases from sealers in the south and settlers in the east could have been expected to lower this level to about two-thirds the precontact level, as an optimistic number.

The arrival of the second smallpox epidemic in about 1829–31 might then have shocked the Aborigines into a drastic loss condition if it meant that not much more than one-third of their precontact numbers survived at the beginning of the 1830s. Even allowing for the possibility of a significant overestimate of loss, the interior Aborigines seem to have been most probably in a considerably worse condition in which to encounter the British than the Botany Bay Aborigines had been.

There was, however, a factor that helped both sides to temporise over large areas of the plains. This was the radical change in resource/population ratios for

Aborigines, allowing them, subject to any losses due to former economies of scale, the prospect of a considerable food surplus. If there had been more disease deaths, there were also fewer mouths to feed. With fewer claims against them, the plant and animal resources would have increased. It is possible that Aborigines, in 1830, were better fed than before 1788. But, in addition, because of resource improvements, it took longer for sheep and cattle to denude the required Aboriginal supplies than it would have done prior to 1830. The Aborigines could prolong their survival somewhat longer than the Aborigines at Botany Bay had been able to do, though they were in the longer run less able to avert the eventual outcome. This experience may have been less true of Western Victoria, where Aboriginal specialisation of eel canals and higher population densities made survivors highly exposed. Sheep and cattle quickly destroyed the network of eel canals, implying starvation for the Aborigines.

The implications are ambivalent. In terms of demographic conditions, the large mass of Aborigines were already close to being submissive remnants when the main British resource takeover was attempted.

This makes all the more remarkable the resistance that was presented by Aborigines. In turn, this resistance was more feasible because of the relative improvement in food supplies. However, the radically reduced numbers may also help to explain why many settlers, large and small, regarded Aborigines as pests and treated them as such. With such small numbers on the ground, they attempted to continue their long-established practices, including firing the bush. To the British, this was at best incomprehensible, since it was believed that Aborigines could easily garner enough food, and at worst an unnecessary and even wanton threat to livestock and other property. For the Aborigines on the other hand, once allowed to remain on and be partly integrated into pastoral properties, sustained closer contact in both submission and integration meant continued exposure to the other introduced diseases that gradually destroyed those surviving the second epidemic of smallpox and the takeover.

Although Queensland is a matter essentially for the second half of the nineteenth century, it is convenient to note that there the second epidemic of smallpox was timed to allow a very considerable recovery in numbers when the Aborigines faced a rapid influx of British settlers. They were also much less exposed to venereal disease, partly from the ending of the convict system and partly from the destruction of their southern compatriots. Moreover, they occupied areas into which British settlers were not so ready to move (a condition that applied even more to the Northern Territory). As movement in occurred, however, there appears to have been a good deal (not clearly specified or counted) of violence combined with pastoral integration. It seems that Queensland cannot be regarded as typical of the Australian experience.

There is no evidence that smallpox affected Van Diemen's Land. The primary relevant disease was venereal, causing reduced rates of reproduction, though there is some suggestion of respiratory problems in the southern half of the island. In this case, however, one must also observe the taking of women by sealers. The two factors together meant an extreme limitation on the ability to sustain tribal existence, even though literally 'half-castes' were produced in sealing settlements.

The implications for Tasmania might then be seen in terms of (a) an increasingly male Aboriginal society confronting the dominantly male British; (b) with a reduced female workforce, the Van Diemen's Land Aborigines depended even more on interchange between the coast and the rivers than they traditionally had; (c) Aboriginal males may increasingly have been induced to engage in gathering in addition to hunting, even further degrading their normal work and social mode; (d) increasingly throughout the 1820s, the average age of Aborigines was rising as fewer children were born during 1800–04. All these features seem much more pronounced in Tasmania as compared with the mainland. In a situation in which Aborigines were offered little prospect of integration, the takeover might then have been seen essentially as a fight to the finish and perhaps a desperate effort at retribution.

In Western Australia, the impact of diseases in the south-west up to 1850 needs to be seen as strongly influenced by the determination of the settlers and the military to free British occupiers of personal risks from Aborigines. Despite so-called 'battles' with Aborigines, it is doubtful whether violence was the prime contributor (fifteen Aborigines were killed at 'the Battle of Pinjarra'). By force, the Aborigines were driven off their lands and into areas of low resource potential. Widespread starvation is reported by the second half of the 1830s, inevitably enhancing the effects of epidemics. By 1841, remnant Aborigines in the south-west were wholly under British control.

In almost every area of contact at which one looks, then, disease coupled with demographic disturbance appears as intimately interrelated with economics (including settler-induced starvation) and the law in determining the ability of British settlers to succeed in the takeover process. Had disease not intervened in such a drastic way and, from the British point of view, at such opportune times, the question could well have become whether the effort would have been worth the cost to the British. Clearly, Aborigines resisted widely unless already shattered by disease prior to exposure to the British. But introduced diseases appear as the dominating factor in simplifying British access to Australian resources. Since several of these diseases spread over long distances while British settlements were closely contained and the settlers were unaware, the effects on Aborigines as a whole were often not apparent.

28

CONCLUSIONS

 $\mathbf{G}$ iven the evolution of European society, economy and technology, it was virtually inevitable by the eighteenth century that some intrusion into Australia should occur. It is possible, indeed, that successive imperial constraints on Javanese maritime activity, at least in the construction of the large vessels that the Javanese were capable of building and handling, prevented a South-east Asian intrusion earlier and on a scale larger than the trepangers visiting from Sulawesi.

One might speculate about the possibility of alternative nationalities invading Aboriginal lands. But from almost every point of view — an isolated location for convicts to deal with domestic social problems, the structure of the British domestic economy, British maritime capability, extending trading interests into the Indian Ocean and to China, the growth of whaling activity into the southern hemisphere, extra- and intra-European conflict and competition, the British inclination to settle distant areas — all made Australia a useful, if incidental, appendage to Britain.

The incoming British were representatives of one of the most recently formed of human societies in the world, colliding with one of the most ancient. The Aborigines had adapted to slow evolution and an attachment to land that was managed rather than exploited; and they had evolved strong preferences for non-material ends. By contrast, British society had been exposed to massive change over a short period, and through external influences and internal dynamics had been projected into the position of the most wealthy and technically advanced society on earth. There was little place in British value systems, technical approaches or preference systems for Aborigines, at any rate when it came to a face-to-face choice of which group was to have access to Australian resources. In terms of exploitative technology, the British had left the Aborigines far behind. The British settlers were soon to leave most of them, literally, for dead. A very ancient society was largely rolled away by a very youthful one, and with substantial indifference, notwithstanding Whitehall's professed desire for Aboriginal welfare. The British in Britain and in Australia had objectives with much higher priority than Aboriginal wellbeing.

The continent, once entered, presented British settlers with a highly advantageous area for pastoral development to supply a basic raw material to a prime British industry. By the mid-1840s, indeed, Australia had become the dominant supplier to Britain, exceeding all other sources combined. Moreover, the wool supplied was of high quality. The possibility of exploiting Australian natural resources in this way had, however, been greatly facilitated by prior resource management over thousands of years by Australian Aborigines. Most importantly, by avoiding exploitative technology and by using fire as a primary means of resource control, Aborigines had laid the foundations of the open woodlands and grasslands on which British livestock thrived.

Those livestock implied the introduction of an exploitative rather than management use of Australian resources. British pastoralism did not depend on high level technology or large-scale fixed investment up to 1850. To that extent, the occupation of Australia was relatively easy. Aborigines had prepared the way and British settlers fell heir to past Aboriginal achievements. But livestock exploitation meant the destruction of much of the ecology that Aborigines had fostered. The British takeover, at this level, was more a confrontation between British livestock on the one hand and Aboriginal mammals and plants on the other rather than a clash between British and Aboriginal persons. The livestock won, hooves down. (In the process, they went on, later in the nineteenth century and into the twentieth century, to destroy the ecology to such an extent that a massive retreat was required. But that is another story.)

At the human level, the confrontation was between two radically different groups, neither understanding the social assumptions or value systems of the other. To Aborigines, attachment to the land went so deep that its loss, more than any other matter, destroyed all purpose. To the British, land was real estate, a source of profit and wealth, an object to be bought and sold in the market. In claiming rights over land, the British were able to control and break up Aboriginal economic activity at many points, any one of which could have had severe effects on the viability of Aboriginal society.

The mutual response did, indeed, lead to a good deal of violence on both sides. Some of this violence was idiosyncratic but underlying it there was a fundamental economic issue. In a few areas, violence may have been a dominant influence on the outcome, but cannot generally be accepted as a prime determinant. On the other hand, there were more efforts at accommodation on both sides than seem to be generally acknowledged.

The basic problem of the Aborigines was their thousands of years of isolation. This isolation was not specially important in terms of social organisation or technology. The British, after all, introduced little in the way of technology in pastoral exploitation, although specialised pastoral use of land conflicted directly with Aboriginal use. The colonists had no special advantage in military technology and possibly often a weakness in military organisation. Nor was British market self interest obviously superior to Aboriginal group behaviour. Indeed, self interest on the part of small settlers depended, in the confrontation, on an appeal to their group authority or their joint (including military) action against Aborigines. The cost of isolation to the Aborigines lay essentially in their exposure to introduced diseases for which they had no immunity, and the impact of these diseases was accentuated by pastoral interference in Aboriginal land use which reduced food supplies. Colonial indifference rather than violence added further to the inroads of disease. The rest was incidental (except in Van Diemen's Land). The takeover was a game in which all the dice were loaded against the Aborigines. Their experience was not unique. It was replicated, in essential form and to a similar degree, throughout the whole of the Americas.

Until their resulting disease-induced weakness is recognised. Aborigines will continue to appear to some of the present beneficiaries of the original British takeover, as ineffectual, inferior and, in the last resort, pests — just as they did to the early British settlers. Some 150 years after the essential destruction of Aboriginal society, Australians today have not yet come to terms with the presence, on the fringes of their society, of remnant Aborigines. The actions of the original settlers may be comprehended in the context of the original takeover, when many felt insecure and threatened. Today, a basic social problem remains in the widespread indifference to the difficulties of a special minority, the descendants of those who preceded us to this continent. Some recognition has been made. Very limited land rights, particularly the recognition of some sacred sites, have been acknowledged. Belatedly, the importance of Aborigines in the pastoral industry of northern Australia has been accepted with a recent pastoral industry award for Aborigines. Aborigines have also recently been accorded voting rights and have ceased to be wards of the state. For their part, many Aborigines continue to be uncertain about whether they wish to be isolated from or integrated with the rest of Australian society.

Whatever limited, hesitant steps may have been taken in the late twentieth century to accommodate Aborigines, one of the crucial lessons of history has not been learned. It is essential that it should be. After World War II it appeared that Aboriginal populations had passed through the nadir of about 90 000 that their populations (as measured) reached in the 1920s and had begun to rise rapidly to a present level of the order of 250 000 (probably using different measures). Though Aboriginal viability is not immediately threatened, this recovery has slackened drastically. It is exposed to the same dominant problems with which British settlement began — health combined with malnutrition and lack of care (Australian Institute of Health, 1986, 1989).

The diseases have changed, but, as usual, the more things change the more they remain the same. We do not have very high quality statistics on Aboriginal health and it is probable that there is a good deal of regional variation. There is widespread malnutrition, at least as bad as anything in Third World countries. Aboriginal life expectancy is at about the level European Australians had attained during the second half of the nineteenth century — about 22 years less than is now experienced by non-Aborigines. Infant mortality is many times that of non-Aborigines and Aboriginal weights from infancy into adulthood are generally significantly below those of non-Aborigines. At adulthood, the weight relativities are reversed, with marked obesity among Aborigines. This is, in fact, the reverse of signs of improvement at adult ages. Indeed, death rates for Aborigines in early adulthood (20–39) are one of the most striking features of the modern Aboriginal health problem.

Aborigines now confront the worst of all worlds — diseases due to underdevelopment and diseases due to advanced development, with several in between these extremes. There is widespread malnutrition. Interestingly, Aborigines are affected widely by a *chronic* form of hepatitis B (perhaps 40 per cent of all Aborigines suffer from this) and by diabetes *not requiring insulin* injections. Both conditions commonly result in early adult death but also in *low performance characteristics prior to death*. Both reflect the destruction of the Aboriginal lifestyle and the handout philosophy (sugar and flour) of non-Aboriginal society. The former is associated with liver diseases, the latter with pancreatic and heart disease. These outcomes may mask another problem, the frequency of streptococcal infections that lead to liver, kidney and heart diseases and radically reduce life expectancy.

Other problems might be listed — including venereal disease, alcoholism, petrol sniffing and so on. This is a sorry tale, wherever one looks, of ignorance, antagonism and rejection by non-Aborigines and lack of resources, opportunity, incentive and direction by Aborigines. Essentially, non-Aboriginal attitudes remain a repetition of those of before 1850 when, at least, early settlers might be recognised as feeling exposed to risk from Aborigines. Torres Strait Islanders are held up as a shining example of what Australian Aborigines might be but are not. In fact the islanders are not nearly so exposed to hepatitis, diabetes, streptococcal or similar debilitating diseases, nor have they been so subject to territorial intrusion. Having occupied a non-European part of the world, present-day non-Aboriginal Australians cannot afford to preserve an old settler tradition, long since irrelevant (except, perhaps, to the profit and loss accounts of exploitative mining companies).

Writing in the centre of Australia near Lake Amadeus in 1873, the explorer Ernest Giles pondered the following:

> The valley is surrounded by picturesque hills, and I am certain it is the most charming and romantic spot I ever shall behold ... (T)his is no doubt an old-established and favourite camping ground ... No creatures of the human race could view these scenes with apathy or dislike, nor would any sentient beings part with such a patrimony at any price but that of their blood. But the great Designer of the universe, in the long past of creation, permitted a fiat to be recorded, that the beings whom it was His pleasure in the first instance to place amidst these lovely scenes must eventually be swept from the face of the earth by others more intellectual, more dearly beloved and gifted than they. Progressive improvement is undoubtedly the order of creation, and we perhaps in our turn may be as ruthlessly driven from the earth by another race of yet unknown beings of an order infinitely higher, infinitely more beloved, than we. On me, perchance, the eternal obloquy of the execution of God's doom may rest, for being the first to lead the way, with prying eyes and trespassing foot, into regions so fair and so remote; but being guiltless alike in act or intention to shed the blood of any human creature, I must accept it without a sigh. (Giles, 1889, vol. 1: 183–4.)

BIBLIOGRAPHY

Abbott, C. G. & N. B. Naim (eds) (1969) *Economic Growth of Australia 1788–1821*, Melbourne: Melbourne University Press

Allchin, B. & R. Allchin (1968) *The Birth of Indian Civilization*, Harmondsworth Pelican

Allen, H. (1972) 'Where the Crow Flies Backwards: Man and Land in the Darling Basin', unpub. PhD thesis, Department of Prehistory, Australian National University

Allen, J. *et al.* (eds) (1977) *Sunda and Sahul: Prehistoric Studies in Southeast Asia, Melanesia and Australia*, London: Academic Press

Allen, J. *et al.* (1988) 'Pleistocene Dates for the Human Occupation of New Ireland, Northern Melanesia', *Nature*, vol. 331

Altman, J. C. (1987) *Hunter-gatherers Today*, Canberra: Australian Institute of Aboriginal Studies

Ashton, P. M. (1972) *Transactions of the Second Aberdeen-Hull Symposium on Malesian Ecology*, University of Hull, Department of Geography, Misc. Sev. no. 13

Atkinson, A. & M. Aveling (eds) (1987) *Australians 1838*, Sydney: Fairfax, Syme & Weldon

Australian Agricultural Company Records, ms, Canberra: Australian National University Archives of Business & Labour

Australian Institute of Health (1986) 'Aboriginal Health Statistics', proceedings of a workshop, Darwin, April 1986

Australian Joint Copying Project, Commissiariat Accounts, reel 3570, pieces 556–579, 1791–1819; reel 1078, piece 5, 1808–9

Australian Joint Copying Project, Governors, Agents, NSW rel 1079, pieces 3, 5

Barton, G. B. (1889) *Historical Records of New South Wales*, Sydney: Government Printer

Barwick, D., in D. J. Mulvaney & J. Golson (1971) *Aboriginal Man and Environment in Australia*, Canberra: Australian National University Press

Basu, R. N. *et al.* (1979) *The Eradication of Smallpox from India*, New Delhi: World Health Organization

Becker, G. S. (1965) 'A Theory of the Allocation of Time', *The Economic Journal*, September

Belcher, M. J. (1982) 'The Child in New South Wales Society, 1820–37', unpub. PhD thesis, Department of History, University of New England

Bellwood, P. (1985) *Prehistory of the Indo-Malaysian Archipelago*, London: Academic Press

Belshaw, J. (1978) in I. McBryde *Records of Times Past*, Canberra: Australian Institute of Aboriginal Studies

Bennett, F. D. (1840) *Narrative of a Whaling Voyage around the Globe*, London: Richard Bentley

Berndt, R. M. & C. H. Berndt (1953) *The First Australians*, Sydney: Ure Smith

Berndt, R. M. & C. H. Berndt (1965) *Aboriginal Man in Australia*, essays in honour of Emeritus Professor A. P. Elkin, Sydney: Angus & Robertson

Berndt, R. M. & R. Tonkinson (1988) *Social Anthropology and Australian Aboriginal Studies*, Canberra: Australian Institute of Aboriginal Studies

Beveridge, P. (1883) 'On the Aborigines inhabiting the Great Lacustrine and Riverine Depression of the Lower Murray, Lower Murrumbidgee, Lower Lachlan and Lower Darling', *Journal of the Royal Society of New South Wales*, no. XVII

Beveridge, P. (1889) *The Aborigines of Victoria and the Riverina*, Melbourne: Hutchinson

Birdsell, J. B. (1972) *Human Evolution*, Chicago: Rand McNally

Blainey, G. (1982) *A Land Half Won*, Melbourne: Macmillan

Blainey, G. (1985) *The Triumph of the Nomads*, Melbourne: Macmillan

Blum, W. M. (1988) 'Late Quaternary Sediments and Sea Levels in Bass Strait and Southeastern Australia — A Preliminary Report', *Search*, vol. 19, no. 2

Boomgaard, (nd) 'Disease, Death and Disasters in Java, 1820–1880', unpub. paper, Canberra: Australian National University

Boserup, E. (1965) *The Conditions of Agricultural Growth*, New York: Aldine

Bowler, J. M. (1978) 'Glacial Age Events at High and Low Altitudes: A Southern Hemisphere Perspective', in van Zanderew Bakker (ed.) *Antarctic Glacial History and World Palaeoclimates*, Rotterdam: Balkema

Bowler, J. M. & R. Jones (1979) 'Australia was a Land of Lakes', *Geographical Magazine*, July

Bride, T. F. (1898) *Letters from Victorian Pioneers*, Melbourne: Government Printer

Broome, R. (1982) *Aboriginal Australians*, Sydney: George Allen & Unwin

Bryson, R. A. & T. J. Murray (1977) *Climates of Hunger*, Canberra: Australian National University Press

Bryson, R. A. & A. M. Swain (1981) 'Holocene Variations of Monsoon Rain in Rajasthan', *Quaternary Research*, no. 16

Burrows, E. H. (1958) *A History of Medicine in South Africa up to the Nineteenth Century*, Capetown: A. A. Balkema

Busby, G. (1974/75) 'Correspondence', *New South Wales Medical Gazette*, vol. V

Butlin, N. G. (1983) *Our Original Aggression: Aboriginal Populations of South-eastern Australia 1788–1850*, Sydney: Allen & Unwin

Butlin, N. G. (1985) 'Macassans and Aboriginal Smallpox: the "1789" and "1829" Epidemics', *Historical Studies*, vol. 21, no. 84

Butlin, S. J. (1953) *Foundations of the Australian Monetary System, 1788–1851*, Melbourne: Melbourne University Press

Caldwell, — (nd) 'The Demographic Evidence for the Incidence and Cause of Abnormally Low Fertility in Tropical Africa', unpub. paper, Australian National University

Campbell, J. (1985) 'Smallpox in Aboriginal Australia, the early 1830s', *Historical Studies*, vol. 21, no. 84

Carr, D. J. & S. G. M. Carr (eds) (1981) *People and Plants in Australia*, Sydney: Academic Press

Castles, A. (1982) *An Australian Legal History*, Sydney: Law Book Company

Chappell, J. & N. J. Shackleton (1988) 'Oxygen Isotopes and sea level', *Nature*, vol. 324

Christie, M. F. (1979) *Aborigines in Colonial Victoria 1835–86*, Sydney: Sydney University Press

Church, J. A. *et al.* 'The Leeuwin Current', unpub. paper, Hobart: CSIRO

Clammer, J. (ed.) (1978) *The New Economic Anthropology*, London: Macmillan

Clarke, D. L. (ed.) (1972) *Models in Archaeology*, London: Methuen

Clarke, D. L. (1979) *Analytical Anthropology*, London: Academic Press

CLIMANZ (1983) *Proceedings of the first CLIMANZ Conference 1981*, Canberra: Australian National University Press

Cline, R. (ed.) (1981) *Seasonal Reconstruction of the Earth's Surface at the Last Glacial Maximum*, Geographical Society of America, Map & Chart Series, MG–36

Clough, S. B. & C. W. Cole (1952) *Economic History of Europe*, Boston: Heath

Coale, A. & Demeny, P. (1966) *Regional Model Life Tables and Stable Populations*, Princeton, NJ: Princeton University Press

Coghlan, T. A. (1918) *Labour and Industry in Australia*, vol. 1, Oxford: Oxford University Press

Collins, D. (1798, 1802) *An Account of the English Colony in New South Wales*, vols 1 & 2, London: Cadell & Davies

Cook, N. D. (1982) *Demographic Collapse, Indian Peru 1520–1620*, Cambridge: Cambridge University Press

Cook, S. E. & W. Borah (1948) *The Population of Central Mexico in the Sixteenth Century*, Berkeley, Cal.: University of California Press

Cox & Greenwood (ni), Ledger 1801–1806, ms, London: Lloyd's Bank Archives

Creighton, C. (1965) *A History of Epidemics in Britain*, London: F. Case

Cumpston, H. H. L. (1940) *The History of Smallpox in Australia*, Melbourne: Government Printer

Cumpston, J. H. (1964) *Shipping Arrivals and Departures, Sydney, 1788–1825*, Canberra: Roebuck

Curr, E. M. (1883) *Recollections of Squatting in Victoria*, Melbourne: G. Robertson

Curr, E. M. (1886) *The Australian Race*, 4 vols, Melbourne: Government Printer

Dawson, J. (1880) *Australian Aborigines*, Sydney

Denevan, W. M. (1976) *The Native Populations of America in 1492*, Madison, Wis.: University of Wisconsin Press

Derbyshire, E. (1987) 'A History of Glacial Stratigraphy in China', *Quaternary Science Reviews*, vol. 6, no. 3/4

de Rossel, E. P. E. (1800) *Voyage in Search of La Perouse*, vol. 1, London

Deutch, C. E. & B. G. Muir (1980) 'Long Range Sighting of Bushfires as a Possible Incentive for Pleistocene Voyages to Greater Australia', *The West Australian Newsletter*, vol. 14, no. 7

Dingle, T. (1988) *Aboriginal Economy*, Ringwood, Vic.: Penguin

Dobyns, H. (1966) 'Estimating Aboriginal American Population: An Appraisal of Techniques with a New Hemisphere Estimate', *Current Anthropology*, vol. VII

Dobyns, H. F. (1983) *Their Numbers Became Thinned*, Knoxville: University of Tennessee Press

Docker, E. G. (1964) *Simply Human Beings*, Brisbane: Jacaranda

Donnell, R. (1983) *European Economic Prehistory: A New Approach*, New York: Academic Press

Dunsdorfs, E. (1956) *The Australian Wheat Growing Industry, 1788–1948*, Melbourne: Melbourne University Press

Elder, B. (1988) *Blood on the Wattle*, Sydney: Allen & Unwin

Evatt, H. V. (1938) *Rum Rebellion*, Sydney: Angus & Robertson

Eyre, E. J. (1845) *Journal of an Expedition of Discovery into Central Australia*, London: T. & W. Boone

Fitzpatrick, B. (1939) *British Imperialism and Australia, 1788–1833*, London: Allen & Unwin

Flanagan, R. (1862) *The History of New South Wales*, London: Sampson Low

Fletcher, B. H. (1976) *Landed Enterprise and Penal Society*, Sydney: Sydney University Press

Flinders, M. (1814) *A Voyage to Terra Australis*, London: G. & W. Nicol

Flood, J. (1980) *The Moth Hunters: Aboriginal Prehistory of the Australian Alps*, Canberra: Australian National University Press

Flood, J. (1983) *Archaeology and the Dreamtime*, Sydney: Collins

Foelsche, — (1882) 'Notes on the Aborigines of North Australia', *Proceedings of the Royal Society of South Australia*, —

Foley, J. C. (1957) *Droughts in Australia: Review of Records from Earliest Years of Settlement to 1955*, Bureau of Meteorology Bulletin no. 43, Melbourne: Bureau of Meteorology

Foster, S. O. *et al.* (1978) 'The Spread of Smallpox Among a Somali Nomadic Group', *The Lancet* no. 14.

Fox, J. J. (1980) *Indonesia: The Making of a Culture*, Canberra: Australian National University Press

Fraser, J. (1882) 'The Aborigines of New South Wales', *Journal of the Royal Society of New South Wales*, no. XVI

Frith, H. J. (1973) *Wild Life Conservation*, Sydney: Angus & Robertson

Frith, H. J. (1976) *Waterfowl in Australia*, Sydney: Angus & Robertson

Galloway, R. W. & M. E. Bahr (1979) 'What is the Length of the Australian Coast?', *Australian Geographer*, vol. XIV, no. 4

Gamble, C. (1986) 'Hunter-gatherers and the Origin of States', in J. A. Hall (ed.) *States in History*, Oxford: Oxford University Press

Gates, W. L. (1971) 'Modeling the Ice-Age Climate', *Science*, vol. 191, March

Gavin, S. M. (1977) 'The History of the Earth's Surface Temperature During the Past 100 Million Years', *American Review of Planet Science*, vol. 5

Gibbons, J. R. H. & F. G. A. Clunie (1986) 'Sea Level Changes and Pacific Prehistory: New Insights Into Early Human Settlement of Oceania', *Journal of Pacific History*, vol. XXI, nos 1–2

Giles, E. (1889) *Australia Twice Traversed*, 2 vols, London: Sampson Low, Marston, Searle and Rivington

Gould, R. A. (1982) 'To Have and Have Not: The Ecology of Sharing Amongst Hunter Gatherers' in N. M. Williams & E. S. Hann, *Resource Managers: North American and Australian Hunter Gatherers*, Boulder, Col.: Westfield Press

Grey, C. (1841) *Journals of Two Expeditions of Discovery in North-west and Western Australia During the Years 1837, 1838 and 1839*, 2 vols, London: T. & W. Boone

Gudeman, S. (1986) *Economics as Culture*, London: Routledge

Hackett, C. J. (1975) 'An Introduction to Diagnostic Criteria of Syphilis, Treponarid and Yaws (Treponematoses) in Dry Bones, and Some Implications', *Virchows Archiv A: Pathological Anatomy and Histology*, vol. CCCLIXX

Hainsworth, D. R. (1972) *The Sydney Traders: Simeon Lord and his Contemporaries, 1788–1821*, Melbourne: Cassell

Hallam, S. J. (1975) *Fire and Hearth*, Canberra: Australian Institute of Aboriginal Studies

Hallam, S. J. (1977) 'The Relevance of Old World Archaeology to the First Entry of Man into New Worlds: Colonization Seen from the Antipodes', *Quaternary Research*, no. 8

Hallam, S. J. (1981) 'The First West Australians' in W. Stannage (ed.) *A New History of Western Australia*, Nedlands, W.A.: University of Western Australia Press

Hallam, S. J. (1985) 'The History of Aboriginal Firing', in J. R. Ford (ed. *Symposium on Fire Ecology and Management in Western Australian Ecosystems*, Perth: University of Western Australia Press

Hanks, P. & — Keon-Cohen (eds) (1984) *Aborigines and the Law*, Sydney: George Allen & Unwin

Harris, D. R. (ed.) (1980) *Human Ecology in Savanna Environments*, London: Academic Press

Hart, C. W. M. & A. R. Pilling (1960) *The Tiwi of North Australia*, New York: Holt, Rinehart & Winston

Hassan, F. A. (1981) *Demographic Archaeology*, London: Academic Press

Hawdon, J. (1952) *The Journey from New South Wales to Adelaide (1938)*, Melbourne: Georgian House

Higgs, E. S. (ed.) (1975) *Palaeoeconomy*, Cambridge: Cambridge University Press

Historical Records of Australia, series 1, vols 1–6

Historical Records of New South Wales, vols 1–7

Horridge, A. *Outrigger Canoes of Bali and Madura, Indonesia*, Honolulu: University of Hawaii Press

Horton, D. R. (1981) 'Water and Woodland: The Peopling of Australia', *Institute of Aboriginal Studies Newsletter*, no. 16

Hunter, J. (1798) *An Historical Journal of the Transactions at Port Jackson and Norfolk Island*, London: printed for J. Stookdale

Joffre, M. E. *et al.* (1976) 'Granuloma Inguinale Simulating Advanced Pelvic Cancer', *The Medical Journal of Australia*, December 4

Jones, F. L. (1970) *The Structure and Growth of Australia's Aboriginal Population*, Canberra: Australian National University Press

Jones, R. (1969) 'Firestick Farming', *Australian Natural History*, vol. XVI, September

Jones, R. (1975) 'The Neolithic, Paleolithic and the Hunting Gardeners: Man and Land in the Antipodes', *Quaternary Studies*, vol. IX, INQUA Congress, 1973, in the Royal Society of New Zealand Bulletin, no. 13, Wellington

Jones, R. (1977) 'Man as an Element of a Continental Fauna: The Case of the Sundering of the Bassian Bridge', in J. Allen, J. Golson & R. Jones (eds) *Sunda and Sahul: Prehistoric Studies in Southeast Asia, Melanesia and Australia*, London: Academic Press

Jones, R. (1977a) 'The Fifth Continent: Problems Concerning the Colonization of Australia', *Annual Review of Anthropology*, vol. 8

Jones, R. (ed.) (1980) *Northern Australian Options and Implications*, Canberra: Australian National University Press

Jones, R. (1980a) 'Hunters in the Australian Coastal Savanna' in D. R. Harris (ed.) *Human Ecology in Savanna Environments*, London: Academic Press

Kennedy, E. B. (1902) *The Black Police of Queensland*, London: Murray

Kirk, R. L. (1983) *Aboriginal Man Adapting*, Melbourne: Oxford University Press

Kirk, R. & E. Szathmary (1985) *Out of Asia*, Canberra: Australian National University Press

Krefft, G. 'Narrative of the Exploring Expedition Led by W. Blandowski 1856–7', ms, Mitchell Library, Sydney

Kroeber, A. L. (1925) *Handbook of the Indians of California*, Bureau of American Ethnology, bulletin 78

Krzywicki, L. (1934) *Primitive Society and Its Vital Statistics*, London: Macmillan

Kukla, G. (1987) 'Loess Stratigraphy in Central China', *Quaternary Science Review*, vol. 6, nos 3–4

Kutzbach, J. E. (1981) 'Monsoon Climate of the Early Holocene Climatic Experiment with the Earth's Orbital Parameters for 9,000 Years Ago', *Science*, vol. 214.

Laidler, P. W. & M. Gelfaud (1971) *South Africa, Its Medical History 1652–1898*, Capetown: C. Struik

Lawrence, R. (1968) *Aboriginal Habitat and Economy*, Occasional Paper no. 6, Department of Geography, School of General Studies, Canberra: Australian National University

Lawrence, R. (1971) 'Habitat and Economy: A Historical Perspective', in D. J. Mulvaney & J. Golson (eds) *Aboriginal Man and Environment in Australia*, Canberra: Australian National University Press

Lessard, G. & A. Chouinard (1980) *Bamboo Research in Asia*, Canada: IDRC

Lewis, H. T. (1982) 'Fire Technology and Resource Management in Aboriginal North America and Australia', in N. M. Williams & E. S. Hunn, *Resource Managers: North American and Australian Hunter Gatherers*, Boulder, Col.: Westfield Press

Lofgren, M. C. (1975) *Patterns of Life*, Perth: Western Australian Museum

Loos, N. (1982) *Invasion and Resistance*, Canberra: Australian National University Press

Lourandos, H. (1977) 'Aboriginal Spatial Organisation and Population of Southwestern Victoria Reconsidered', *Archaeology and Physical Anthropology in Oceania*, vol. XII, no. 3

Lourandos, H. (1980) 'Change or Stability? Hydraulics, Hunter Gatherers and Population in Temperate Australia', *Archaeology and Physical Anthropology in Oceania*, vol. 11

Lourandos, H. (1980a) 'Forces of Change: Aboriginal Technology and Population in Southwestern Victoria', unpub. PhD thesis, Department of Anthropology, University of Sydney

Macknight, C. C. (1976) *The Voyage to Marege: Macassan Trepangers in Northern Australia*, Melbourne: Melbourne University Press

McBryde, I. (1978) *Records of Times Past*, Canberra: Australian Institute of Aboriginal Studies

McCarthy, F. D. & M. McArthur (1960) 'The Food Quest and the Time Factor in Aboriginal Economic Life', in C. P. Mountford (ed.) *Records of the Australian-American Scientific Expedition to Arnhemland*, vol. 2: 'Anthropology and Nutrition', Melbourne

McLure, F. A. (1966) *The Bamboos: A Fresh Perspective*, Harvard: Harvard University Press

Manguin, P. V. (1987) 'The Southeast Asian Trading Ship: An Historical Approach', *Journal of South-east Asian Studies*

Manning, J. (1882) 'Notes on the Aborigines of New Holland', *Journal of the Royal Society of New South Wales*, no. XVI

Meehan, B. (1975) 'Shell Bed and Shell Midden', unpub. PhD thesis, Department of Prehistory, Australian National University

Meehan, B. (1977) 'Man does not Live by Calories Alone: The Role of Shellfish in a Coastal Cuisine', in J. Allen *et al.* (eds), *Sunda and Sahul: Prehistoric Studies in Southeast Asia, Melanesia and Australia*, London: Academic Press

Misra, V. N. & S. N. Rajaguri (1986) 'Environment et Culture de l'Homme Prehistorique dans le Desert du Thar, Rajasthan, Inde', *L'Anthropologie*, vol. 90

Mitchell, B. R. (1988) *British Historical Statistics*, Cambridge: Cambridge University Press

Mitchell, T. L. (1839) *Three Expeditions into the Interior of Eastern Australia*, London: T. & W. Boone

Mooney, J. (1928) 'The Aboriginal Populations of America North of Mexico', Smithsonian Miscellaneous Collections, no. LXXXX

Morton, S. R. & K. G. Brennan (nd) 'Birds', mimeo chapter to be published in C. D. Haynes *et al.*, *Monsoonal Australia: Landscape, Ecology and Man in the Northern Lowlands* (forthcoming)

Mulvaney, D. J. (1975) *The Prehistory of Australia*, Ringwood, Vic.: Penguin

Mulvaney, D. J. & J. Golson (eds) (1971) *Aboriginal Man and Environment in Australia*, Canberra: Australian National University Press

Mulvaney, D. J. & J. P. White (eds) (1987) *Australians to 1788*, Sydney: Fairfax, Syme & Weldon

Nanson, G. C. & R. W. Young (1987) 'Comparisons of Thermoluminescence and Radiocarbon Age-determinations from Late-Pleistocene Alluvial Deposits near Sydney, Australia', *Quaternary Research*, vol. 27, 1987

Nanson, G. C. & R. W. Young (1988) 'Fluvialite Evidence for the Period of Late-Quaternary Pluvial Climate in Coastal Southeastern Australia', *Palaeogeography, Palaeoclimatology, Palaeoecology* vol. 66

Nanson, C. G. *et al.* (1986) 'Coexistent Mud Braids and Anastomosing Channels in an Arid-zone River: Cooper Creek, Central Australia', *Geology*, vol. 14

New South Wales (1845) 'Report from the Select Committee on the Conditions of the Aborigines, with Appendix, Minutes of Evidence and Replies to a Circular Letter', New South Wales V & P Legislative Council, Sydney

New South Wales (1845a) 'Reports from the Committee on Immigration with Appendix, Minutes of Evidence and Replies to Circular Letter on the Aborigines', New South Wales V & P Legislative Council, Sydney

Nix, H. A. (1974) 'Environmental Control of Breeding, Post-breeding Dispersal and Migration of Birds in the Australian Region', *Proceedings of the 16th Ornithological Congress*

Pardoe, C. (1988) 'The Cemetery as symbol', *Archaeology in Oceania*, vol. 23, no. 1

Peterson, G. M. *et al.* (1979) 'The Continental Record of Environmental Conditions 18,000 years BP: An Initial Evaluation', *Quaternary Research*, vol. 12

Peterson, N. (ed.) (1976) *Tribes and Boundaries in Australia*, Canberra: Australian Institute of Aboriginal Studies

Petrie, C. C. (1904) *Tom Petrie's Reminiscences of Early Queensland*, Brisbane: Watson Ferguson

Plomley, N. J. (ed.) (1966) *Friendly Mission: The Tasmanian Journals and Papers of George Augustus Robinson 1929–34*, Hobart: Tasmanian Historical Research Association

Presland, G. (ed.) (1977, 1980) *Journals of G. A. Robinson*, Records of the Victorian Archaeological Society, nos. 5, 6 & 7

Price, T. D. & J. A. Brown (1985) *Prehistoric Hunter Gatherers: The Emergence of Cultural Complexity*, New York: Academic Press

Pryor, F. L. (1977) *The Origins of the Economy*, New York: Academic Press

Radcliffe-Brown, A. R. (1930) 'Former Numbers and Distribution of the Australian Aborigines', *Official Yearbook of the Commonwealth of Australia*, Canberra: Australian Government Publishing Service

Radford, R. A. (1946) 'The Economic Organisation of a P.O.W. Camp', *Economics*

Reece, R. H. W. (1974) *Aborigines and Colonists*, Sydney: Sydney University Press

Reid, A. (—) 'The Pre-colonial Economy of Indonesia', *Bulletin of Indonesian Economic Studies*, vol. XX, no. 2

Reynolds, H. (1981) *The Other Side of the Frontier*, History Department, James Cook University, Townsville

Roberts, S. H. (1924) *History of Australian Land Settlement, 1788–1920*, Melbourne: Macmillan

Roberts, S. H. (1935) *The Squatting Age in Australia*, Melbourne: Melbourne University Press

Robson, L. (1983) *A History of Tasmania*, vol. 1, Melbourne: Oxford University Press

Rose, F. G. G. (1987) *The Traditional Mode of Production of the Australian Aborigines*, Sydney: Angus & Robertson

Rosenblat, A. (1945) *La Poblacion indigena de America desde 1492 hasta la actualidad*, Buenos Aires: Institution Cultural Espanola

Rowley, C. D. (1972) *The Destruction of Aboriginal Society*, Ringwood, Vic.: Penguin

Ryan, L. (1981) *The Aboriginal Tasmanians*, St Lucia, Qld: Queensland University Press

Sahlins, M. (1972) *Stone Age Economics*, London: Tavistock

Salway, P. (1981) *Roman Britain*, Oxford: Oxford University Press

Schrire, G. (1982) *The Alligator Rivers: Prehistory and Ecology in Western Arnhemland*, Canberra: Australian National University Press

Shann, E. O. G. (1930) *Economic History of Australia*, Cambridge: Cambridge University Press

Shao-Wu Want (1984) 'El Nino and Summer Temperatures in Northeast China, 1860–1980', *Tropical Ocean Atmosphere Newsletter*, May

Singh, G. *et al.* (1974) 'Late Quaternary History of Vegetation and Climate of the Rajasthan Desert, India', *Philosophical Transactions, Royal Society*

Singh, G. & E. Geissler (1985) 'Late Cainozoic History of Vegetation, Fire, Lake Levels and Climate at Lake George, New South Wales, Australia', *Philosophical Transactions of the Royal Society*

Smith, E. A. (1983) 'Anthropological Applications of Optimal Foraging Theory: A Critical Review', *Current Anthropology*, vol. 24

Smith, L. R. (1980) *The Aboriginal Population of Australia*, Canberra: Australian National University Press

Smyth, R. Brough (1878) *Notes Relating to the Habits of the Natives of Other Parts of Australia and Tasmania*, 2 vols, London

Spate, O. H. K. (1979, 1983) *The Pacific Since Magellan*, vol. 1: 'Spanish Lake'; vol. 2: 'Monopolists and Freebooters', Canberra: Australian National University Press

Stannage, W. (1981) *A New History of Western Australia*, Nedlands, WA: University of Western Australia Press

Starr, C. G. (1974) *A History of the Ancient World*, New York: Oxford University Press

Stearn, E. W. & Searn, A. E. (1945) *The Effect of Smallpox on the Destiny of the Amerindians*, Boston: Bruce Humphries

Steven, M. (1965) *Merchant Campbell 1763–1846*, Melbourne: Oxford University Press

Steven, M. (1983) *Trade, Tactics and Territory. Britain in the Pacific: 1783–1823*, Melbourne: Melbourne University Press

Stewart, T. D. (1973) *The People of America*, London: Weidenfeld & Nicolson

Stormon, E. J. (ed.) (1978) *The Salvado Memoirs*, Nedlands, WA: University of Western Australia Press

Street, F. A. & A. T. Grove (1979) 'Global Maps of Lake-level Fluctuations since 30,000 BP', *Quaternary Research*, no. 12

Sturt, C. (1833) *Two Expeditions into the Interior of Southern Australia*, London: Smith, Elder & Co.

Sturt, C. (1849) *Narrative of an Expedition into Central Australia*, 2 vols, London: Boone

Swain, A. M. *et al.* (1983) 'Estimates of Holocene Precipitation for Rajasthan, India, Based on Pollen and Lake-level Data', *Quaternary Research* vol. 19

Tench, W. (1961) *Sydney's First Four Years* (with introduction and annotations by L. F. Fitzhardinge), Sydney: Angus & Robertson

The Muster of New South Wales and Norfolk Island, 1805–6 (1989) Sydney: ABGR

Thompson, D. F. (1939) 'The Seasonal Factor in Human Culture', *Journal of the Prehistoric Society*, no. 10

Thompson, H. P. (1966) 'Estimating Aboriginal American Population: A Technique Using Anthropological and Biological Data', *Current Anthropology*, October

Thorne, A. & R. Raymond (1989) *Man on the Rim*, Sydney: Angus & Robertson

Tindale, N. B. (1974) *Aboriginal Tribes of Australia*, Canberra: Australian National University Press

Tolcher, H. M. (1986) *Drought or Deluge: Man in the Cooper's Creek Region*, Melbourne: Melbourne University Press

Torgerson, T. *et al.* (1983) 'General Bathymetry of the Gulf of Carpentaria and the Quaternary Physiography of Lake Carpentaria', *Palaeogeography, Palaeoclimatology, Palaeoecology*, vol. 2, no. 5.

Turnbull, C. (1974) *Black War: The Extermination of the Tasmanian Aborigines*, Melbourne: Sun Books

Vamplew, W. (ed.) (1987) *Australians: Historical Statistics*, Sydney: Syme, Weldon & Fairfax

Van Diemen's Land (1856) *Statistical Account of Van Diemen's Land or Tasmania*, Hobart: Government Printer

Walker, D. (ed.) (1972) *Bridge and Barrier*, Canberra: Australian National University Press

Walker, D. & Sun Xiangjun (nd) 'Vegetational and Climatic Changes at the Pleistocene-Holocene Transition Across the Eastern Tropics', mimeo

Wasson, R. J. (1983) 'Late Quaternary Palaeoenvironments in the Desert Dunefields of Australia', *SASQUA*

Wasson, R. J. *et al.* (1983) 'Geomorphology, Late Quaternary Stratigraphy and Palaeoclimatology of the Thar Dunefield', *Zoology and Geomorphology*, NF Suppl-bd 45

Watson, F. (1914–) *Historical Records of Australia*, vols. 1–4, 10–15

Webb, S. G. (1987) 'A Palaeodemographic Model of Late Holocene Central Murray Aboriginal Society, Australia', *Human Evolution*, vol. 2, no. 5

Wentworth, W. C. (1824) *A Statistical Account of the British Settlements in Australia*, London: G. B. Whittaker

White, J. P. & J. F. O'Connell (1982) *A Prehistory of Australia, New Guinea and Sahul*, New York: Academic Press

Whitmore, T. C. (ed.) *Biogeographical Evolution of the Malay Archipelago*, Oxford: Oxford University Press

Wickler S. & M. Spriggs (1988) 'Pleistocene Occupation of the Solomons', *Antiquity*, vol. 62

Williams, E. (1987) 'Complex Hunter-gatherers: A View from Australia', *Antiquity*, vol. 61

Williams, N. M. (1987) *Two Laws*, Canberra: Australian Institute of Aboriginal Studies

Williams N. M. & E. S. Hunn (eds) (1982) *Resource Managers: North American and Australian Hunter Gatherers*, Canberra: Australian Institute of Aboriginal Studies

Williamson, J. & R. G. Barry (1974) 'Simulation of the Atmospheric Circulation Using the NCAR Global Circulation Model with Ice Age Boundary Conditions', *Journal of Applied Meteorology*, April

Wilson, D. (1978) *The Anglo-Saxons*, Harmondsworth: Penguin

Wiseman, J. 'Markets and Trade in Pre-Majapahit Java', *Michigan Papers on South and South East Asia*, no. 13

Wright, J. (1981) *The Cry for the Dead*, Melbourne: Oxford University Press

Wyrtki, K. (1961) *Physical Oceanography of the South East Asian Waters*, NAGA report no. 2, California

Zubrowe, E. (1990) 'The Depopulation of Native America', *Antiquity*, vol. 64

APPENDIX 1

PRELIMINARY 'MODEL/CHECKLIST' OF ABORIGINAL MIGRATION TO AUSTRALIA

At the moment, this preliminary 'model/checklist' is merely for ordering data and exposition. Its size may seem to be unwieldy even for descriptive purposes but in many areas or periods several variables collapse to zero. It is presented here essentially as a checklist.

Notes

(a) There are 22 exogenous variables marked with *, 13 endogenous variables and 13 equations expressed in a provisional form (note that if it were to be developed as a model, the equations would need to be used in incremental and differential terms to deal with spatial contrasts and incremental temporal changes). Throughout i = ith region; t = tth period.

(b) It is also important to note that the underlying approach permits the acceptance or rejection of Malthusian population theory and that several variables may have, in different regions and periods, either a positive or a negative sign. Obviously, one could make all variables in equations 12 and 13 endogenous but this is complex enough as it stands.

Equations

1. Nit = f(Nx*, g, m, F)it

   where N = population & Nxit = base populations
   g = birth rate
   m = death rate
   F = emigration

2. Rit = f(Rx*, M*, A*, L*, T*)it

   where R = total natural resources
   Rxit = base natural resources
   M = glacier masses
   A = aridity
   L = land added by sea subsidence
   T = temperature (ambient)

3. Yit = f(R, I, S, K)it

   where Y = output/income
   R = total natural resources (supplies)
   I = information
   S = (labour) search time
   K = capital

4. Iit = f(G*, Z*, J*, V*)it

   where I = information
   G = level of intelligence
   Z = learning by doing
   J = tastes
   V = resource dispersion

5. Sit = f(J*, V*, KI)it

   where S = (labour) search time
   J = tastes
   V = natural resource dispersion in any gathering area
   K = capital
   I = information

6. Kit = f(B*, E, G*, Y, N)it

   where K = capital
   B = cultural diffusion
   E = trade
   G = level of intelligence
   Y = income/output
   N = population

7. git = f(a*, fx*, c*)it

   where g = birth rates
   a = reproductive females
   fx = fertility rate by age
   c = average age at marriage

8. mit = f(d*, ex*)it

> where m = death rates
> d   = age structures
> ex = life expectancy by age

9. Eit = f(Yj, Yk, G*, a*)it

> where E = trade
> Yj = income/output of jth region
> Yk = income/output of kth region
> G = level of intelligence
> a   = natural resource disparities

10. Xit = f(Yj, Yj + 1, Nj, Nj + 1, C, U*, D*)it

> where X = inducement to leave region
> Yj, Yj + 1 = income/output of jth and adjoining region
> Nj, Nj + 1 = population of jth and adjoining region
> C = internal/external conflict
> U = infrequent physical upheavals
> D = (frequent) personal accident

11. Cit = f(Nj, Nj + 1, Rj, Rj + 1, Kj, Kj + 1, Wj*, Wj + 1*)it

> where C = conflict
> Nj, Nj + 1 = population of the jth and adjoining region
> Rj, Rj + 1 = natural resources of the jth and adjoining region
> Kj, Kj + 1 = capital of the jth and adjoining region
> Wj*, Wj + 1* = social/power structures of the jth and adjoining region

12. $Qit = f(\dfrac{Yj + 1 - Yj}{Nj}, H^*, O^*, P)it$

> where Q = costs of transfer
> Yj, Yj + 1 = income/output of the region of emigration and its neighbour
> Nj = population of the region of emigration
> H* = distance covered in transfer
> O* = ocean conditions
> P   = maritime capability

13. $Fit = f(\dfrac{Yj}{Nj}, X, Q)it$

> where F = migration flow
> X = inducements to depart
> Q = transfer cost
> Yj = output/income of the region of emigration
> Nj = population of the region of emigration

APPENDIX 2

NOAA DEPTH CONTOUR MAPS

These contours are derived from computer tapes of the Digital Relief of the Surface of the Earth from the US National Oceanographic and Atmospheric Administration. These are organised on a uniformly gridded database with a grid spacing of 5' latitude by 5' longitude. This means that, approximately, one degree of latitude is 111 kilometres throughout (there are slight differences by latitude due to the shape of the earth). One degree of longitude varies as follows:

Longitude 0 degrees, 111.3 km; 10 degrees, 109.6 km; 20 degrees 104 km; 30 degrees 96.4 km; 40 degrees 85.4 km; 50 degrees 71.7 km; 60 degrees 55.8 km; 70 degrees 38.2 km; 80 degrees 19.4 km.

Oceanic bathymetry was carried out by the US Naval Oceanographic Office as at 1988. The tape data are sonar soundings corrected by echo-sounding correction tables to account for variable sea conditions (chiefly water temperature), combined with Admiralty Charts and national soundings together with land topography measured from satellites. This grid system, despite its coarseness, presents far more detail in important areas than is available on the Admiralty Charts, which show large gaps in soundings in both the Java Sea and the Gulf of Thailand. Nevertheless, the NOAA tapes should be read as only pointing to phenomena that seem worth much closer investigation. Taken on that basis, they are an excellent beginning. The maps presented relate to key points in the ice age.

INDEX

For EU product safety concerns, contact us at Calle de José Abascal, 56–1°,
28003 Madrid, Spain or eugpsr@cambridge.org.

www.ingramcontent.com/pod-product-compliance
Ingram Content Group UK Ltd.
Pitfield, Milton Keynes, MK11 3LW, UK
UKHW012200180425
457623UK00020B/312